D1055680

Critical Essays on
Robert Burns

The Scottish Series

General editor: Alexander Scott

The Scottish Series will include in its range books on every aspect of Scottish literature and social history from the earliest times to the present, including anthologies (both poetry and prose), new editions of Scottish classics, scholarly studies, critical surveys, and collections of essays. These volumes will be designed for the general reader and the serious student alike, and the editors of the various volumes will be recognized authorities in their different fields.

The following volumes have already been published:

The Hugh MacDiarmid Anthology, edited by Michael Grieve (MacDiarmid's son) and Alexander Scott. Issued in honour of the poet's eightieth birthday, this constitutes the most representative selection of his work published to date, illustrating the full scope of Scotland's greatest living writer.

A Scottish Ballad Book, edited by David Buchan.

Religion and Social Class, by A. Allan MacLaren.

The general editor of the series, Alexander Scott—the poet, dramatist, critic and biographer—is Head of the Department of Scottish Literature in the University of Glasgow.

The Scottish Series

Critical Essays on Robert Burns

Edited by
Donald A. Low

Department of English Studies
University of Stirling

Routledge & Kegan Paul
London and Boston

First published in 1975
by Routledge & Kegan Paul Ltd
Broadway House, 68-74 Carter Lane,
London EC4V 5EL and
9 Park Street,
Boston, Mass. 02108, USA

Set in Monotype Bembo
and printed in Great Britain by
T. & A. Constable Ltd
Hopetoun Street, Edinburgh
Copyright Routledge & Kegan Paul Ltd 1975

ISBN 0 7100 8109 X

Published with the support of the Scottish Arts Council

Contents

Acknowledgments

The idea of producing this collection of critical essays on Burns arose out of friendly and stimulating discussion in the Universities Committee on Scottish Literature. The editor's warm thanks are due to Professor T. A. Dunn and to Mr Alexander Scott, respectively Chairman and Secretary of UCSL since its inception in 1968.

The editor and publishers wish to thank Mr Thomas Crawford for kindly granting them permission to reprint, with minor changes in annotation, part of his book *Burns: A Study of the Poems and Songs* (Oliver & Boyd, 2nd edition 1965, pp. 82-104); and Professor James Kinsley, for kindly granting them permission to reprint, with minor changes in annotation, part of his article 'The Music of the Heart', based on the Gregynog Lectures delivered at the University College of Wales at Aberystwyth in February 1963, and originally published in *Renaissance and Modern Studies* (edited by James Kinsley and R. S. Smith, University of Nottingham), volume VIII (1964), pp. 25-36.

Chronological Table

1759   Robert Burns born at Alloway, near Ayr, 25 January.

1766   Burns's father becomes tenant of Mount Oliphant, a farm near Alloway.

1774   Burns writes his first song at harvest-time, 'Thus with me began Love and Poesy'.

1777   The family move to Lochlea Farm, by Tarbolton.

1780   Burns is active in founding a Bachelors' Debating Club at Tarbolton.

1782–3   Reads Fergusson's *Poems*.

1784   His father dies at Lochlea. Burns and his brother Gilbert move to Mossgiel Farm, near Mauchline, leased from Gavin Hamilton.

1785   Meets Jean Armour, begins to 'puzzle Calvinism with . . . heat and indiscretion', and writes much poetry.

1786   Runs into trouble with Jean Armour's family, vainly tries to forget her in 'all kinds of dissipation and riot', parts from 'Highland Mary', and makes plans to emigrate to Jamaica. *Poems, Chiefly in the Scottish Dialect* published in Kilmarnock (July). Burns gives up the idea of emigration, and goes to Edinburgh (November).

1787   First Edinburgh and London editions of *Poems*. Tours the Borders and the Highlands of Scotland, begins his sustained contribution to James Johnson's *Scots Musical Museum*, and meets Mrs M'Lehose, 'Clarinda'.

1787–8   Much of this winter spent in Edinburgh.

1788   Burns acknowledges Jean Armour as his wife ('and so farewell Rakery!'), leases the farm of Ellisland, near Dumfries, and is commissioned as an exciseman. From now on, writes more songs than poems.

1789   Begins work in the Excise at a salary of £50.

1790   Writes 'Tam o' Shanter'.

1791   Gives up Ellisland in favour of full-time excise work, and moves to Dumfries. On a visit to Edinburgh says farewell to Clarinda.

1792   Burns is asked to contribute to George Thomson's *A Select Collection of Original Scotish Airs* (1793-1818). He is accused of political disaffection. This charge blows over, but 'I have set, henceforth, a seal on my lips, as to these unlucky politics.'

1793   Second Edinburgh edition of *Poems* and first set of Thomson's *Select Collection* published.

1794   Appointed Acting Supervisor of Excise.

1795   Joins in organizing the Dumfries Volunteers. Severely ill with rheumatic fever.

1796   Burns dies at Dumfries, 21 July.

Note on Abbreviations

Kinsley   *The Poems and Songs of Robert Burns*, edited by James Kinsley (3 volumes, Clarendon Press, Oxford, 1968). In the essays which follow, poems and songs are referred to by their title, first line, or number in this fully annotated edition. Where only these details and Burns's text are sought, reference can equally be made to Kinsley's one-volume Oxford Standard Authors edition (Oxford, 1969). Other references are to page numbers in Kinsley, volume 3 (Commentary).

Letters   *The Letters of Robert Burns*, edited by J. De Lancey Ferguson (2 volumes, Clarendon Press, Oxford, 1931). Reference is to volume and page numbers of this edition.

Other abbreviations are explained in the text and notes of the essays in which they occur: for those used in Cedric Thorpe Davie's essay 'Robert Burns, Writer of Songs', for example, see note 1, p. 184.

Introduction

Donald A. Low

There have been so many editions of Burns that J. W. Egerer, author of the most recent *Bibliography of Robert Burns*, believes his popularity last century may have been greater even than Shakespeare's,[1] while the number and size of modern editions, translations and reprints show a further massive extension of interest in the twentieth century. Translation into more than twenty languages has created a world-wide public. In several European countries, in Russia, and in parts of the Far East several versions compete for the attention of enthusiastic readers. Nor are Burns's works known only by the printed page. 'Tam o' Shanter' and many other poems are recited aloud in most countries at least once every year. Live song recitals, broadcasts and numerous records help to meet the seemingly insatiable demand for Burns's songs in performance. It is not so with other poets and song-writers.

Paradoxically, it was against all the odds that Burns became known in his own country, let alone elsewhere. He was born a poor tenant-farmer's son in 1759, only a few years after Thomas Gray had written in his *Elegy* of how gifted men who might have

> wak'd to extacy the living lyre

were denied the chance to do so because of ignorance and chill penury which

> repress'd their noble rage,
> And froze the genial current of the soul.

By the time he was writing poetry in early manhood Burns had known such hard physical toil on uneconomic small farms that his health was damaged—this was to be the cause of his early death. His first collection of poems was published in 1786 in a small edition in Kilmarnock, a town in Ayrshire, when he was on the point of giving everything up and emigrating to the West Indies. A local press is not a promising point of origin for an ambitious writer, which Burns at that time was. Moreover, the title *Poems, Chiefly in the Scottish Dialect* was no guarantee of success. As a natural poet, he had sought to communicate with other versifiers, one or two local patrons of such activity, and eventually a wider public; but the chance of his work being noticed outside his own region was slight. In Edinburgh, a typical man of letters of the day wrote of himself that he was not 'partial to the productions of the vulgar rhymers in the Scottish dialect, of whom every district has its favourites'.[2]

Beyond Scotland, Burns's use of the vernacular was obviously a potential disqualification for success as a poet—but any such consideration was wildly hypothetical. Then by chance his poems were commended to Edinburgh friends by a stranger, the blind Ayrshire poet Thomas Blacklock. He was taken up by leading critics, and in a matter of weeks was famous.

The true nature of his poetic gift was so misunderstood, however, that within two years Burns quietly turned his back on this early fame. 'His reputation is vastly faded', a journalist noted in 1789.[3] He had been urged to write long poems, and plays, but instead went back to oral inspiration and folk-song. The first appearance of 'Tam o' Shanter' in book form in 1791 was as a footnote to a book of antiquities by a friend. He allowed his songs to be published obscurely, often unsigned, in serial song collections, which of course were not reviewed in the usual way. Immediately popular when sung, but counting for little at the time in the conventional hierarchy of poetic 'kinds', the songs had to await collection until after he was dead. More damaging still to appreciation of his art, the first collected edition of his work in 1800 excluded 'The Jolly Beggars', 'Holy Willie's Prayer' and other satires which were judged to be too offensive to print, although nearly all of them had been published at various times in separate, sometimes anonymous, editions, broadsides and chapbooks. Quite apart from this was the fact that not for 150 years would the complete and unexpurgated text of Burns's other and bawdy song collection, *The Merry Muses of Caledonia*, take its place on library shelves along with the rest of his writings.

Not only poverty but also Burns's use of dialect, the amount of critical misdirection he had to put up with, his casualness in publishing his songs, and prolonged censorship, all appeared to stand in the way of lasting fame.

What is the unique quality that enabled him to reach and captivate so many people? Wordsworth identified 'the presence of human life' in his poetry. Scott believed that of all the authors he had known only Burns and Byron wrote with complete spontaneity. Burns himself wrote of 'stringin' blethers up in rhyme':

Some rhyme a neebor's name to lash;
Some rhyme, (vain thought!) for needfu' cash;
Some rhyme to court the countra clash,
    An' raise a din;
For me, an *aim* I never fash;
    I rhyme for *fun*.

('To J. S****', ll. 25-30)

It is characteristic of him to have expressed this, the central truth, in words which disarm criticism. Fun is accepted or rejected; it cannot be argued with! Like Byron—and Scott—Burns refuses to be confined by the limiting terms of any literary theory. He stands for life, not for abstractions which get in the way. His apparent *naïveté* conceals subtle poetic art. Hence this book. But unless Burns's sheer delight in experience, his need to please himself and others, is accepted at face value, the essential spirit of his writings is missed.

By an irony which would have amused him, his very popularity and distrust of anything but life itself have produced a reaction of disdain on the part of many recent 'critic folk' and 'college asses'. The excesses of the Burns Cult usually get blamed; but that is a stale complaint and an absurdly inadequate excuse. The fact that in 1970 there were over 300 Burns Clubs and Societies on the roll of the far-flung Burns Federation is no kind of justification for a *trahison des clercs*. Burns is not only the most widely enjoyed of poets. He receives much less than his fair share of discussion in schools and universities.

This is partly because his 'highkilted Muse' makes some educators uncomfortable. 'To a Mouse' is acceptable in the classroom, but 'The Jolly Beggars' disrupts theoretical models of what literature ought to be about. Besides, it is bawdy! But may not Burns's kind of bawdiness, alight with humour, be altogether more wholesome than either censorship which gags, or pulp fiction which is displayed in station bookstalls and corner cafés, and which certainly gets read?

Burns is an improviser of genius. Improvisation in art proves disconcerting to people accustomed to impose a tidy conceptual framework on what they study. (That is why criticism of Byron and Scott also lags behind the study of other Romantic writers who are more susceptible to philosophically orientated inquiry.) This characteristic is found in all of Burns's work. It is especially notable in the epistles:

Sae I've begun to scrawl, but whether
In rhyme, or prose, or baith thegither,

Or some hotch-potch that's rightly neither,
    Let time mak proof;
But I shall scribble down some blether
    Just clean aff-loof.

              ('Second Epistle to Lapraik', ll. 37-42)

and in the songs. The epistles and songs make up what is in the strict sense a body of occasional poetry. They are the two largest single groups in Burns's entire output. As the satires, and they are the next largest group, were also produced spontaneously by particular occasions rather than written deliberately according to a long-term plan of a Miltonic or Wordsworthian kind, it can be seen that a neatly schematic critical approach to Burns's poetry is impossible. This, which can be accepted as an enjoyable challenge, deters 'douse folk' who think by rule.

So far from being the unlettered peasant he was for long held to be, the 'Heaven-taught ploughman' of legend, Burns drew, as David Murison shows, on wide knowledge of two literatures, and also on oral tradition. Much has still to be done to explore his creative borrowings, and his affinities with other authors. Maria Riddell noted in a 'Character Sketch' of Burns in 1796 that there was a resemblance between the sudden sallies of humour and sentiment in his work and the writings of Sterne, which he knew well. This topic has not yet been investigated, no doubt because it means crossing academic boundaries between English and Scottish literature and between poetry and fiction. And critics of late eighteenth-century literature have been still less willing to interest themselves equally in books, folk-song and country talk. Yet the complex nature of Burns's actual cultural setting demands no less. John Baird writes, ' "Only connect." No poet stands to gain more from the sympathetic application of Forster's precept than Robert Burns.' There is an obvious need for other papers on Burns's literary relationships with particular contemporaries.

Basic questions remain open, undecided, and in most places of learning, unasked. How, for example, does Burns's poetry connect with Romanticism, the most memorable phase of artistic expression in Europe since the Renaissance? This question is evaded not because it is too simple to bother with, or irrelevant, but because once again it involves stepping over narrow academic frontiers which have become an obstruction to understanding.

Burns did not have a transcendental attitude towards Nature. He knew fields as taskwork too well to develop such an outlook. His was a shrewd, practical vision of the countryside, that of a farmer. On high-days, holidays and when courting, he rejoiced in natural beauty, but his delight was different in kind from the response to Nature of Coleridge and Wordsworth, which was essentially a religious one. The opening of 'The Holy Fair' illustrates Burns's way of enjoying the countryside:

> Upon a simmer *Sunday morn*,
>   When Nature's face is fair,
> I walked forth to view the corn,
>   An' snuff the callor air:
> The rising sun, owre GALSTON muirs,
>   Wi' glorious light was glintan;
> The hares were hirplan down the furrs,
>   The lav'rocks they were chantan
>   Fu' sweet that day.

These lines convey a mood of intense pleasure in the scene, with the poet strolling in the morning air, noting the state of his cornfield, and anticipating a day with no work ahead. He describes the light as 'glorious', but this is a Scottish farmer's conversational phrase, not an intimation of eternity. The stanza contrasts with most of Wordsworth's famous poetic statements about the renewing power of Nature, including this passage from 'Lines Composed a Few Miles above Tintern Abbey':

> And I have felt
> A presence that disturbs me with the joy
> Of elevated thoughts; a sense sublime
> Of something far more deeply interfused,
> Whose dwelling is the light of setting suns,
> And the round ocean and the living air,
> And the blue sky, and in the mind of man:
> A motion and a spirit, that impels
> All thinking things, all objects of all thought,
> And rolls through all things.

Burns delighted in the beauty of the external world, but he did not describe it in a way which suggests any mystical experience.

It is also plainly evident that he did not develop a theory of the Imagination as the power which 'half-creates the world it sees'. He had no need of it, because the interaction of his mind with the objects of sense was a consistently vital process, something he accepted as simply part of being alive. It is pointless, therefore, to look in his poetry for that technique which came into being along with Romantic ideas of Imagination, the frequent use of symbolism to denote what Coleridge called 'the translucence . . . of the universal in the general; above all . . . the translucence of the eternal through and in the temporal'.

Faith in Nature, a theory of the poetic Imagination, and symbolism are integral to some definitions of Romantic art. But does this dispose of the possibility that, by virtue of other qualities which his poetry shows, Burns is nevertheless one of the earliest poets in the British Isles to participate in the spirit of Romanticism?

Blake apart, Burns was the first British poet of his century to stress as dynamic values freedom, both personal and national, simplicity and joy. These, no less than the Coleridgian concepts already described, are all primary attributes of Romanticism. Confident self-expression is fundamental to the very idea; freedom in some form was to be celebrated by every Romantic poet, composer and artist in Europe; and, as M. H. Abrams has recently pointed out, the keynote of their work is joy.[4] With Blake, Burns made poetry an instrument of joy in the decade 1786-96, which was, significantly, one of revolutionary hopes.

Further, Burns anticipated Wordsworth in employing 'language really used by men' in his poetry, and Wordsworth was ready to recognize his success in doing so. There is again a distinction to be made between formulating a set of ideas to justify a process one has carried out, and carrying out the process quite unselfconsciously. 'The Vision' begins:

> The sun had clos'd the *winter-day*,
> The Curlers quat their roaring play,
> And hunger'd Maukin taen her way
>   To kail-yards green,
> While faithless snaws ilk step betray
>   Whare she has been.
>
> The Thresher's weary *flingin-tree*,
> The lee-lang day had tir'd me;
> And when the Day had clos'd his e'e,
>   Far i' the West,
> Ben i' the *Spence*, right pensivelie,
>   I gaed to rest.

> There, lanely, by the ingle-cheek,
> I sat and ey'd the spewing reek,
> That fill'd, wi' hoast-provoking smeek,
>   The auld, clay biggin;
> And heard the restless rattons squeak
>   About the riggin.
>
> All in this mottie, misty clime,
> I backward mus'd on wasted time,
> How I had spent my *youthfu' prime*,
>   An' done nae-thing,
> But stringin' blethers up in rhyme
>   For fools to sing.

This is a man speaking to his fellow-men in his own real language, and its difference from the poetic diction Burns and Wordsworth knew so well is illustrated at another point in 'The Vision' when Burns makes Coila speak in dignified English. Burns was ahead of his time in breaking from artificiality and finding the way back to a direct mode of poetry. The authentic use of Scots marked the innovation.

A Romantic poet, bringing in a new age of emotional affirmation, Burns none the less shared certain values which belong distinctively to the Enlightenment. He was sceptical, ironic, and grounded in Reason. Satire was no less natural a medium for Burns than for Pope, whose work he admired. He had read, too, some of the noted philosophical prose of his age. Patronizing acquaintances in Edinburgh discovered that, while most things amused him, it was impossible to fool him with a bad argument.

Scepticism on the subject of superstition prevails in his letters and in the prose introduction to 'Hallowe'en', in which he stands outside the folklore of his district and suggests that the practices which the poem describes are of objective interest to the 'enlightened' inquirer into social customs. But there was much more to his response to supernatural country lore than a rational and tutored disbelief. His comments on this subject are those of an Enlightenment thinker—but with a difference! He could readily put himself in the position of believing tales of cantraips, bogles and ghosts. As a child, he had listened to such stories in wonder, and he never lost the habit of surrendering in imagination to dark possibilities of local legend. It was his lasting ability to identify in feeling with the subjects of supernatural happenings which made it possible for him to write 'Tam o' Shanter'. Tam's vividly presented consciousness is at the heart of the poem. And what *did* happen to Meg's tail? There is the direct humour of Tam's final bewilderment, and also the allusive humour of an ironist sceptical both of the value of searching the external world for 'the evidence of miracles'—a prominent topic in eighteenth-century theological debate—and, in the end, of unaided reason itself. Tipsy, credulous man certainly does not live up to the possibilities of reason. Burns also implies, however, that the supernatural cannot be wholly explained away by rational investigation. Such a point of view, and the controlling stress in the poems and songs on being true to emotional experience, allow Burns to transcend the Enlightenment tradition on which he draws.

Burns's egalitarianism can partly be understood as a poetic expression of what Carl Woodring has described as 'the universalist bias of the Enlightenment in Scotland'.[5] But this is only one element behind his distinctive belief in a new social order. Popular democratic feeling in Scotland contributed much, as did Burns's familiarity with a vernacular literature noted since the fourteenth century for its expression of ideas of freedom and equality. Barbour, Henryson and Lyndsay had all been convinced of the equality of men before their Maker. All this was transformed for Burns by the fact that he lived in an Age of Revolution. It matters less to follow the course of his interest in party politics, which to some extent was frustrated in later years by his having an official post in the Excise, than to recognize the breadth and depth of his concern with man as a social being.

'His way of universality,' writes Carl Woodring, 'was not the way of Blake or Shelley. To the end, he saved love for the bed or the rushes.'[6] This is at best a half-truth, and sets up false contradictions. Burns's life was physically orientated, certainly; but he put the knowledge which he derived from experience to the service of an ideal of tolerance ultimately derived from the Christian concept of charity, and historically related, through a common debt to the revolutionary climate of the 1780s, to Blake's radical emphasis on liberty in love:

> Then gently scan your brother Man,
>   Still gentler sister Woman;
> Tho' they may gang a kennin wrang,
>   To step aside is human.

As these lines show, his poetry is informed by a warmly affectionate vision of individuals as interdependent. It is true that Neoplatonism and transcendental interests, which distinguish Shelley's poetry, are largely absent; but not even the complete absence of these qualities would be synonymous with the absence of love.

Geniality is a hallmark of Burns's work, just as it is of Chaucer's. The poet who wrote

> It's coming yet for a' that,
> That Man to Man the warld o'er
> Shall brothers be for a' that

had penetrated to an insight whose simplicity makes systematic thought and metaphysics alike unnecessary. Here as elsewhere geniality shades into love for humanity at large. Significantly, the idea in these lines is that of Tom Paine in *The Rights of Man*. Neither their political colouring nor Burns's characteristic pride accounts for their full power, however. Burns produces a mood which can exist independently of considerations of politics, class or race. Its source lies in something more dynamic than any of these, a variant of the approach to life which theologians call 'agape'.

This is in no sense to deny that Burns is also a poet of eros. He celebrates the life of the senses—in *The Merry Muses*, quite uninhibitedly. But that is not all. In his finest love-songs passion will usually be found to exist along with humorous acceptance:

> O Wha my babie-clouts will buy,
> O Wha will tent me when I cry;
> Wha will kiss me where I lie,
> The rantin dog the daddie o't

or with the more measured expression of a fully personal concern:

> Till a' the seas gang dry, my Dear,
> And the rocks melt wi' the sun:
> I will love thee still, my Dear,
> While the sands o' life shall run.

Burns's sense of the inclusiveness of love leads him to find words which, in Scott's phrase, contain 'the essence of a thousand love tales':

> Had we never lov'd sae kindly,
> Had we never lov'd sae blindly!
> Never met—or never parted,
> We had ne'er been broken-hearted.

Similarly, it was not merely physical attraction or an interest in 'the bed or the rushes' which elicited his tender tribute to Jessie Lewars, who nursed him in his last illness. No doubt there is gallantry in these lines, but there is in addition a deeper protective feeling, a sense of one person apprehending another in relationship:

> Oh wert thou in the cauld blast,
>   On yonder lea, on yonder lea;
> My plaidie to the angry airt,
>   I'd shelter thee, I'd shelter thee:
> Or did misfortune's bitter storms
>   Around thee blaw, around thee blaw,
> Thy bield should be my bosom,
>   To share it a', to share it a'.

The last line sums up not only this stanza but also the whole direction of Burns's life and of his poetry.

The chronology of Burns's literary career explains the arrangement of this collection of essays on his work, the first for more than twenty-five years. The first three essays view the poet in the broad context of his life, his relationship with his original public, and his linguistic situation. In 'Robert Burns: A Self-portrait', G. Ross Roy describes the character of the man who is so frankly revealed by his Commonplace Books, journals and letters. He finds Burns to have been witty and earthy, a sometimes lonely figure who nevertheless loved company and who had the gift of helping people to rise above themselves. Ian Campbell identifies as crucial for an interpretation of Burns the difference between his intimate knowledge of his native community in Ayrshire and his strained attempt in 1786-7 to communicate with 'polite' Edinburgh readers. The argument he goes on to develop is supported by examples from 'Death and Doctor Hornbook' and later poems. David Murison, editor of the *Scottish National Dictionary*, examines in 'The Language of Burns' not only the poet's linguistic and cultural heritage, but also his use of words in particular poems. His essay enriches appreciation of what he aptly describes as Burns's 'ability to fix in the vivid concrete terms of ordinary experience a universal truth'.

Next, there are separate essays on the epistles and satires, the two kinds of poem to which Burns devoted more time and energy than to any other form except song. In 'The Epistles', Thomas Crawford isolates for discussion the characteristic qualities of Burns's varied experiments in this genre, noting among other features the social dichotomy Burns posits between career-minded 'douse folk' and the 'hairum-scairum, ram-stam boys' with whom he feels himself naturally to belong. For Crawford, the 'self-dramatizations of the epistles express a mind in motion'. This is an essential point, and one with implications for the reading of Burns's other work. Local events provided the poet with the inspiration to write most of his satirical poems, and Burns's reputation as a satirist in his lifetime was largely gained 'underground' because of a censorship which made orthodox publication impossible. Alexander Scott assesses the satires with these facts in mind, and convincingly demonstrates that Burns's underground poetry has power and relevance beyond narrow limits of time or place. His essay adds substance to Carlyle's opinion: a satirist must be 'a good hater', but in the case of a major poet 'the Indignation which makes verses is, properly speaking, an inverted Love'. The most popular of all the poems during Burns's life time was 'The Cotter's Saturday Night'. Some reasons for the widespread appeal of this poem when first published form one part of John D. Baird's inquiry in his essay on Burns and Cowper. He also draws attention to differences between these two, the most noted Scottish and English poets of their day. His breadth of reference establishes the value of adopting a comparative literary approach in the study of Burns.

Burns's songs have suffered from critical neglect in the past. Here they receive equal attention with the poems. In 'The Music of the Heart', James Kinsley explores the richly idiosyncratic background against which poetry and song flourished together in eighteenth-century Scotland. 'Robert Burns and Jacobite Song', by David Daiches, concentrates on Burns's lyrical treatment of one major and perennially fascinating theme, and in so doing illustrates Scott's remark that Burns had 'the *tact* to make his poetry tell by connecting it with the stream of public thought and the sentiment of the age'. Finally, Cedric Thorpe Davie draws on a lifetime's experience of musical composition, arrangement and performance in his comprehensive survey, 'Robert Burns, Writer of Songs'. His professional ability to define the ways in which words and music match each other as parts of a single entity answers a long-standing need. He invites the reader to listen, rather than to remain content with words on the page, and, as Master of Music in St Andrews, Scotland's 'singing university', never loses sight of Burns's over-riding aim, which was to create pleasure.

Notes

1 J. W. Egerer, *A Bibliography of Robert Burns* (Edinburgh, 1964), viii.
2 Robert Anderson to James Currie, 27 October 1799. Quoted in *Burns Chronicle* (1925), xxxiv, p. 13.

3 Quoted in *Burns Chronicle* (1940), new series xv, p. 16.
4 M. H. Abrams, *Natural Supernaturalism: Tradition and Revolution in Romantic Literature* (London, 1971), p. 431.
5 Carl Woodring, *Politics in English Romantic Poetry* (Cambridge, Mass., 1970), p. 56.
6 *Ibid.*, p. 59.

Chapter 1

Robert Burns: A Self-portrait

G. Ross Roy

More than most authors we come to know Burns through the letters he wrote and received. True, there are some contemporary accounts of the poet, but these are mostly to be found piecemeal, scattered through journals and reminiscences of those who had met him, usually during the two years from late 1786 until 1788 when he was a familiar sight on the streets of Edinburgh. The picture which we form of the poet through these glimpses of him is that of a man riding the crest of a wave of universal admiration; if he had faults these were either glossed over or excused as the quite forgivable eccentricities of genius. Unfortunately he had no Boswell; the accounts of him in Edinburgh are by different observers with quite other standards from those few who gave us details about him after he had left the capital.

Although he kept no systematic journal, he twice—on his Border tour and on a Highland tour—kept a sort of running diary for a short space of time. These diaries are so cryptic that, while they form a valuable record of the people he met and the places he visited, they do not afford a detailed view of the poet's thinking or the process that would turn sense-impression into poetry. I deliberately wrote first of the people he met because one has the impression that for Burns the most important aspect of these journeys was the meeting of people; he was above all else a social being. He loved company—in part as an escape from the gnawing loneliness within but in part, too, because he could help people to rise above themselves, to share his vision of a better world.

Burns's first Commonplace Book covers the period from April 1783 to October 1785. It thus contains almost the earliest surviving record in the poet's hand (there are a few letters of earlier date) during a crucial two and a half years of his life, a time when he was ripening as a poet. This is not to suggest that Burns began writing poetry only in 1783 when he commenced the Commonplace Book—the book itself tells us that 'I never had the least thought or inclination of turning Poet till I got once heartily in Love, and then Rhyme & and [sic] Song were, in a manner, the spontaneous language of my heart.'[1] In his autobiographical letter the poet tells us that this first venture into verse came in his 'fifteenth autumn', some ten years before the Commonplace

Book was begun. But though he was known locally as a versifier, capable of turning a rhyme with mordant wit, he apparently addressed himself seriously to poetry at about the time that he began his entries in the Commonplace Book.

The opening paragraph of that work shows us a self-conscious novice admitting that he was 'but little indebted to scholastic education', who excused his 'performances [which] must be strongly tinctured with his unpolished, rustic way of life'.[2] The paragraph is followed by two quotations from Shenstone, a writer for whom Burns had a very high regard, and whom he mentions frequently in the Commonplace Book. Though his intentions may have been good, Burns was probably still only incubating his poetic gift for the first year of the Commonplace Book—the first eleven months, to March 1784, occupy only five and a half pages, one of which is blank. Suddenly in March and April we have twelve pages of MS., and as suddenly we get a glimpse of the maturing of Burns's genius. Citing Shenstone to the effect that 'love-verses writ without any real passion are the most nauseous of all conceits', Burns adds,[3]

> As I have been all along, a miserable dupe to Love . . . I put the more confidence in my critical skill in distinguishing foppery & conceit, from real passion & nature.—Whether the following song will stand the test, I will not pretend to say, because it is MY OWN.

Stand the test it most certainly did—the song was 'My Nanie, O'.

In another entry made in April 1784 Burns devotes about a page and a half to the beginning of an essay which sought to divide young men into two classes: grave and merry. The next entry is dated August, and opens thus:[4]

> The foregoing was to have been an elaborate dissertation on the various species of men; but as I cannot please myself in the arrangement of my ideas, I must wait till farther experience & nicer observation throw more light on the subject.—In the mean time I shall set down the following fragment which, as it is the genuine language of my heart, will enable any body to determine which of the Classes I belong to ——

Here follows 'Green grow the Rashes—O'.

While there are unmistakable signs of the emergence of Burns's genius as a song-writer—on the whole probably the greatest in the

English-speaking world—there are some pedestrian performances too, witness:[5]

> O Thou, Unknown, Almighty Cause
>   Of all my hope & fear,
> In whose dread presence ere an hour
>   Perhaps I must appear.

And so on. The piece is prefaced: 'A prayer, when fainting fits, & other alarming symptoms of a Pleurisy or some other dangerous disorder, which indeed still threaten me, first put Nature on the alarm.—' While Henley and Henderson suggest December 1781 as the date of composition,[6] the fact that Burns chose to include it in his Commonplace Book in 1784 points to a still-forming critical faculty in the poet.

But on the whole the poems get better as we go along: in September we find 'Tibbie I hae seen the day' and the first proof we have of Burns's writing of bawdry, 'My girl she's airy'.

Exactly half the entries were made between June 1785 and October of that year, when he abandoned the Commonplace Book. On these pages we find an artist who is confident of his work. Here are 'The Death & Dyin' Words o' Poor Mailie', the two 'Epistles' to Lapraik with their deft handling of Standard Habbie, as well as others. Here too under the date of August we have a first glimpse of Burns calling for a more truly national poetry:[7]

> We have never had one Scotch Poet of any eminence, to make the fertile banks of Irvine, the romantic woodlands & sequestered scenes on Aire and the heathy, mountainous source, & winding sweep of Doon emulate Tay, Forth, Ettrick, Tweed, &c. this is a complaint I would gladly remedy, but Alas! I am far unequal to the task, both in native genius & education.—

On this modest estimate he was gloriously wrong.

Burns kept a second Commonplace Book between 9 April 1787 and at least the spring of 1789, perhaps later. Although editors from Currie onwards have used the MS., and although all the contents of the MS. have been published, the work has never been published in its entirety at one time. Most of the MS. is filled with transcripts of poems. On page 2 Burns declares that 'I will sketch every character that anyway strikes me, to the best of my observation, with unshrinking justice'.[8]

In the early pages we do find comments on some of the people Burns had met. These entries are intensely human: we have Burns complaining of a person of rank being showered with attention 'that is forgot to the

Son of Genius and Poverty' (p. 4); we have Burns writing that the 'noble G—— [Glencairn] has wounded me to the soul' because he favoured a 'blockhead' rather than the poet in dinner conversation (p. 5); and on the same page, while displaying his liking for Hugh Blair, Burns is severe in his judgment of the doctor's abilities—he says, in fact, that he is 'meerly [*sic*] an astonishing proof of what industry and application can do'. Of Dugald Stuart the poet wrote that he was 'the most perfect character I ever saw' (p. 6) and he gives us also a fine short sketch of his publisher William Creech (pp. 7-8). Although he suggests Creech's tight-fistedness, he does not openly mention it. Burns was to know a good deal more of his publisher's fondness for money before he finally got a settlement with him!

Unfortunately Burns did not keep to his stated intent to sketch those people he met during his protracted Edinburgh stay—and what a pity that is. For Burns was not taken in by those he met, as we see from the trenchant remarks he made in some of his letters.

When Burns had a little money from the unexpected success of his Edinburgh volume of poems (he eventually cleared about £450, a tidy sum in those days)[9] he treated himself to what was probably the first real holiday of his life. Leaving Edinburgh on 5 May 1787, Burns went on an extended tour of the Border which lasted until 1 June. The journal which the poet kept while on this trip is the longer of two he is known to have kept. The tour came when Burns's fame was at its zenith, and we can sense the poet's enjoyment of the flattery he received. Thus on 7 May: 'My reception from Mr. & Mrs. Brydon extremely flattering'.[10] On 9 May: 'Dine with Captn. Rutherford. The Captn . . . showed a particular respect to My Bardship—.' On 11 May: 'Was waited on by the Magistrates and presented with the freedom of the burgh' (Jedburgh).

At the same time Burns was enjoying the pretty, and not-so-pretty, women (of sisters he wrote [8 May] that they had 'too much of the Mother's half-ell mouth & hog-like features'). The next day he was 'within a point and a half of being damnably in love'. And Burns the practical farmer is impressed with the land, or comments on the price of a fox-hunter (11 May), or attends the sale of an unfortunate farmer's stock (25 May) and calls on 'rigid Economy & decent Industry' to preserve him from such a fate. Although this last entry is cryptic we feel the shudder of recollection of his own experience at Lochlea.

Towards the end of June Burns made a second tour; this time he visited the West Highlands as far as Inverary for a week. He kept no journal that is known, although we have a fragment of a letter to

Robert Ainslie from Arrochar and a long letter to James Smith of Linlithgow upon the completion of the trip on 30 June.

Later that summer Burns and his friend William Nicol, classics master at the High School of Edinburgh, toured the Highlands from 25 August until 16 September. Burns started well, but the journal[11] soon becomes little more than a catalogue of places visited and people seen; almost one-third of the journal is devoted to the first two days of the trip. When he visited Linlithgow on the first day he was moved by the sight of the room where Mary Queen of Scots was born. He liked the Gothic church, too, with its 'infamous stool of repentance standing, in the old Romish way, on a lofty situation. What a poor, pimping business is a Presbyterian place of worship, dirty, narrow and squalid, stuck in a corner of old Popish grandeur such as Linlithgow and, much more, Melrose!' We can feel the poet's indignation; he knew the ignominy of the cutty stool and the counterfeit piousness of the world's Holy Willies.

Although he was a brilliant man, Nicol was no easy travelling companion. Burns complained in a letter to his cousin, James Burness of Montrose, that his friend had decided on another route so that they could not renew the acquaintance of the previous evening.[12] Still, the two men remained friends even after the trip which the poet felt was an unqualified success. 'My journey through the Highlands', he wrote to Patrick Miller on 28 September, 'was perfectly inspiring; and I hope I have laid in a good stock of new poetical ideas from it.'[13] One of the sights which most moved Burns was the field of Bannockburn, which he visited on 26 August:[14]

Come on to Bannockburn . . . the field of Bannockburn—the hole where glorious Bruce set his standard. [Here no Scot can pass uninterested.—I fancy to myself that I see my gallant, heroic countrymen coming o'er the hill and down upon the plunderers of their country, the murderers of their fathers; noble revenge and just hate glowing in every vein, striding more and more eagerly as they approach the oppressive, insulting, blood-thirsty foe! I see them meet in gloriously-triumphant congratulation on the victorious field, exulting in their heroic royal leader and rescued liberty and independence!]

There can be little doubt that this scene was in his mind when he wrote 'Scots wha hae' six years later.

But these journals and Commonplace Books, interesting though they may be, give us a bare glimpse of Burns the man and artist. For most of our first-hand information we have to turn to the letters which survive either in MS. or in early printed form taken from MSS. which can no longer be traced. Unfortunately these latter are suspect both for what early editors have, through the use of ellipsis, shown to be omitted, and what they have silently added. The classic example of this sort of tampering is to be found in Letter 604[15] and concerns Burns's collection of bawdy poems and songs, first printed in 1799. The letter was first published by Currie in 1800, and was dated by him December 1793. In the letter, as published by Currie and all subsequent editors including Ferguson, we find the sentence 'A very few of them are my own'. Unfortunately for Currie's reputation, when the MS. turned up it contained no such sentence! Before a copy of the *Merry Muses* was discovered with a complete title page allowing us to date it positively, I had argued that it must have appeared in 1799 or very early in 1800 (both known copies contain leaves with watermarks dated 1799 and 1800)—early enough for Currie to become aware of its existence and insert 'A very few of them are my own', in order, as he thought, to protect the poet's reputation.[16] Although the collection alluded to by Burns has disappeared (or been destroyed, as has been alleged) we have ample proof that Burns did, in fact, write and collect bawdry. So in the long run it has been Currie's reputation which has suffered, not Burns's.

Even an engraved facsimile is not beyond being tampered with. I have seen one such from which an entire sentence has been deleted and the two remaining parts of the letter brought together to look as though that was how Burns had penned it. The only reliable transcript then must be one which has been made directly from the MS. Fortunately we have a large number of these and occasionally another MS. turns up which had been lost sight of for as much as a century; less frequently a completely new letter is uncovered.

In all we have slightly over 750 letters to help set the record straight. This sounds like a goodly number, but partly because of their distribution they are not quite as helpful in reconstructing Burns's life as one might suppose. For example, only about forty letters survive which were written before 31 July 1786—the date of publication of the Kilmarnock volume—and of these one-half came from the six months preceding that date. In other words, less than two dozen letters survive which were written before the poet was twenty-seven.

In the next, or Edinburgh, period from August 1786 to November 1788, we find about 250 letters. As we should expect, this is proportionately the largest number. They come at a time when Burns was the toast of Edinburgh, and his busy social life required an increase in his letter-writing. Then, too, one supposes, people were more inclined to keep the letters they received from this ploughman with the ready sally and the flashing eyes who had written poems which set the whole of Scotland astir.

The not-quite-three years, from December 1788 to October 1791, during which Burns worked the soil at Ellisland and rode about 200 miles a week as an exciseman, find our poet penning about 200 letters, and finally during the Dumfries period, from November 1791 until his death in July 1796, there are about 260 letters.

Thus we account for about 750 letters, but I feel quite certain that 50 per cent or so of those he wrote either have not survived, or have not come to light. Certainly the humble people who subscribed to all the 612 copies of the Kilmarnock edition of the poems in the three and a half months from the time Burns first began circulating the subscription list (15 April) until the volume actually came out, would not be ones to preserve letters. Like the edition itself, of which I estimate not more than seventy-five copies survive, the poet's letters were soon illegible, victims alike of damp, smoke and crowded living-space which were the commonplaces of peasant life at that time. Parenthetically, I might note that, just as far more letters were preserved by correspondents who came from a higher social order once Burns went to Edinburgh, so a correspondingly higher number of copies of the Edinburgh (1787) edition of the poems survive. Most of the people who purchased a copy of Burns's poems in sturdy French grey boards at six shillings had libraries.

I base my estimate, however, on firmer ground than supposition. There are, for example, in Burns's own letters, and in letters to him, unmistakable references to letters which are now lost. As late as the 1860s there was an important sale of Burns MSS. in which letters were listed by date and addressee—and some of these letters, too, are now lost. But the most important evidence of lost letters is to be found in a document which first came to light in the 1930s when J. C. Ewing published it in the *Burns Chronicle*: a list of the letters which were sent to the poet, which Currie prepared when he was gathering material for his edition of the poet's life and works. This list does not include the letters from George Thomson, Mrs Dunlop, Mrs M'Lehose and Mrs Maria Riddell, all of whom had requested the return of their letters shortly after Burns was dead. In all, the document lists 300 letters written to Burns by 135 correspondents. What is most interesting about this list, perhaps, is that, of these 135 names, we have letters by

Burns to only 80; thus we add 55 names to the list of the poet's correspondents (assuming that these letters were answers to Burns or called forth answers), bringing the total of correspondents to 225.

Before discussing the contents of the letters, it may be interesting to examine briefly the history of their publication. The earliest printed letters were sent to newspapers, and one, to the Earl of Buchan, was published in 1791 in the *Bee*. The letter was accompanied by Burns's 'Address to the shade of Thomson'. No significant number of letters was published during the poet's life; it was not, in fact, until Currie's four-volume edition that we find a fairly large number: 178 in all, including 50 to George Thomson and most of those to Mrs Dunlop. Two years later, 25 letters to Mrs Agnes M'Lehose (Clarinda) were published in Glasgow and were the cause of a lawsuit which forced their removal from the market, but not before a certain number of copies had been purchased.

R. H. Cromek's *Reliques of Robert Burns* added 74 in 1808; Hogg and Motherwell added 9 in their edition of 1834-6; Cunningham added 42 to his eight-volume edition of 1834, as well as completing the Border tour, which had been published in part by Currie, and also adding the journal of the Highland tour. In 1843 Mrs M'Lehose's grandson added 23 Burns letters, as well as publishing his grandmother's letters to Burns. Robert Chambers added 23 and 14 letters in his editions of 1851 and 1856; Hatley Waddell added 30 in 1867, and Scott Douglas published 98 new letters and completed 22 in his edition of 1877. In 1896 William Wallace, revising the Chambers edition, printed another 42 for the first time, and then two years later he published the Burns–Dunlop correspondence, with 33 new letters, 10 completed which had previously only been partially published; he also added Mrs Dunlop's letters to Burns. In this century 13 were first published in 1926, and Ferguson's edition of 1931 added about 70. Finally, the edition on which I am working will add about 30 and complete quite a large number.

When we turn to the letters themselves, one person deserves particular attention, although Burns only sent him eight letters which survive. He is Dr John Moore (1729-1802) of Stirling, who was living in London when his friend Mrs Dunlop sent him a copy of the Kilmarnock edition. In 1779 Moore had published *A view of society and manners in France, Switzerland, & Germany*, a work which was in its sixth edition by 1786. An equally successful work *A view of society and manners in Italy* appeared in 1781. Moore was full of advice to Burns—including his insistence that the poet abandon Scots for English and 'make himself master of the heathen mythology'—advice which Burns fortunately did not follow. This is not to suggest that Burns did not admire Moore; when Moore published a novel, *Zeluco*, in 1789, Burns was ecstatic over it, calling it 'a most sterling performance'.[17] In his copy of the novel, which was sent to him by the author, Burns declared that passages were worthy of Fielding.

By far the most important item in the Burns–Moore correspondence is the long autobiographical letter the poet wrote on 2 August 1787, for this famous letter supplies a good deal of what would be otherwise unknown information about Burns—especially about his earlier years. Unfortunately it has been used several times to prove that Burns's reading was only a thin veneer, but a glance at it will show that he was, in fact, well-read. In it he wrote:[18]

My knowledge of ancient story was gathered from Salmon's and Guthrie's geographical grammars; my knowledge of modern manners, and of literature and criticism, I get from the Spectator.— These, with Pope's works, some plays of Shakespeare, Tull and Dickson on Agriculture, The Pantheon, Locke's Essay on the human understanding, Stackhouse's history of the Bible, Justice's British Gardner's directory, Boyle's lectures, Allan Ramsay's works, Tayler's scripture doctrine of original sin, a select collection of English songs, and Hervey's meditations had been the extent of my reading.

What people so often forget is that Burns is here recounting his life to the age of about twenty! Elsewhere in the letter he told Moore that the first two books he ever read 'in private' were 'the life of Hannibal and the history of Sir William Wallace.—Hannibal gave my young ideas such a turn that I used to . . . wish myself tall enough to be a soldier; while the story of Wallace poured a Scotish prejudice in my veins which will boil along there till the flood-gates of life shut in eternal rest.—'[19] At another point he mentions reading *Pamela* and *Ferdinand, Count Fathom* which gave him 'some idea of novels'. Then it was 'the very important addition of Thomson's and Shenstone's works; I had seen mankind in a new phasis';[20] or again it was his 'great pleasure' from reading *Tristram Shandy* and *The Man of Feeling*.[21] A turning-point came when 'meeting with Fergusson's Scotch Poems, I strung anew my wild-sounding, rustic lyre with emulating vigour.—'[22] An interesting printed announcement lists some of the books in Burns's library at the time of his death. In it we find, to name just a few, Blair, Kames, Adam Smith, Homer, Virgil, Tasso, Chaucer, Ramsay, Ossian, Fergusson, Percy's *Reliques*, Smollett, Fielding, Henry Mackenzie,

Shakespeare, Molière in French, and a translation of Schiller's *Robbers*. This last work was published only in 1792.

We gather other facts from this letter too—information which helps us better to understand the poet. Here, for instance, we are introduced to the conflict between the stern Calvinist father and the gifted misunderstood son which was to colour much of his life. Here, too, we see his introduction to the tales and songs of 'devils, ghosts, fairies, brownies, witches, warlocks, spunkies, kelpies, elf-candles, dead-lights, wraiths, apparitions, cantraips, giants, inchanted [*sic*] towers, dragons and other trumpery'[23] by an old maid of his mother's, who must surely have sowed the seeds of 'Tam o' Shanter' in the youngster's mind—perhaps the tale itself came from her.

So although Moore does not appear to have influenced Burns to any noticeable extent, we must be grateful that this literary friendship prompted Burns to write his long, rambling autobiographical letter, surely one of the most important Burns documents in existence.

The letters which Burns exchanged with Frances Anna Wallace Dunlop (1730-1815) form the largest collection extant. Originally preserved at Lochryan, both sides of the correspondence are now at the Morgan Library in New York. Mrs Dunlop first wrote to Burns shortly after the publication of the Kilmarnock edition, ordering a half-dozen copies. The poet held Mrs Dunlop in high esteem, and certainly enjoyed her company—for instance after spending four days as her guest in December 1792, he wrote that these were 'four of the pleasantest I ever enjoyed'. But Mrs Dunlop was an elderly widow with a grown family, and was inclined to look upon Burns as a wayward son who needed constant reminders to be on his best behaviour, reminders mixed with pious exhortation. This motherly feeling was perhaps increased owing to the fact that Mrs Dunlop was estranged from her eldest surviving son, who was married to Eglintoune Maxwell, sister to the Duchess of Gordon. So, fond though he may have been of her, Burns no doubt found her letters something of a bore. One is constantly struck by the unequal length of the letters: to Mrs Dunlop's three-, four-, five-, and even eight-page missives, Burns frequently sent off a one-page reply, scrawled in haste, and promising a long letter soon, which was never written. This is not to suggest that only the poet's letters are interesting: Mrs Dunlop was a highly intelligent woman; her letters are full of politics, literature, gossip, and fascinating details about day-to-day life. Nor are Burns's letters to her all short notes; one of the finest letters he wrote was to his friend and patron on New Year's Day 1789.

A good deal of what Burns had to say to Mrs Dunlop concerned politics. He felt that he could share his innermost thoughts with her; for instance he wrote more openly to her of his true feelings about the French Revolution than he did to any other correspondent. It was, in fact, this unguardedness which led him to dismiss the guillotining of Louis XVI and Marie-Antoinette as 'the delivering over a perjured Blockhead & an unprincipled Prostitute to the hands of the hangman'.[24] This was more than friendship could bear, and an estrangement clouded the last eighteen months of the poet's life. It should be said that four of Mrs Dunlop's sons served in the army and two of her daughters had married French Royalists.

More interesting to the student of literature are Burns's comments on what he is reading and on his poems, copies of which he frequently enclosed. He sent her the first recorded copy of 'Auld Lang Syne' on 7 December, 1788, with the enigmatic comment, 'Light be the turf on the breast of the heaven-inspired Poet who composed this glorious Fragment!'[25] It is generally accepted that Burns reworked the 'fragment', although how much of the song is his own is far from clear. He also sent her the first recorded copy of 'Tam o' Shanter' although it seems likely that Captain Francis Grose was sent an earlier MS. Among other great poems the poet sent to his friend are 'Scots wha hae', the 'Lament of Mary Queen of Scots' and 'Flow gently sweet Afton'.

Burns's letters to George Thomson (1757-1851) form the second great collection. In 1792 Thomson began collecting material for *A Select Collection of Original Scotish Airs*, and enlisted Burns's aid in the task, offering to pay him 'any reasonable price' for his contributions. Thomson's request was that Burns should remake old songs and add new ones to airs which had no words, or for which the words were, in Thomson's phrase, 'absolutely indecent'. It should be recalled that Burns had, since 1787, been sending new and rewritten songs to James Johnson for his *Scots Musical Museum*; in fact Burns was, to all intents, editor of the work. But Johnson's work was unpretentious, whereas Thomson spoke of an elegant collection—historically we recognize that the *Scots Musical Museum* is by far the more significant work.

With his characteristic enthusiasm Burns promised Thomson as many songs as he should need, provided that the words were Scots. 'If you are for *English* verses,' he wrote, 'there is, on my part, an end of the matter.'[26] Nor would he hear of accepting money, saying that his songs were 'either *above*, or *below* price'. Thomson was not the one to pass up a good thing, and, apart from a few trifling gifts, Burns only once received any payment for the songs he sent.

The Burns–Thomson correspondence was first published in the fourth volume of Currie's edition of Burns in 1800. Thomson got his letters back from the poet's widow shortly after Burns's death, and by the time Currie was putting together the edition of Burns's works, he had to rely on Thomson for Burns's letters to him, and for copies of his letters to Burns. Now Thomson was a vain man, and after Burns's death he wished to appear in the best possible light, so he made a selection of his own letters and heavily scored through passages in Burns's which would reflect poorly upon him. He later claimed that he had destroyed the copies of his own letters; it seems probable that he also destroyed some of Burns's. Otherwise how would we explain the fact that we have in August 1793 seven letters, some of several pages, five in September, then one on 29 October, one some time in December, and the next some time in May 1794, and this at a time when Burns was sending many songs to Thomson—in one letter he discusses seventy-four songs with the editor. To be at this pitch of creativity and then to write one letter in six months, followed by one or more letters a month, is just not believable. Internally, too, there is strong evidence that there were other letters—letters which, no doubt, Thomson did not wish to see published.

Time has not been kind to Thomson, and the ink which he used to score out passages in Burns's letters has faded unequally with the ink used by Burns, so that we can now make out almost all of these cancelled passages. Many of them refer to Johnson's *Scots Musical Museum*, a publication of which Thomson was apparently jealous. One example will suffice. On 19 October 1794, Burns wrote to Thomson as follows:[27]

My dear Friend,
By this morning's post I have your list, & in general, I highly approve of it.—I shall, at more leisure, give you a critique on the whole: in the meantime, let me offer you a new improvement, or rather, restoring old simplicity, in one of your newly adopted songs.—

O when she cam ben she bobbit, (a crochet stop here)
                                        —[Burns's comment]
O when she cam ben she bottit; (a crochet stop)
And when she cam ben, she kist Cockpen,
And syne denied that she did it.—(a crochet stop)

24

This is the old rhythm, & by far the most original & beautiful.—
Let the harmony of the bass, at the stops, be full; & thin & dropping through the rest of the air; & you will give the tune a noble &
striking effect.—Perhaps I am betraying my ignorance; but
Mr. Clarke is decidedly of my opinion.—He goes to your
town. . . .

The interesting point in this passage, it seems to me, is that it shows
Burns to have possessed a not inconsiderable knowledge of music,
although he modestly deferred to Thomson in the field. The latter
apparently felt he would look better with such passages altered, so that
we find it appearing thus:

By this morning's post I have your list, and, in general, I highly
approve of it. I shall, at more leisure, give you a critique on the
whole. Clarke goes to your town. . . .

Other passages show Thomson tampering with the texts Burns had
sent him. The most outrageous example of Thomson's meddling
concerns 'Scots wha hae' which Burns first sent him about 30 August
1793. In its first form the final line of each stanza was short:

> Scots, wha hae wi' WALLACE bled,
> Scots, wham BRUCE has aften led,
> Welcome to your gory bed,—
>   Or to victorie.—

The final lines of the five subsequent stanzas are:

> 2 Chains & Slaverie.—
> 3 —Let him turn & flie:—
> 4 Let him follow me.—
> 5 But they *shall* be free!
> 6 Let us DO—or DIE!!!

Thomson's answer, which he dated 5 September in his copy to Currie,
speaks of Burns as sending 'verses that even Shakespeare might be
proud to own'.[28] He did not like the tune Burns had proposed ('Hay,
tuttie taitie') and proposed instead 'Lewie Gordon'. He also added:[29]

Now, the variation that I have to suggest upon the last line of each
verse (the only line too short for the air) is as follows:—

> Verse 1 Or to [*glorious*] victory.
>   2 Chains [*chains*] and slavery.
>   3 Let him [*let him*] turn and flee.

4 Let him [*bravely*] follow me.
5 But they shall [*they shall*] be free.
6 Let us [*let us*] do or die.

If you connect each line with its own verse, I do not think you will find that either the sentiment or the expression loses any of its energy.

The only line which I dislike in the whole of the song is 'Welcome to your gory bed!' Would not another word be preferable to 'welcome'?

To this Burns answered, in a letter postmarked 3 September 1793:[30]

I am happy, my dear Sir, that my Ode pleases you so much.— Your idea, 'honor's bed,' is, though a beautiful, a hacknied idea; so, if you please, we will let the line stand as it is. I have altered the song as follows—

Burns then copied out the poem once more with the following changes:

1 Or to glorious victorie
2 Edward, Chains & Slaverie!
3 Traitor! Coward! turn & flie!
4 Caledonian! on wi' me!
5 But they shall be—shall be free!
6 Forward! Let us Do, or Die!!!

The date of this letter is puzzling, for the poet is here answering on 3 September a letter which Thomson did not write until 5 September. We can only assume that Thomson, either through a slip or for some unknown reason, misdated the copy of his letter which he supplied to Currie. The sequence of the exchange can, of course, be doubted.

Thomson's reply, dated 12 September, is as follows:[31]

One word with regard to your heroic ode. I think, with great deference to the poet, that a prudent general would avoid saying anything to his soldiers which might tend to make death more frightful than it is. 'Gory' presents a disagreeable image to the mind; and to tell them 'Welcome to your gory bed,' seems rather a discouraging address, notwithstanding the alternative which follows. I have shewn the song to three friends of excellent taste, and each of them objected to this line, which emboldens me to use the freedom of bringing it again under your notice, I would suggest:—

> Now prepare for honour's bed
> Or for glorious victory!

Exasperated, Burns came back with a near ultimatum: use the song the way he wanted it, or omit it from the collection:[32]

'Who shall decide when Doctors disagree?'—My Ode pleases me so much that I cannot alter it.—Your proposed alterations would, in my opinion, make it tame.—I am exceedingly obliged to you for putting me on reconsidering it; as I think I have much improved it.—Instead of 'Soger! hero!' I will have it to be—'Caledonian! On wi' me!'—I have scrutinized it over & over; & to the world, some way or other, it shall go as it is.—At the same time, it will not in the least hurt me, tho' you leave the song out altogether, & adhere to your first idea of adopting Logan's verses.—

Several months later Burns put it bluntly to Thomson, 'Pray are you going to insert "Bannockburn," . . . in your Collection? If you are not, let me know; as in that case I will give . . . [it] to Johnson's Museum.'[33]

Reading the exchanges, it becomes evident that Thomson 'edited' the copies of his letters which he sent to Currie; nowhere, for example, do we see him mention the 'Soger! hero!' to which Burns objected. Burns apparently sent the song to Johnson, where it appeared in Vol. 6 of the *Scots Musical Museum* in 1803, set to a ballad tune by William Clarke.[34] Thomson, who first published it in 1799, used 'Lewie Gordon' as the air. When James Currie published his *Works of Robert Burns* in 1800 the public became aware of the disagreement between Burns and Thomson and, according to James C. Dick, the public 'demanded that the original words should be printed with its own tune',[35] so in a subsequent volume of his *Select Collection* (1801) Thomson reverted to the original words to the tune 'Hey tuttie, taitie'. Never one to admit gracefully that he had been wrong, Thomson prefixed the words with this note: 'The Poet originally intended this noble strain for the Air . . . but, on a suggestion from the Editor . . . who then thought "Lewie Gordon" a fitter tune for the words, they were united . . . . The Editor, however, having since examined the Air "Hey tuttie, taitie" with more particular attention, frankly owns that he has changed his opinion. . . .' And so at last this great song of Burns's was joined with the tune which the poet had so unerringly chosen for it.

So that I do not appear unduly prejudiced against Thomson, it should be pointed out that both Haydn and Beethoven, who were enlisted to arrange music for this collection, had difficulties with the editor, who felt that he could improve on their settings. At one point Thomson requested changes in Beethoven's melodies, whereupon the composer replied on 19 February 1813 (the original letter is in French).

I am put out that I have not been able to comply with your wish. I am not used to retouching my compositions; I have never done this, as I am convinced of the truth that any partial change alters the character of the composition.

Incidentally, it is perhaps as well that Burns agreed to produce songs for Thomson free of charge, because Beethoven also had financial difficulties with his Scottish editor. For example, on 29 February 1812, he complained to Thomson that, whereas he was being paid only three ducats per song, Haydn had personally assured him that he was receiving four. He added, 'As for Mr. Kozeluch who delivers you each song with accompaniment for two ducats, I compliment you and the English and Scottish editors when they have seen them.' Thomson did, in fact, send £5 to Burns on 1 July 1793, with the comment:

As I shall be benefited by the publication, you must suffer me to enclose a small mark of my gratitude, and to repeat it afterwards when I find it convenient. Do not return it for, by Heavens! if you do, our correspondence is at an end.

Scott Douglas aptly suggests in a footnote to the letter that Thomson probably added the last sentence *ex post facto*.[36] The poet's reply was characteristic of his pride and at the same time shows us how deeply concerned he was that this should really be a labour of love—'either *above*, or *below* price' as he had said.[37]

I assure you, my dear Sir, that you truly hurt me with your pecuniary parcel.—It degrades me in my own eyes.—However, to return it would savour of bombast affectation; But, as to any more traffic of that Dr & Cr kind, I swear, by the HONOUR which crowns the upright Statue of ROBT BURNS'S INTEGRITY!—On the least motion of it, I will indignantly spurn the by-past transaction, & from that moment commence entire Stranger to you!—BURNS'S character for Generosity of Sentiment, & Independance [*sic*] of Mind, will, I trust, long outlive any of his wants which the cold, unfeeling, dirty Ore can supply: at least, I shall take care that such a Character he shall deserve.—

Thomson sent no more money. We can imagine the anguish it cost Burns to write Thomson on 12 July 1796, a few days before his death, 'After all my boasted independance [sic], curst necessity compels me to implore you for five pounds.—' The MS. is docketed in Thomson's hand, for Currie's use, 'This idea is exaggerated—he could not have been in any such danger at Dumfries [Burns had written that he was threatened with jail over a debt] nor could he be in such necessity to implore aid from *Edinr.*'[38]

The Burns–Thomson exchange did one thing for the poet—it made him re-examine some of his work more critically and thus helped him to become even more master of his art. Johnson allowed Burns a completely free rein in the *Scots Musical Museum*; Thomson sometimes forced Burns to better a song. Unfortunately most of Thomson's collection appeared after the poet's death, and, in fitting words to tunes, Thomson paid little attention to Burns's instructions. It should be noted here that he always wrote a song with a particular tune in mind, which he even noted on the MS. In an often-quoted passage, Burns told Thomson how he wrote songs:[39]

> untill I am compleat [sic] master of a tune, in my own singing, (such as it is) I never can compose for it.—My way is: I consider the poetic Sentiment, correspondent to my idea of the musical expression; then chuse my theme; begin one Stanza; when that is composed, which is generally the most difficult part of the business, I walk out, sit down now & then, look out for objects in Nature around me that are in unison or harmony with the cogitations of my fancy & workings of my bosom; humming every now & then the air with the verses I have framed: when I feel my Muse beginning to jade, I retire to the solitary fireside of my study, & there commit my effusions to paper; swinging, at intervals, on the hind-legs of my elbow-chair, by way of calling forth my own critical strictures, as my pen goes on.—

The letter from which this excerpt was taken contains the poet's comments on seventy-four songs; it affords us one of several opportunities to assess Burns's meticulousness in collecting and rewriting the traditional songs of Scotland, and at the same time to appreciate the breadth of the poet's knowledge about his country's songs and music. Considered as a whole, the letters Burns wrote to Thomson form the most important single collection in existence; their value is only slightly marred by the pretty obvious tempering of Thomson in the versions he claimed to have sent to the poet.

James Johnson (d. 1811), to whom Burns wrote twenty-one letters which survive, was a much more obscure figure than Thomson. He was by trade an engraver and music-seller, and began publication of his *Scots Musical Museum* in 1787. The work on Vol. 1 was probably well advanced before Burns met him, for the poet contributed only three songs to it; subsequently Burns was virtually the editor, contributing some 200 songs to the remaining five volumes. Neither Johnson nor Thomson paid Burns for his contributions, and as we have seen Burns did not want payment. Although, as was mentioned, Thomson's *Select Collection* was a much more prestigious publication, within himself Burns knew that the *Museum* was a far more important work. A few weeks before his death he wrote to Johnson:[40]

> Your work is a great one; & though, now that it is near finished, I see if we were to begin again, two or three things that might be mended, yet I will venture to prophesy, that to future ages your Publication will be the text-book & standard of Scotish Song & Music.—

Burns never wrote anything like that to Thomson. Nearly 200 years later this is still the greatest single collection of Scottish songs with music.

This complete frankness on the part of Burns is what makes these letters to Johnson more human in a way than are those to his other musical editor. We always sense a certain wariness on the poet's part when he is addressing himself to Thomson. With Johnson he could be quite uninhibited; there was not the barrier of position and money to stand between them.

When he was about to leave Edinburgh in May 1787, Burns wrote Johnson, regretting that they had not come to know each other better, for, he added, 'I have met wt few people whose company & conversation gave me so much pleasure, because I have met wt few whose sentiments are so congenial to my own.—'[41] They obviously met again, for in his last letter, quoted above, Burns wrote: 'Many a merry meeting this Publication has given us.'

Johnson apparently kept a look-out for song books which he passed on to Burns. On 28 [July?] 1788, the poet says he hopes to get 'some fine tunes from among the Collection of Highland airs which I got from you'.[42] In another letter he inquired if Johnson had any other tunes to send him.[43] About October 1792, he asked Johnson to have a copy of the *Museum* (by this time four of the six volumes had been published) interleaved and bound up as he had had done for Robert Riddell, so that he could 'insert every anecdote I can learn, together with my own criticisms and remarks on the songs', adding, 'A copy of this kind I shall leave with you, the Editor, to publish at some after period, by way of making the Museum a book famous to the end of time, and you renowned for ever.'[44]

The best thing that can be said of this friendship is that Johnson made no attempt ever to have his way over Burns in matters of songs, or the music to which they were to be set. At one point the poet exclaimed, 'I have sent you a list that I approve of, but I beg & insist that you will never allow my opinion to overrule yours.'[45] Johnson must have recognized, however, that Burns's genius was the surest guide, and published the songs which Burns had written or collected just as the poet sent them to him. In this he differed, of course, from Thomson; it is his use of Burns's text as it was sent which makes the *Museum* a more reliable source than the *Select Collection*.

The third largest group of letters from Burns are those he wrote, mostly under the pen name of Sylvander, to Nancy M'Lehose, who used the name Clarinda. Burns met her in Edinburgh in December 1787, where she was living under the patronage of her cousin, Lord Craig, after unsuccessfully trying to make a go of life with her wastrel husband. It was love at first sight on both sides, with Clarinda trying to dampen the poet's ardour. For a while they exchanged daily letters— at the height of the infatuation four letters passed between them in twenty-four hours. Apart from a bit of Edinburgh gossip, we gain little from those letters; in fact they are somewhat of an embarrassment to serious Burns scholars. The late Professor Ferguson has called the Edinburgh relationship a 'hot-house atmosphere' and he was right. Almost immediately after leaving Edinburgh we find the poet's letters dropping off so completely that it was a year before he wrote her. In 1791 there was a brief flurry of letters from Burns, but by this time he was safely married and settled into his Excise position in Dumfries. One letter stands out above all the rest: written on 27 December 1791, it consists of a short paragraph and three songs: 'Behold the hour, the boat arrive', an undistinguished song; 'Thou gloomy December' which opens with the lines

> Ance mair I hail thee, thou gloomy December!
> Ance mair I hail thee wi' sorrow and care!
> Sad was the parting thou makes me remember:
> Parting wi' Nancy, O, ne'er to meet mair!

The third song was also written for Clarinda, and is one of the greatest
love songs in the language—'Ae fond kiss', with its superb lines:

> Had we never lov'd sae kindly,
> Had we never lov'd sae blindly!
> Never met—or never parted,
> We had ne'er been broken-hearted.—

But these lines were written after Burns realized that nothing could
ever come of his feelings for Clarinda; with great art he avoided over-
stepping the bounds of nostalgia into maudlin sentimentality. How
time and distance had enabled Burns to shape his feelings can be judged
by reading Burns's letter of 12 January 1788:[46]

> You talk of weeping, Clarinda: some involuntary drops wet your
> lines as I read them. Offend me, my dearest angel! You cannot
> offend me—you never offended me. If you had ever given me the
> least shadow of offence, so pardon me my God as I forgive
> Clarinda. I have read yours again; it has blotted my paper . . . .
> Forgive, my dearest Clarinda, my unguarded expressions. For
> Heaven's sake, forgive me, or I shall never be able to bear my own
> mind.

The impression one gathers in reading this correspondence is that the
poet struck a pose; as Burns himself wrote to Agnes M'Lehose, 'I like
the idea of Arcadian names in a commerce of this kind'.[47] And this is
what the entire relationship was: an imaginary pastoral, insubstantial
and unreal, the stuff of dreams.

Another woman to whom Burns wrote quite frequently (twenty-
three letters) was Maria Riddell (1772-1808) who was the sister-in-law
of Robert Riddell, for whom Burns prepared the Glenriddell MSS.
Maria was a woman of taste and charm and, until he was banished by
both Riddell families for some drunken misbehaviour of which we have
no details, she exerted a considerable influence on him. Unfortunately,
Maria's letters to Burns do not appear to have survived—she requested
their return after the poet's death.

The earliest correspondence we have between Maria and Burns is
probably of February 1792, at which time they were apparently
already on quite friendly terms. An interesting early note on vaccina-
tion is found in Burns's question, 'has little Mademoiselle been
innoculated with the Small-pox yet? If not let it be done as soon as it is
proper for the habit of body, teeth, &c.'[48] In playful mood Burns wrote

to tell her that he had managed to obtain for her (he was an Excise officer, remember) a pair of French gloves which she coveted but was unable to get: 'You must know that French gloves are contraband goods, and expressly forbidden by the laws of this wisely-governed realm of ours.'[49]

At times Burns appears almost jealous of Maria; there certainly was a flirtation between them if nothing more serious. A falling out over Burns's outrageous behaviour occurred late in 1793 or early in 1794, and led Burns at one point to address her in the third person and even to write one of the most unworthy pieces he ever composed, 'Pinned to Mrs R——'s carriage':

> If you rattle along like your Mistress's tongue,
>   Your speed will outrival the dart:
> But, a fly for your load, you'll break down on the road,
>   If your stuff be as rotten's her heart.——

One can only hope that Maria never saw such an unworthy product of the poet's pen; in any case, by about March 1795 the friendship was resuming its earlier cordiality; later that spring the poet sent a miniature of himself for Mrs Riddell to inspect, and some months later she sent him some poetry of hers to peruse. Immediately after the poet's death Maria published a memoir of her friend which T. F. Henderson has called 'the best thing written of him by [a] contemporary critic'.[50]

These then are the major collections of letters by Burns which survive. His letters to his superiors and patrons are neither more nor less fawning than those of any other petty employee of the century. These letters could be roughly classified as official correspondence and dismissed.

A less extensive series of letters, which are, however, most interesting, are those from Burns to Peter Hill (1754-1837), a man whom Burns had met as a clerk in Creech's bookshop, and who later went into business for himself as a bookseller. Burns's letters to him give us a good idea of the works the poet wanted to read. In a letter of March 1790, for instance, he ordered for the local library which Robert Riddell supported the following items:[51]

The Mirror—The Lounger—Man of feeling—Man of the world (these for my own sake I wish to have by the first Carrier) Knox's history of the Reformation—Rae's history of the Rebellion 1715— Any good history of the Rebellion 1745—A display of the Secession Act & Testimony by Mr. Gibb—Hervey's Meditations— Beveridge's thoughts—& another copy of Watson's body of Divinity.

At the same time he asked Hill to send him for his own use[52]

> second-handed or any way cheap copies of Otway's dramatic works, Ben Johnson's [sic], Dryden's, Congreve's, Wycherly's [sic], Vanbrugh's, Cibber's, or any Dramatic works of the more Moderns, Macklin, Garrick, Foote, Colman, or Sherridan's.— A good Copy too of Moliere in French I much want.— Any other good Dramatic Authors in their native language I want them; I mean Comic Authors chiefly, tho' I should wish Racine, Corneille, & Voltaire too.—

Even more interesting are the letters to his friends, some a little above him, some a little below him on the social scale. To those people, as to no one else, Burns could write as he really thought; they could neither give him anything nor take anything from him, so there was no need to write painfully correct letters. Nevertheless, these letters are almost always in English rather than Scots. To one or two intimate friends he occasionally wrote in the vernacular; among these was William Nicol. The best of these letters came to the High School master from Carlisle during his Border tour:[53]

> Kind, honest-hearted Willie,
> I'm sitten down here, after seven and forty miles ridin, e'en as forjesket and forniaw'd as a for foughten cock, to gie you some notion o' my landlowper-like stravaguin sin the sorrowfu' hour that I sheuk hands and parted wi' auld Reekie.—
>
> . . .
>
> I hae dander'd owre a' the kintra frae Dumbar [sic] to Selcraig, and hae forgather'd wi' monie a guid fallow, and monie a weel-far'd hizzie.—I met wi' twa dink quines in particlar, ane o' them a sonsie, fine fodgel lass, baith braw and bonie; the tither was a clean-shankit, straught, tight, weel-far'd winch, as blythe's a lintwhite on a flowerie thorn, and as sweet and modest's a new blawn plumrose in a hazle shaw.—
>
> . . .
>
> I was gaun to write you a lang pystle, but, Gude forgie me, I gat myself sae notouriously bitchify'd the day after kail-time that I can hardly stoiter but and ben.—
>
> . . .
>
> I'll be in Dumfries the morn gif the beast be to the fore and the branks bide hale.—
>> Gude be wi' you, Willie! Amen—
>> ROBT BURNS

34

It may be that the Bard was a wee bit fou', but in his cups or not he had an unsurpassed command of the vernacular.

Among other correspondents to whom there are a dozen or so surviving letters is Alexander Cunningham (d. 1812), a Writer to the Signet and friend of his Edinburgh days, who played a leading role in promoting a subscription for Burns's family. Of the 'great folk' we can single out James Cunningham, fourteenth Earl of Glencairn (1749-91), an early patron of Burns, whose death removed a man who had managed to help without offending. For him Burns wrote his fine 'Lament for James Earl of Glencairn'. There was also Robert Graham, twelfth Laird of Fintry (1749-1815), who, as Commissioner of the Scottish Board of Excise, secured the poet's appointment to the Excise. It was to him that Burns turned when he was informed that his conduct with respect to his political views was being investigated. In a letter dated 31 December 1792, Burns implored Graham, on behalf of his family, more than for his own sake, to spare him from dismissal. It is an embarrassing letter to read even at this distance in time; Burns was obviously distraught at the prospect that he could be almost summarily dismissed, and humbled himself to avert disaster. In a letter written five days later he denied point by point the allegations that he was 'disaffected', and we have no doubt he was telling the truth. Certainly Burns was sympathetic to the ideas of parliamentary reform and Republicanism (little distinction was made between the two at this time) and he was dissatisfied with the government, not as conceived but as it at that time functioned. Put succinctly, Burns was not disloyal; he was imprudent.

What sort of man, then, emerges from the letters? Those to his patrons and men whom he considered well above himself are certainly the least human, couched, as they are, in the formal language of proper letter-writing so admired and copied in that period. Beneath the formal style, however, one can detect a man who is not without a sense of his own dignity, a pride which would not let him stoop to servility. He lived at a time when the humble-born could expect nothing except through patronage, and so he asked help of those he respected. His letter to the Earl of Glencairn of February 1788 requesting the earl to secure him an Excise post is a good example of Burns's style. He finishes the letter: 'I am ill-qualified to dog the heels of Greatness with the impertinence of Solicitation, and tremble nearly as much at the idea of the cold promise as the cold denial.'[54] The poet had sized up his man, and the post was secured without Burns having to humble himself.

To his friends, and occasionally, as to Thomson once or twice, we have the real Burns emerging. He was one of the great conversationalists of his age, and to intimates his letters were an extension of this talent. He was generous, sometimes to a fault, but he was also canny, as every tenant farmer had to be to survive. He had an inexhaustible love and tenderness for his children—legitimate and 'love-begotten' alike. He was only mildly radical in his political views, although he is frequently quoted out of context to try to place him in a posture he would never have adopted. Above all he was witty and earthy; he made no secret to his friends of his interest in bawdy poetry. To reject this is to deny part of what made him a great humorous poet and a great love poet.

Finally there is something intangible which attracts us to Robert Burns. 'Who touches this book, touches a man', Walt Whitman said of his *Leaves of Grass*, and this is the feeling we take away with us after reading Burns's letters. Across the centuries a living presence reaches out and touches our hearts with wonder that this simple man could find so much beauty in his harsh world.

Notes

1 *Robert Burns's Commonplace Book, 1783-1785*, ed. James Cameron Ewing and Davidson Cook (Glasgow, 1938), p. 3. Of the several editions of the *Commonplace Book* this is the only completely accurate one, consisting of a printed transcript of the MS. as well as a facsimile of the original. It was reissued in 1965. Henceforth cited as *Commonplace Book, 1783*.

2 *Commonplace Book, 1783*, p. 1.

3 *Ibid.*, pp. 11-12.

4 *Ibid.*, pp. 15-16.

5 *Ibid.*, p. 18.

6 *The Poetry of Robert Burns*, ed. W. E. Henley and T. F. Henderson, 4 vols (Edinburgh, 1896-7), I, p. 375.

7 *Commonplace Book, 1783*, p. 36.

8 William Jack published the prose sections of this Commonplace Book in *Macmillan's Magazine* from March to July 1879 (Vols 39, 40). Annotations have been taken from this source, but the page numbers will be those of the MS.

9 See Burns's letter to Mrs Dunlop of 25 March 1789.

10 'The Journal of the Border Tour', ed. De Lancey Ferguson, in *Robert Burns His Associates and Contemporaries*, ed. Robert T. Fitzhugh (Chapel Hill, 1943), pp. 108-22. This is the only reliable edition of the journal. Subsequent references will be to date of entry only.

11 *Journal of a Tour in the Highlands made in the Year 1787*, ed. J. C. Ewing (London & Glasgow, 1927). This edition combines a printed transcription of the journal and a facsimile of the MS. References will be to date of entry.

12 *The Letters of Robert Burns*, ed. J. De Lancey Ferguson, 2 vols (Oxford, 1931), I, p. 124. Henceforth cited as *Letters*. The letter in question is of 13 September 1787.

13 *Letters*, I, p. 126.

14 The bracketed part is not with the MS. There was apparently an expanded version (location not now known) which was first used by Lockhart in 1828. The present text is from the printed portion of Ewing's edition of the journal.

15 *Letters*, II, p. 222.

16 See my review of *The Merry Muses*, ed. G. Legman, in *Studies in Scottish Literature*, II (April 1965), pp. 267-70.

17 *Letters*, I, p. 360.

18 *Ibid.*, p. 109.

19 *Ibid.*, pp. 106-7.

20 *Ibid.*, p. 111.

21 *Ibid.*, p. 112.

22 *Ibid.*, p. 113.

23 *Ibid.*, p. 106.

24 *Letters*, II, p. 281.

25 *Letters*, I, p. 280.

26 *Letters*, II, p. 122.

27 *Ibid.*, pp. 264-5.

28 *The Works of Robert Burns*, ed. William Scott Douglas, 6 vols (Edinburgh, 1877-9), VI, p. 283. Henceforth cited as Scott Douglas.

29 Scott Douglas, VI, pp. 283-4. The words added by Thomson are bracketed and italicized.

30 *Letters*, II, pp. 196-7.

31 Scott Douglas, VI, p. 286.

32 *Letters*, II, pp. 206-7.

33 *Ibid.*, p. 252.

34 See William Stenhouse's note in *The Scots Musical Museum*, ed. James Johnson, 4 vols (Edinburgh, 1853), pp. 493-6.

35 James C. Dick, *The Songs of Robert Burns* (London, 1903), p. 449.

36 Scott Douglas, VI, p. 254.

37 *Letters*, II, p. 181.

38 *Ibid.*, p. 329.

39 *Ibid.*, pp. 200-1.

40 *Ibid.*, p. 322.

41 *Letters*, I, p. 89.

42 *Ibid.*, p. 239.

43 *Ibid.*, p. 275.

44 *Letters*, II, p. 129.

45 *Letters*, I, p. 325.

46 *Ibid.*, p. 162.

47 *Ibid.*, p. 149.

48 *Letters*, II, p. 111.

49 *Letters*, II, p. 173.
50 Henley and Henderson, *op. cit.*, II, p. 421.
51 *Letters*, II, p. 15.
52 *Ibid.*, p. 15.
53 *Letters*, I, pp. 94-5.
54 *Ibid.*, p. 178.

Chapter 2

Burns's Poems and their Audience

Ian Campbell

Robert Burns announced himself to the world as a rustic genius. In the preface to the 'Kilmarnock Burns', he begged his readers, 'particularly the Learned and the Polite, who may honor him with a perusal, that they will make every allowance for Education and Circumstances of Life'. The learned and the polite took him at his word, and the tradition of the noble peasant Burns has grown from that day to this. Recent criticism has balked at this oversimplification; critics like David Daiches and Tom Crawford have pointed out Burns's learning, his reading, his very subtle understanding of society, of human nature, of the relationship between words and music, between folk-tales and the acceptable literary forms of his time. Burns emerges from his letters a man fully conscious of his very considerable gifts and learning, yet fully aware of the limitations his environment and station in society placed on the full development of these powers. The critical exploration of a poem like 'Tam o' Shanter' is a fine process of disentangling the genuinely naïve from the subtle and well-engineered manipulation of the reader's response, the rhetorical (in the technical sense) from the *simpliste* or merely inspired.

Burns's visit to Edinburgh was the great testing-point of the image of the humble but heaven-taught peasant which he wished to present to the world. His poems were published, they had achieved a modest success, Henry Mackenzie had been captivated by them and in the *Lounger* he had given them a lengthy notice which put their commercial success beyond doubt. At this point the author emerged from western obscurity, and made a public appearance under eastern eyes. It was November 1786. Edinburgh was prepared to be charmed by Burns, and it was. His social career was hectic, as he wryly noted to Gavin Hamilton. 'By all probability I shall soon be the tenth Worthy, and the eighth Wise Man, of the world.'[1] His acquaintance ranged through all parts of Edinburgh, including not only those eminent in literature (such as Dugald Stewart and Dr Blacklock) but also those socially eminent. His behaviour and deportment were universally admired.[2]

His manners were then, as they continued ever afterwards, simple, manly, and independent; strongly expressive of conscious genius

39

and worth; but without anything that indicated forwardness, arrogance, or vanity. He took his share in conversation, but not more than belonged to him; and listened with apparent attention and deference, on subjects where his want of education deprived him of the means of information.

This behaviour delighted his Edinburgh hosts, for to many it seemed that he not only wrote as one conscious of his social station, and not trying to break out of it, but also that he had sufficient 'natural breeding' in real life to keep within his social station while being lionized. Yet it is here that a closer look at this familiar tale may reveal a useful critical point. Dugald Stewart, even while describing Burns's well-judged social behaviour, did quibble that 'If there had been a little more of gentleness and accommodation in his temper, he would, I think, have been still more interesting'.[3] Burns, it is very clear from the descriptions of him which were made at the time of this Edinburgh visit, lost not a bit of his reserve or self-sufficiency under the glare of publicity, or the pressure of city life. He went there self-possessed, and to a large extent self-made, and he remained thus through it all. Walter Scott, only sixteen, noticed 'a strong expression of sense and shrewdness in all his lineaments'.[4] Dugald Stewart opined that although 'the attentions he received during his stay in town from all ranks and descriptions of persons, were such as would have turned any head but his own', Burns survived unscathed. 'He retained the same simplicity of manners and appearance which had struck me so forcibly when I first saw him in the country.'[5]

There is an ironical appearance to these descriptions now. The literati were pleased to see how little difference their city had made to the rustic genius. Burns's place, after all, was in their eyes to remain in the country, and there to produce more poems of the same general kind, although tempered in their excess by the literary advice of Edinburgh critics. Burns's respectful bearing, his power of remaining untouched by the experience of city life, were hopeful signs. Yet the modern reader, with the advantage of hindsight, sees these things in a different light. The modern reader is helped too by Burns's correspondence, which shows how little overawed he was by the company of literati and social eminences he met in Edinburgh. Commonplace romantic stories tell how he moved from mingling with the great and famous to the company of some disreputable lover, but the real point of his social mobility is not to emphasize Burns the Great Lover, but to show how intensely self-possessed he was. Edinburgh affected him with excitement, with understandable pride at being lionized for his talents, but it did not shine before him as any promised land. The low literary quality of 'Edina, Scotia's Darling Seat' is some indication of this. Others might be quoted from his correspondence. Even while still there, on his first visit, he wrote home clear-sightedly.[6]

> Novelty may attract the attention of mankind a while; to it I owe my present eclat: but I see the time not distant far when the popular tide which has borne me to a height of which I am perhaps unworthy shall recede with a silent celerity and leave me a barren waste of sand, to descend at my leisure to my former station. —I do not say this in the affectation of modesty; I see the consequence is unavoidable and am prepared for it.—I had been at a good deal of pains to form a just, impartial estimate of my intellectual Powers before I came here; I have not added, since I came to Edr, any thing to the account; and I trust, I shall take every atom of it back to my shades, the coverts of my un-noticed, early years.

So little was he bowled over by Edinburgh life, which he was later to describe as 'houses building, bucks strutting, ladies flaring, blackguards sculking, whores leering, &c. in the old way'.[7] To Mrs Dunlop he was very scathing, too, in writing of the 'pomp of Princes street',[8] and the ridiculous pride of many he saw there. Although he met many people in Edinburgh whose friendship he admired and appreciated: 'I am afraid my numerous Edin[r] friendships are of so tender a construction that they will not bear carriage with me.'[9] No, Burns kept his head in Edinburgh. 'In reality,' he wrote, 'I have no great temptation to be intoxicated with the cup of Prosperity.'[10] When he got back to Mauchline, he felt an initial depression very understandable after the excitement of Edinburgh, aggravated, as he told William Nicol, by 'the stateliness of the Patricians in Edin[r], and the servility of my plebeian brethren, who perhaps formerly eyed me askance, since I returned home'.[11] Burns was genuinely hurt, as the letters show, to find that he might be no longer part of the community from which he had produced the poems which made him famous.

Burns's early story is a familiar one; he was well known all round his part of Ayrshire for his powers of speech, his conviviality (which led to the Tarbolton Bachelors), a great popularity in Masonic circles which opened doors to him (even among the Canongate masons, in Edinburgh), his strenuous social and amorous pursuits, his activities as a local poet and punster whose reputation spread out from local beginnings to national recognition. Burns was very firmly rooted in his locality, and criticism of his work must take continuous account of this fact, or poems like 'Holy Willie's Prayer' and 'Tam o' Shanter' lose enormously. To remove to Edinburgh was to gain experience, to receive just critical acclaim for work done in Ayrshire. He was not to settle in Edinburgh, but to enjoy himself and return to the scene of his labours. To find himself eyed askance by his friends and equals thus stung as much as the patronage of some of the literati. What is very interesting indeed is to see that he was (in the letter just quoted) quite aware of patronage, which stung him. Yet the literati testify to the fact that he did not show his chagrin, but bore himself with perfect good manners during his stay in Edinburgh. Once again, we come to the point of Burns's self-control and self-possession. It was fitting that, when he felt out of sorts on his return to Dumfriesshire, he should try to console himself with *Paradise Lost*, particularly admiring 'the dauntless magnanimity; the intrepid unyielding independence; the desperate daring, and noble defiance of hardship, in that great personage, Satan'.[12] 'I have very little dependance on mankind', he added later in the same paragraph,[13] and completed the testimony to his own independence of mind.

Along with independence went acute sociability. Burns, in his famous autobiographical letter to Dr John Moore, wrote of his[14]

> strong appetite for sociability, [and] . . . a constitutional hypocondriac taint which made me fly solitude, add to all these incentives to social life, my reputation for bookish knowledge, a certain wild, logical talent, and a strength of thought something like the rudiments of good sense, made me generally a welcome guest; so 'tis no great wonder that always 'where two or three were met together, there was I in the midst of them'.

In short, Burns was the centre of his social community in Ayrshire, a sociable man who loved fun and conviviality. He looked at life, often, from inside such a community, and he had the power of adapting his world-view to the values of that community, without *limiting* it to the values thus expressed. An outstanding example is the opening section of 'Tam o' Shanter', in which the world is seen from the cosy shelter of a convivial group by the inn fireside. The first four lines

> When chapman billies leave the street,
> And drouthy neebors, neebors meet,
> As market-days are wearing late,
> An' folk begin to tak the gate

are purely descriptive of the conditions *leading up to the opening*—the opening itself is in the fifth line,

> While we sit bousing at the nappy,

a line actually descriptive of the conditions in the poem at the time, as they affect Tam. The other things belong to the world outside the social group, and by the time Tam actually ventures into the outside world, in the story of this poem, the day has gone, it is dark, and none of the initial description is of any relevance. What counts is what is going on in Tam's own social circle, and it is this which is introduced in the fifth line. Very significantly, it is introduced with the word 'we'— 'While *we* sit bousing at the nappy'. At once, the audience is drawn in, for it is necessary for the reader to share Tam's world-view in order fully to appreciate his contempt for the world-values outside the howff, and particularly for him to share in the drunken contempt Tam feels for the devil and the witches. Insulated from the full horror (a horror still real to Burns's contemporaries) of witchcraft and wizardry, Tam sees it all through an alcoholic haze, which lasts undisturbed till his drunken

> Weel done, Cutty-sark!

breaks the spell, and simultaneously the witches become aware of his presence as an onlooker, and his drunken stupor gives way to fear, and flight. A dramatic monologue-rendering of 'Tam o' Shanter' would reinforce this interpretation very strongly. Tam is unaware of the danger of the world—

> The storm without might rair and rustle,
> Tam didna mind the storm a whistle.

—not till he sees the witches actually heading for him does he turn in flight, and Burns makes the pace of the remainder of the poem (up to the mock *sententia*) headlong flight, expressive of the real pace of life which replaces the drunken maundering, the half-stultified looking around and noting of lurid detail without actual comprehension. The pace of the poem, in short, is not tied to the real-life situation described, or to real-life events, but to the subject's powers of comprehension: as the subject is drunk, or half-drunk, this means that the poem has to convince the reader to see things at this pace, if he is to share in the re-creation of the story. We know that Burns composed the poem at speed, re-living with delight the action as he embodied it in verse;

the reader is invited to share in this delighted re-creation, and in order to achieve this is invited to see the action through the drunken eyes of Tam, and to share his befuddled incomprehension.

This point is an important one, I believe, in the proper criticism of Burns. We know Burns enjoyed drink—his powers in this field belong to the folklore of Scottish literature—and much of his poetry emerges from the human contact he achieved in the social situation which accompanied this drinking. This does not so much apply to Edinburgh, where Burns was on his best behaviour, at least part of the time, but to the Ayrshire community to which he was proud to belong, and from which he drew his inspiration and poetical strength. The community embraced all orders, holy and unholy, sober and drunken, rich and poor, but we have a good idea from poems such as 'The Twa Dogs', 'Tam o' Shanter' and 'The Holy Fair' what part of the community pleased Burns most. He felt he belonged to it, and his hurt when he returned from Edinburgh and found himself alienated is proof of this.

In a small country like Scotland, the power of the community is not one to be underestimated. In the tenth and eleventh chapters of *The House with the Green Shutters*, George Douglas Brown brilliantly evokes the closed nature of these communities. In this specific example, an outsider, formerly a member of the community, returns to his childhood scenes, and is met by the hostility of the outstanding member of the community—John Gourlay. The resulting enmity is one of the mainsprings of the hostility which eventually brings about the downfall of the House with the Green Shutters. Yet throughout the book the community is brilliantly used by the author, who was himself estranged from his childhood community by prosperity (although to surprisingly small an extent), and who grew up never quite accepted by it, as a result of illegitimate birth and a proud independence which made him unpopular. Brown was hypersensitive to this feeling of being apart from his community,[15] and he used it throughout his book to show how characters could be rebuffed by a village, in its corporate form of the 'bodies'. A stranger, or someone unpopular, need not necessarily be met with rudeness, but with bland politeness, by perfect civility, yet by a complete lack of communication. Within themselves the gossips of the community share their news impartially, they communicate with little reserve and (in this case) startling spite,[16] yet when confronted by a stranger the shutters go up. The result is not rudeness; it is perfect civility and politeness, yet complete self-possession. The stranger is not rebuffed, he is simply excluded from the community, treated with complete self-possession and reserve. In chapter five Jock Gilmour is dismissed from the service of John Gourlay in the House with the Green Shutters, and as he staggers down the hill, his chest on his shoulder, the first persons he meets are the 'bodies', who treat him exactly in this way. He is not one of them, but he is interesting (he has gossip they would like to share) so he is humoured and his information is extracted deftly.

> 'Aye man, Dyohn!' lisped Deacon Allardyce, with bright and eagerly enquiring eyes. 'And what did he thay to that, na? *That* wath a dig for him! I'the warrant he wath angry.'
> 'Angry? He foamed at the mouth! But I up and says to him, "I have had enough o' you," says I, "you and your Hoose wi' the Green Shutters," says I, "you're no fit to have a decent servant," says I. "Pay *me my* wages and I'll be redd o' ye," says I. And wi' that I flang my kist on my shouther and slapped the door ahint me.'
> 'And *did* he pay ye your wages!' Tam Wylie probed him slily, with a sideward glimmer in his eye.
> 'Ah, well; no; not exactly,' said Gilmour, drawing in. 'But I'll get them right enough for a' that. He'll no get the better o' me.' Having grounded unpleasantly on the question of the wages he thought it best to be off ere the bloom was dashed from his importance, so he shouldered his chest and went. The bodies watched him down the street.
> 'He's a lying brose, that,' said the baker. 'We a' ken what Gourlay is. He would have flung Gilmour out by the scruff o' the neck, if he had daured set his tongue against him!'
> 'Faith, that's so,' said Tam Wylie and Johnny Coe together.

As soon as the stranger has gone, the community lets down its barriers, and free interchange is again possible. The process operates elsewhere in the book, even when members of the community are alone. It could be seen at work, too, in the works of Lewis Grassic Gibbon where, in *Sunset Song*, the inhabitants of Kinraddie act with composure and self-possession in the presence of strangers because they are conscious of belonging to a community, whose values they uphold (while freely criticizing individual members). Incomers meet with cool polite reserve, and they withdraw baffled. John Guthrie confronting the rich motorist, the villagers confronting the minister (especially Long Rob), Chris dealing with strangers after her father's death, all display the calm and the self-possession of people who know the way of life of their community intimately, and find that by conforming to its values they can face the unexpected with calm.

What relevance has this to the study of Burns? The point has already been made that Burns belonged to such a community as Barbie and Kinraddie, and that he valued his membership of it highly. It has been suggested that Tam o' Shanter sees the world from the cosy intimacy of such a community, and that the best position a reader may adopt is to place himself in the position of such a person, and try to follow Tam's thought-processes at their own speed. I believe that the premises outlined so far, applied to 'Death and Doctor Hornbook', illustrate how such an application of biography and social history may assist the criticism of literature.

'Death and Doctor Hornbook' tells, in thirty-one six-line stanzas, of an encounter between a tipsy farmer, on his way home, and a supernatural creature, who is shown as the poem progresses to be Death. After a wary initial exchange of pleasantries and threats, for the narrator (whom we can call, for convenience, Burns) is more than a little befuddled, the two sit down to chat, and after much recorded conversation a sudden warning of dawn (in the form of a clock striking) makes the ghostly figure of Death retreat precipitately to the nether regions whence he came. The poem is light-hearted, sufficiently so for the supernatural being never to assume terrifying proportions. Like Tam's witches, he is too distanced by Burns's befuddlement to be seen as the Grim Reaper, but rather as a chance passer-by who has a crack with a stranger on the road.

The resemblances between 'Tam o' Shanter' and 'Death and Doctor Hornbook' are well developed. Both poems are a form of the dramatic monologue; in both cases the speaker is a little drunk, in both he meets with supernatural beings who emerge as figures of fun and folk-tale, but with their gruesome aspects not quite submerged beneath the glazed drunken understanding of the teller. Tam's catalogue of gruesome sights in Kirk-Alloway is matched by the bloody exploits of Death in this poem. To Burns's readers, as much as to the modern ones (perhaps more), Death would be a familiar visitant, with life-expectancies low and wars a frequent occurrence. Death was no joke, however light-heartedly Burns could treat it.

The poem opens on a note of ambiguity; a passing dig at ministers is part of the ironic protestation that this poem is serious, matching perfectly the mock pulpit-seriousness of the ending of 'Tam o' Shanter'. Burns protests, too much, that this is a serious poem; at once we suspect its bona fides. This suspicion is heightened by the description of befuddlement. The self-excusing tone—

> I was na fou, but just had plenty:
> I stachered whiles, but yet took tent aye
> To free the ditches;
> And hillocks, stanes, an' bushes, kend aye
> Frae ghaists an' witches—

convinces no one; Burns clearly was tipsy. Yet he was not altogether drunk; rather he was initially garrulous, and in a right mood to talk to any passing stranger. Death cannot be taken seriously in these circumstances. Burns is not fit to take him seriously, and as we are being told what happened through Burns's eyes, we can no more be terrified by the apparition than Burns was. Yet Burns's artistry is at its finest here, for he borrows the ballad technique in his initial description of Death—

> I there wi' *Something* does foregather—

leaving the details absolutely to the reader's imagination, till he offers a few clues in the following stanza. The effect is very much like (quite possibly borrowed from)

> About the middle o' the night,
> They heard the bridles ring—

What bridles, what horses, we never find out. The details are entirely supplied from the darker depths of the reader's imagination. Admittedly, Burns does add a few touches about the thinness of Death, and the length of his sickle, but the description is vague. Artistically, this is excellent; and it is in keeping with Burns's dull state that he does not look more closely, nor remark on it more than that it had

> The queerest shape that e'er I saw.

He greets it with openness, without effusiveness.

> 'Guid-een,' quo' I; 'Friend! hae ye been mawin,
> When ither folk are busy sawin?'

The reference to the sickle is boorish, the reader laughs, the potential tension is removed. The whole situation is reduced to two country people talking of the weather, of the crops. It could be one of a thousand Scottish short stories, instead of a supernatural event. (It is noticeable that Stevenson employs just the same low-level technique in the similar confrontation in *Markheim*.)

Death does not fit into this tone.

> It spak right howe: 'My name is Death,
> But be na fleyed.' Quoth I, 'Guid faith,
> Ye're maybe come to stap my breath;
> But tent me, billie:
> I red ye weel, take care o' skaith,
> See, there's a gully!'

Two points concern Burns's retort to Death. One is the drunken stupidity of it (of course death is incorporeal); the other is the devaluing of death in the whole poem, for the announcement of Death's identity is greeted not by awestruck silence, or anguished cries, but by calm *insouciance*, followed by a self-possessed threat. It may be drunken, but there is no mistaking the self-possession of Burns's attitude. Death does not worry him. He is on home ground (emphasized in stanzas 3, 4 and 5) and he fears nothing.

Death and Burns sit down together for a crack. From stanza 10 onwards, the poem is occupied by an increasingly querulous monologue by Death, punctuated by occasional half-ironic observations by Burns. Several comic techniques are employed: the catalogue of experiences and of medical remedies, rising to the ridiculous (and falling to the pathetic by over-emphasis and over-detailed repetition); the ironic juxtaposition on Burns's part of local gossip and old-wives'-tales with Death, the Great Reaper, and with local gossip winning. Death cannot get the better of local medicine, however primitive or ridiculous. The Jonsonesque terms of alchemy and the ridiculously local are put side by side:

> Forbye some new, uncommon weapons,
> *Urinus spiritus* of capons;
> Or mite-horn shavings, fillings, scrapings,
> Distill'd *per se*;
> *Sal-alkali* o' midge-tail-clippings,
> And monie mae.

The two languages, like the two sciences, clash ludicrously, and as there is so much emphasis, repetition and catalogue, the effect is finally pathetic. And it comes from Death, into whose mouth the ridiculous catalogue is put. Burns's speeches are, by comparison, calm, cool and collected; he is the drunkard, supposedly half-tipsy, but it is Death who babbles.

Why this unexpected division of speeches? Surely it is because

Burns's calm self-possession drives Death to more and more self-justification, more and more detail in an effort to impress. Twenty-two stanzas pass, and the death-figure is still talking, too much, too fluently, too exaggeratedly. Burns's reply shows how completely unimpressed he is. All that concerns him is the possible effect on a neighbour's field, which may be ploughed up to provide all the doctor's remedies. The effect on his neighbour affects Burns much more strongly than Death's vision of a world where people live to old age because Death's power has been cancelled out. Burns's philosophical calm, of course, drives the death-figure to still wilder claims and more extravagant speeches. He points out how Hornbook kills as well as cures—usurping his own prerogative:

> Whare I kill'd ane, a fair strae death
> By loss o' blood or want o' breath,
> This night I'm free to take my aith,
>   That Hornbook's skill
> Has clad a score i' their last claith
>   By drap an' pill.

Ironic examples follow. Again there is excess everywhere, too many examples, too ridiculous, all drawn from local gossip, rich in Ayrshire allusion. Death is almost apoplectic.

His last thrust is a pathetic one:

> But hark! I'll tell you of a plot,
> Tho' dinna ye be speakin' o't:
> I'll nail the self-conceited sot,
>   As dead's a herrin;
> Niest time we meet, I'll wad a groat,
>   He gets his fairin!

But alas, he has no chance to elaborate. At this point the clock strikes, and, again borrowing from ballad tradition, the death-figure is made to shift uneasily, to see that his hour is almost past and he must return to his proper place. It might be, if it were more serious, 'The Wife of Usher's Well'. But it is not serious. It is the last thrust at the death-figure, who can only go off uttering empty threats, leaving Hornbook in victorious possession of the field.

It is a doubly ridiculous plot. In the first place, Hornbook's local fame as dilettante apothecary is too insubstantial to bear the fabric of a thirty-one-stanza poem, too local and unimportant to take seriously. This poem is a *jeu d'esprit*, using a snatch of local gossip and parodying larger forms, larger ideas, by ironic contrast with the littleness of the subject. Gray's 'Ode on the Death of a Favourite Cat' employs the same technique, as does Fielding's *Tom Thumb*. In the second place, it is a ridiculous poem because it inverts the expected order. Death makes an appearance on earth, an event which in a ballad would have been recognized for what it was, an omen of evil and a matter for real fear, because actual human death was sure to follow. Here the situation is the same, but the reaction is all wrong. Burns takes it too calmly; he fails to respond to Death's speeches, and so Death literally talks himself out of the audience's respect.

The point to note is that the effect, in both ways, is achieved by taking the reader into the position of the writer as member of a small and closed community. As in 'Tam o' Shanter', Burns is inviting (indeed, forcing) the reader down to the level of a tipsy crony, one of Souter Johnnie's friends, and making him see the events through the blurred and sleepy eyes of a man just this side of drunkenness. This is the intention of the poem, and the artistic means used to achieve it, if less obvious than in the opening of 'Tam o' Shanter', are no less clever.

If the individual perception is that of a half-drunk individual, the perceptions surrounding the story—the world-values, they might be called—are those of the other members of the community, probably those who share his love of sociable drinking and story-telling. The manner of the poem is that of a story retold to friends, among friends; the elaborate self-justification and explanation of the third stanza is that of a crony explaining to his cronies that they knew how much drink he had had, that he was not drunk, and so that the following was a true story and the details were to be trusted. Yet the attitude is faithfully maintained. He was half-drunk, and unable to provide close detail of Death's description. What he can remember is the details of local gossip, ribald, bawdy, ridiculous to a close group who would be familiar with the personalities involved, and would relish the long drawn-out joke on Doctor Hornbook. It is a tissue of jokes to be told to friends, in a local situation; it is told in the manner of a convivial recitation, lubricated by drink; its teller, and its audience, are in the same group, share the same values and knowledge.

Death does not. This is the ultimate comic device of the poem. Death tries in vain to break down this self-sufficient, self-complacent barrier which Burns, as part of his friendly group, erects in his way. Burns cannot be impressed. He is prevented by tipsiness, by rustic reserve in the presence of strangers. It is something the reader would quite easily recognize; he would see what Burns was trying to portray; he would take the poem, indeed he still can take the poem, in this sense. Burns is approaching a familiar situation, familiar because of its ballad associations, namely the confrontation of a mortal with Death. 'Thrawn Janet' derives its central situation from exactly the same confrontation. Burns could have dramatized it, he could have added horrendous details, but instead he chose to limit the poem to the world-values of his clique, and make it comic, which he succeeds in doing, marvellously simply, by the limitations he deliberately imposes on the world-values of the poem, and the techniques of narration. It is a friendly clique poem, and by employing these techniques succeeds in being a great comic one. It is a technique, and a success, which is shown also in the 'Address to the Deil'.

Which brings us back to Burns in Edinburgh. A man slightly aloof, slightly reserved, definitely a man self-possessed and not swept off his feet by the adulation and the sudden contact with both literary high-life and social intercourse of a kind quite outwith his common experience. He retained through it his earlier possession of what he had brought to Edinburgh, a sense of belonging to a community. It is perhaps significant that 'Death and Doctor Hornbook' was written before the visit to Edinburgh, and 'Tam o' Shanter' afterwards. Both display, consistently, the same artistic poise which Edinburgh neither gave nor destroyed. He looked forward to rejoining this community; he felt hurt when a barrier rose between him and it on his return from Edinburgh. Both before and after his first visit, he was noted for his conviviality, his love of sociable drinking. Edinburgh extended his experience, but he viewed it from outside. His aloofness, his sense of belonging to what he had known earlier, a social group in which he felt at ease, arguably extends the reader's understanding of 'Death and Doctor Hornbook', by showing how it is based on a set of values not quite central to the reader of wider experience, yet certainly not a set of values denied to him.

Perhaps this is one reason, apart from causing local offence, why Burns omitted 'Death and Doctor Hornbook' from the Kilmarnock volume—because this was his bid for fame in a wider market, and this was such a localized poem. Yet I do not think we should take the localization as a serious bar to a modern cosmopolitan appreciation of the poem. After the details become forgotten history, the technique remains, and the point, once made, can be applied to the analysis of many of Burns's finest comic poems, such as 'Tam o' Shanter' and 'Holy Willie's Prayer'. This is a point to be taken seriously, for with it one arrives at a justification for taking localized literature, particularly localized Scottish literature, seriously. The language problem is not important. Here the broad, rustic language is merely an intensification of an atmosphere which is created by details, by the attitudes of the two speakers. In this poem, as in Hogg's *Confessions of a Justified Sinner*, one of the most important things a critic must take into account is the conflict between localized values, localized references and the wider references in the poem. The reader, armed with the wider references, such as the implicit references to the border ballads, and the traditions of revenants, possibly also half-unconscious mental references to the Angel of Death in the Book of Exodus, sees this comic poem as a well-finished satire *disguised* as local. The wider reader sees both sides, Death's and Burns's, and he sees how Burns is holding off Death, making a fool of him, by his complacent local rustic reserve. The reader can also see how Burns is employing local reference and satire to deflate the situation, in the classic traditions of mock-heroic poetry. As in Hogg's novel, both a knowledge of the local situation and the ability to see and judge it as local widen the reader's appreciation of the finished work appreciably. In 'Death and Doctor Hornbook' Burns has produced a fine poem which, suitably adorned with *apparatus criticus*, can be understood by anyone as local satire. Implicitly, he has given it a fine mock-heroic shape and form which ensures for it a place in the tradition of the literature of demonology. By a nice balance of provincial and national, Burns has shown that he can be national, and international, in a poem which seems at first sight confined to satire of the most local variety. And this, in Burns's successful poems, is a strong argument in favour of granting him the international stature as poet which seems increasingly to be regarded as his by right.

Notes

1 *The Letters of Robert Burns*, ed. J. De Lancey Ferguson (Oxford, 1931), I p. 55.
2 Quoted from D. Daiches, *Robert Burns* (London, 1952), pp. 235-6.
3 Quoted from Daiches, *op. cit.*, p. 236.
4 Scott's description to Lockhart, quoted from Daiches, *op. cit.*, p. 237.
5 Quoted from Daiches, *op. cit.*, p. 236.
6 *Letters*, I, p. 71.
7 *Ibid.*, p. 182.
8 *Ibid.*, p. 311.

9 *Letters*, I, p. 87.
10 *Ibid.*, p. 71.
11 *Ibid.*, p. 96.
12 *Ibid.*, p. 97.
13 *Ibid.*
14 *Ibid.*, p. 110.
15 See, for example, the episode in Brown's youth described in J. Veitch, *George Douglas Brown* (London, 1952), p. 66.
16 For an example, see *The House with the Green Shutters* (1901), ch. 15.

Chapter 3

The Language of Burns

David Murison

No small part of a poet's business is the manipulation of words, and the great poets have usually been great creators also in the use of language. But even the greatest have to work within the general limits of the language they begin with, its vocabulary, its idiom and its rhythms, and Burns is no exception. In his case the picture is complicated by the fact that for historical reasons he had two languages at his disposal, whose relations to one another have to be understood before we can appreciate his technique and achievement.

Scots and English are essentially dialects of the same original language, Anglo-Saxon, and the differences between them are far outweighed by their similarities, and, for reasons that will appear, the differences, once marked and predictable, are becoming more and more blurred as far as Scots is concerned. But differences there are, not only purely linguistic but also stylistic and thematic. There is of course a large common vocabulary, but Scots has a considerable Norse element and some Dutch, French and Gaelic not shared with English; the vowel and to a lesser extent the consonant systems are different; the grammatical forms, especially in the verbs, vary somewhat; and there are a great many subtle distinctions in syntax and idiom. These differentiae had established and consolidated themselves by the late fifteenth century, and from then on it was as possible to speak of two distinct languages, as it was of two distinct nations. But, as is well known, a series of historical accidents inhibited the growth of the northern tongue and left the field open for the ultimate triumph of the other over the whole island. The Reformation of 1560 and the circulation of the English Bible, in default of a Scots one which never materialized, gave English a spiritual prestige as the language of solemnity and dignity, for the more serious affairs of life, while Scots remained the speech of informality, of the domestic, the sentimental and, significantly enough, the comic, a dichotomy well seen in 'The Cotter's Saturday Night'. The Union of the Crowns in 1603 took the Scottish court and the patrons of culture to London, and almost immediately the results were seen, not only in the language of literature in the works of the poets Drummond, Alexander and Mure, and prose-writers like Urquhart, but in the official documents of state and burgh, and the private papers of the nobility which become more and more anglicized as the century advances, so that English was now gaining also in social prestige at the expense of Scots.

The seventeenth century is in fact the period of transition from Scots to English, and the cope-stone to the process was put on by the Parliamentary Union of 1707, when thenceforth the laws of Scotland would be promulgated from London in the King's English and all administrative pronouncements and documentation would be in the official language of the legislature. It was the process of 1603 over again in a more thorough and final form. Scots prose now lost all status, was reduced to the level of a dialect, and in the eighteenth century hardly exists as a literary form.

In verse, however, all was not lost. The popular tradition of the Middle Ages that we find in 'Christ's Kirk on the Green', 'Peblis to the Play', 'Rauf Coilzear', 'The Wyf of Auchtermuchty', carried on through the seventeenth century, along with the ballad and folk-song and such genre pieces as Sempill's elegy on 'Habbie Simson', notable for its stanza form, the verse epistle, the testament poem, and much more of the sort that was republished by the Edinburgh printer James Watson in his *Choice Collection* of 1706-11. This undoubtedly inspired Allan Ramsay to carry on in the same vein both with anthologies of medieval and contemporary poems, the *Ever Green* and the *Tea-Table Miscellany*, and with a considerable volume of work of his own. And not only was this tradition, because it was of its nature popular, in the vernacular, but also Ramsay himself adopted Scots as the first language of his poems from his own strong nationalist sympathies, later seen in his preface (in Scots) to his collection of proverbs. So it was Ramsay who laid the trail and struck the keynote for this revival of Scottish literature and language as a kind of spiritual compensation for the political eclipse which had overtaken the nation. But it was not a full-scale revival of either. In the eighteenth century as compared with the early sixteenth there was no prose in Scots of a serious, philosophical or scientific nature—the day for that was past. Poetry and its language are on a more popular and less intellectual level; there is no epic, no metaphysical verse, nothing like Dryden or Pope. The vocabulary is much more restricted and personal, more realistic and down to earth, and hence, in Scotland, more regional, because, in the absence of a standard form of speech and of a national and literary centre, local dialects inevitably rise into prominence, as indeed happened in the north-east of Scotland with poets like Skinner, Alexander Ross and Robert and William Forbes, whose works are in some measure linguistic *tours de force*. The efforts to extend the scope and usage of Scots vocabulary, as with Gavin Douglas in 1513 and the *Complaynt of Scotland* in 1548, had long been abandoned, and of course there was none of the polishing and refining that went on in English under the Augustans.

After 1700 the unrestricted penetration of Scotland by English through the Bible and the Church, legal and bureaucratic usage, news-papers and the educational system, produced, especially among those most exposed to it, a kind of mixed informal language in which English words and forms could be grafted on to the vernacular in whatever degree the speaker or writer wished: a state of affairs not so very different from that of today, only the basic Scots vocabulary has become so much thinner and English has replaced it.

Every speaker has various 'registers' or modifications of speech, according to the company he is in or the topic he is discussing, or the atmosphere or manner in which he is discussing it, distinguishing the language of, say, sport from that of politics; though the more educated or socially exalted one is, the more the limits of variation tend to become restricted. In eighteenth-century Scotland the fluctuations were as between more or less Scots and less or more English, the beauties of American and Soho 'in-talk' not having yet struck us. In effect the Age of Enlightenment and Philosophy and the beginnings of the Industrial Revolution were being superimposed on the old feudal and rural culture of Scotland, and in speech terms this corresponds roughly to the functional demarcation line between English as the language of abstract and formal thought and Scots as the language of immediacy and intimacy at a lower intellectual pitch.

The social prestige of English, besides, steadily increased throughout the century, and a mastery of it came to be the aim of at least the upper classes, not merely in writing, as in the case of David Hume, but also in speech, for the English of Scotland was still distinct enough from that of England to be only half-intelligible, as the Scots MPs found to their mortification when they took their seats in the new Westminster. This led later to the somewhat ludicrous elocution classes run in Edin-burgh by an Irishman for the Select Society 'for Promoting the Reading and Speaking of the English Language' in 1761.

It was into this confused and unstable linguistic situation that Burns was born. Both influences, Scots and English, were at work on him from his earliest youth, for he himself was the child of two diverse characters who in themselves epitomize the history and culture of Scotland. It was his father who insisted on a good education for his sons; who represented the Scotland that had descended from the

Reformation by way of the Kirk, that had had its wits sharpened and its philosophy deepened on the frozen logic of the Shorter Catechism; from John Murdoch, the dominie at Alloway, Burns came to know the great works of English literature, Shakespeare, Milton, Pope and other Augustans, and was given a thorough drilling in formal English composition and style. William Burnes himself had written a short religious treatise for family use, in impeccable English.

But there was his mother too and her people and his old nurse, representing the native force in Burns, the element which is of the soil of Scotland, of the folk and their lore, their daily lives, their superstitions, their delight in the fields and woods of Ayrshire, in banks and braes and running water so characteristically Scottish, their shrewd mother-wit, their proverbs, all expressed in their pithy forceful Scots tongue. It is in fact in the blending of the two strains in the Scottish heritage, the intellectual and the traditional, that Burns and his poetry stand out as the voice of Scotland.

Besides the rigorous discipline of Murdoch's emphasis on style, we know from brother Gilbert that the young poet was reading the *Spectator* and Pope's translation of Homer[1] so that the influence of Augustan English was in full play, and there is an even more important note in his autobiographical letter to Dr Moore where he describes his close study of 'a collection of English songs'. 'I pored over them driving my cart, or walking to labour—song by song—verse by verse; carefully noting the true, tender, or sublime, from affectation and fustian; and I am convinced I owe much to this of my critic-craft, such as it is.'[2] Undoubtedly Burns's uncanny flair for the right word in the right place was in part at least the outcome of this.

Another more immediate result was the production of the Mount Oliphant period, a particularly unhappy phase of his life when he developed teenage melancholia and wrote elegies and odes all in somewhat stilted English about 'fickle Fortune', and even attempted a tragedy, of which only the dismal fragment 'All devil as I am, a damned wretch' survives.

Fortunately, about this time he picked up a copy of Ramsay's *Tea-Table Miscellany* and tried his hand at song-writing in Scots, or rather in that half-Scots half-English form that goes back to the early eighteenth or even late seventeenth century, when there was a craze for Scots songs, in London as well as in Scotland. The very first piece he ever wrote, 'Handsome Nell', was in this vein, and also the clever 'Tibbie, I hae seen the day', which is in pretty straight Scots with an English rhyme here and there, as in stanza 2.

Meanwhile his formal if fitful education was progressing; he had read Locke's *Essay concerning Human Understanding*, attended a course in trigonometry and his reading[3]

was enlarged with the very important addition of Thomson's and Shenstone's Works. I had seen mankind in a new phasis; and I engaged several of my schoolfellows to keep up a literary correspondence with me. This last helped me much on in composition. I had met with a collection of letters by the Wits of Queen Anne's reign, and I pored over them most devoutly.

All this goes to show the strict training Burns gave himself in language, the careful weighing up of each word, the ordering of the thought, the choice of imagery as in one of his next songs, 'The Lass of Cessnock Banks', which is self-confessedly an exercise in the use of similes, and above all in 'Mary Morison', which the indefatigable Ritter has shown to be full of echoes of Shakespeare, Pope, Thomson, Shenstone, Mackenzie among others,[4] but these have been woven into a perfect conceptual unity and, what is more, rendered into Scots, despite one or two English forms like *those*, *poor* and *shown*, *canst* and *wilt*, and anglicized spellings like *trembling*, *thought*, and the *-ed* of the past participles. We see the same process at work again a little later in 'Corn Rigs' and much later in 'A Red Red Rose'. Both have motifs and phrases from earlier folk-songs both Scottish and English. 'Corn Rigs', though pitched at a lower and earthier level, is extraordinarily deft in its use of the plainest Scots, with the exception of the one line 'I lock'd her in my fond embrace'; the whole thing reads like an ordinary conversation, and yet by sheer word-music and the evocation of the harvest moonlight produces an almost magical effect. Well might Burns say of it himself, 'The best stanza that ever I wrote, at least the one that pleases me best, and comes nearest to my *beau ideal* of poetical perfection, is this—

> I hae been blythe wi' Comrades dear; I hae been merry
>   drinking;
> I hae been joyfu' gath'rin gear; I hae been happy thinking;
> But a' the pleasures e'er I saw, tho' three times doubl'd fairly,
> That happy night was worth them a', amang the rigs o'
>   barley.

It was about this time (1782), however, that the vital incident occurred in Burns's poetic career. 'Meeting with Fergusson's Scotch Poems I strung anew my wildly-sounding lyre with emulating vigour.'[5]

Later, in his Commonplace Book of August 1784, he links 'the excellent Ramsay and the still more excellent Fergusson' as between them inspiring him to concentrate on celebrating the scenery and life of his native Ayrshire, a theme he reiterates in verse in his 'Epistle to William Simpson'. Burns had in fact found himself as a dedicated Scottish poet.

It was out of this that the Kilmarnock edition sprang. The models are obvious, Fergusson's dialogue between 'Plainstanes and Causey' for 'The Twa Dogs'; 'Caller Water' for 'Scotch Drink'; 'Leith Races' for 'The Holy Fair'; and even more directly 'The Farmer's Ingle' for 'The Cotter's Saturday Night'. 'The Twa Dogs' is a remarkably successful experiment in social criticism in straight conversational Scots. Because of the restricted nature and scope of eighteenth-century Scots, there has to be a certain reduction in focus, the abstract has to be seen in terms of the concrete, the sophistication of an all-purpose language has to be forgone, but within these limits the vigour and vivacity of the concepts are hard to better and the humour adds to the verve:

> There, at Vienna, or Versailles,
> He rives his father's auld entails;
> Or by Madrid he takes the rout,
> To thrum guittarres an' fecht wi' nowt;
> Or down Italian Vista startles
> Whore-hunting amang groves o' myrtles;
> Then bowses drumlie German-water,
> To mak himsel look fair an' fatter,
> An' clear the consequential sorrows,
> Love-gifts of Carnival Signioras.

The last two lines from the Edinburgh edition, substituted for the original couplet, 'An' purge the bitter ga's an' cankers, / O' curst Venetian bores an' chancres', show a further improvement in linguistic polish and wit. 'The Holy Fair', one of Burns's greatest poems, shows the same masterly command of language, by turning the simplest and most natural of conversational prose into poetry. The marvellous evocation of a summer morning in stanza 1 in plain direct Scots, with just a nod of concession to the Augustans in the second line:

> Upon a simmer Sunday morn,
> When Nature's face is fair,
> I walked forth to view the corn
> An' snuff the callor air:

> The rising sun, owre Galston muirs,
>   Wi' glorious light was glintan;
> The hares were hirplan down the furrs
>   The lav'rocks they were chantan
>   Fu' sweet that day

leads on to the well-conceived and concretely rendered vision of the three allegorical women, Superstition, Hypocrisy and Fun, and the utter naturalness of the half-recognition of the last:

> Wi' bonnet aff, quoth I, 'Sweet lass,
>   I think ye seem to ken me;
> I'm sure I've seen that bonie face,
>   But yet I canna name ye.'

And so on through memorable phrase and epigram, 'Screw'd up, grace-proud faces', 'Common-sense has taen the road, / An' aff, an' up the Cowgate', 'There's some are fou o' love divine, / There's some are fou o' brandy', to the broad chuckle at the end.

The same skill in manipulating colloquial Scots is seen at its best in the Epistles, modelled on the verse correspondence between Ramsay and Hamilton of Gilbertfield in the 'Habbie Simson' stanza, so well adapted to the sententious nature of folk-speech, with the frequent sardonic afterthought or phrase of finality conveyed neatly in the 'bob-wheel' at the end:

> 'But faith! he'll turn a corner jinkan, / An' cheat you yet';
>   'The last sad cape-stane of his woes; / Poor Mailie's dead';
>   'I see ye upwards cast your eyes— / Ye ken the road';
>   'Wha does the utmost that he can, / Will whiles dae mair';
>   'A rousing whid at time to vend, / And nail't with Scripture'.

When we come to the 'Epistle to a Young Friend', we find a somewhat different type of Scots. The easy spontaneous style of the Epistles to John Lapraik or William Simpson is more formalized into a series of moral apothegms, still in Scots but in a strongly anglicized variety of it, a homiletic Scots such as must have been heard from many an early eighteenth-century pulpit from the old-fashioned school of preachers of the Moderate faction in the Kirk. It is not unlike Blair, and the poem probably contains more lines quoted from Burns than any other. 'Still keep something to yoursel, / Ye scarcely tell to ony'; 'The glorious privilege of being independent'; 'The fear o' Hell's a hangman's whip, / To haud the wretch in order'; 'A correspondence

fix'd wi' Heav'n / Is sure a noble anchor'. The classic instance of this
is in 'Tam o' Shanter'. The narrative proceeds with gathering speed in
good rich Scots (and nowhere is Burns's facility with the language in
better evidence), when at a natural pause in the story he introduces the
series of similes 'But pleasures are like poppies spread', which has given
critics such a time of it. But surely this is simply the moral homily once
again, interpolated with a certain mock solemnity and the tongue well
in the cheek, and of course in English, as such homilies were bound to be.

This style in fact in different contexts reappears in 'The Cotter's
Saturday Night' and 'The Vision'. In the former the language switches
from Scots to English as the theme fluctuates between the descriptive
and domestic and the stagy moralizing which the majority of critics
delight in execrating. But linguistically the most significant part is
when, 'the chearfu' supper done', the Scots of the chatter at table almost
insensibly and by degrees slides into English as the father takes down the
Bible and worship begins. This is essentially the matter of historical
tradition, and the inveterate association of the Bible and liturgical
language in general in Scotland with English. The setting of 'The
Vision' is not dissimilar, having the same homely vivid vernacular
description of the inside of the cottage and even of Coila in the first
part, and a thoroughly classical English ode in the second when he
meditates on the abstractions of the social order and the function of the
poet, with some good lines in it, especially the succinct and profound
'But yet the light that led astray, / Was light from Heaven', which
sums up in a few words the whole problem and matter of moral
philosophy. But he said more or less the same thing in his Epistles to
John Lapraik and Willie Simpson more directly and simply and un-
affectedly in Scots, and they are worth, and will stand, comparison
with 'The Vision' on this very point.

In 'Holy Willie's Prayer' the same technique is employed, but with
a much more serious purpose; liturgical English and down-to-earth
Scots are woven together and made to alternate with consummate skill
in bringing out the two facets of Willie's character so that he is condemned out of his own mouth:

> Yet I am here, a chosen sample,
> To shew thy grace is great and ample,
> I'm here, a pillar o' thy temple
>   Strong as a rock;
> A guide, a ruler and example
>   To a' thy flock. . . .

> Besides, I farther maun avow,
> Wi' Leezie's lass, three times I trow;
> But Lord, that Friday I was fou
>   When I cam near her,
> Or else, thou kens, thy servant true,
>   Wad never steer her.

Again a comparison of the Scots 'Mouse' with the more Englified 'Daisy' reinforces the general judgment that Burns, in the words of Scott,[6]

> never seems to have been completely at his ease when he had not the power of descending at pleasure into that which was familiar to his ear, and to his habits. . . . His use of English when assumed as a primary and indispensable rule of composition, the comparative penury of rhimes, and the want of a thousand emphatic words which his habitual acquaintance with the Scottish supplied, rendered his expression confined and embarrassed.

Scott, who was much in the same boat himself, knew the lack of un-inhibited fluency that comes of using a stepmother tongue.

So much for the stylistics of the Kilmarnock edition, that mixture, in varying degrees, of Scots for the particular in description and narrative, in which the poet intimately participates, and English or Englified Scots for the more reflective and philosophical passages, when the poet steps back as a commentator and adopts a persona more remote from his subject. This becomes his general practice, and even his songs, in so far as the theme permits, present the same linguistic pattern, as we shall see.

But Burns's Scots itself is worth examining more closely. The poet himself, no doubt with a view to an audience of anglicized Scots, itself a recognition of the linguistic changes in eighteenth-century Scotland, provided to his first edition a glossary, which he much enlarged in his second, of the Scots words he thought needed explanation, and to these he added notes on the pronunciation which all reciters of Burns would do well to heed. He noted also that in Scots the present participle ends in -an (from an earlier -and) and the past participle in -t. The first must be based on the observation of his own ears, detecting a distinction between the participle and the verbal noun which was already dying out in the central dialects of Scotland, but is historically founded and still survives in the northern and southern peripheries of Scots, though long abandoned in literary Scots. He does not apply it rigorously in his own text, and gave it up in his later work. His Scots vocabulary is copious; in his complete works he employs over 2,000 peculiarly Scots words (the average Scots speaker today would have about 500 at the most); his definitions are accurate, and not without humour: *blink*, a glance, an amorous leer, a short space of time, a smiling look, to look kindly, to shine by fits; *clachan*, a small village about a church, a hamlet; *fetch*, to stop suddenly in the draught and then come on too hastily; *hoddan*, the motion of a sage country farmer on an old cart horse; *houghmagandie*, a species of gender composed of the masculine and feminine united; *whid*, the motion of a hare running but not frighted, a lie.

He has of course the vocabulary of the farmer in *aiver, bawsont, fittie-lan, fow, icker, ket, luggie, outler, pattle, stibble-rig, stimpart, risk, thrave, thack* and *raep*; the 'Inventory' is in fact one of many such Scots poems in the tradition of the medieval 'Wowin of Jok and Jenny' where lists of words are versified for their own sake; 'Halloween' again is a richly dialectal catalogue of rustic folklore; the terminology of curling appears in 'Tam Samson's Elegy'. He had an interest in words as such, as his usage and the glossary show and as his few random notes on Border dialect during his tour by the Tweed in 1787 bear out; and to Robert Anderson he admitted the advantages in having 'the *copia verborum*, the command of phraseology which the knowledge and use of the English and Scottish dialects afforded him'.[7]

His native dialect was of course that of Kyle, which is in a debatable land between the dialect region of Strathclyde and that of Galloway, and there are a few words which are specifically from that area, words like *crunt, daimen, gloamin shot, ha bible, icker, jauk, kiaugh, messan, pyle, raucle, rockin, roon, shangan, thummart, wiel, winze, wintle*, all from the rural or local poems; but, by and large, his vocabulary is eclectic, avoiding the purely provincial, and so remaining in the broad stream of traditional literary, one might even say, metropolitan Scots, such at least as had survived the seventeenth-century break-up. For this he is considerably indebted above all to Ramsay, and in part to some others of his poetical predecessors, Sempill, Skinner, Hamilton of Bangour, Ross of Lochlee, whom he mentions several times, and of course Fergusson.

Ritter and others have painstakingly accumulated instances of borrowing and adaptation[8] till one is tempted to wonder if Burns ever wrote an original line, and there is neither need nor space to detail these here. Furthermore, Burns's native command of Scots was such as to make it difficult to distinguish borrowings from spontaneous uses.

But Burns made no secret of his indebtedness to others in the free-masonry of poetry—and, of course, in the songs adaptation was his stated policy and practice—and in his use of some words the borrowings are plain and palpable. It is obvious that he knew passages of Ramsay and Fergusson by heart, and echoes of their phraseology are found in him. The rhymes 'awfu, unlawfu' and 'a winsome wench and walie' in 'Tam o' Shanter' are straight from Ramsay's 'Tale of Three Bonnets'; Ramsay preceded him with *aspar, auld-farran, bellum, beet, Land o' Cakes, clishmaclaver, collieshangie, cooser, dink, donsie, fair fa', flewit, goave, grunzie, jockteleg, ripple, sculdudderie, shaul, whigmaleerie, wimple*; in many cases the contexts are close enough to suggest direct borrowing. Fergusson had been at the same source himself and had passed on to Burns *bughtin time, cheek for chow, drant, doylt, glamour, gloamin, hoddan gray, lyart, oergang, rowt*. It is worth noting incidentally how the poetic quality improves with each borrowing.

Katharine Ogie (a seventeenth-century song) in Ramsay, *Tea-Table Miscellany* (1876), I, 69:

> O were I but some shepherd swain!
>   To feed my flock beside thee,
> At boughting-time to leave the plain,
>   In milking to abide thee.

Fergusson *Hallowfair*, vi:

> Now, it was late in the ev'ning,
>   And boughting-time was drawing near,
> The lasses had stench'd their griening
>   Wi' fouth o' braw apples and beer.

Burns *The Lea-Rig*, i:

> When o'er the hill the eastern star
>   Tells bughtin-time is near, my jo,
> And owsen frae the furrowed field
>   Return sae dowf and weary, O.

To old Scots proverbs and traditional sayings Burns is indebted for 'the stalk o' carl help', 'to stand abeigh', 'sturt and strife', 'moop and mell', and *rigwoodie* from 'Tam o' Shanter' is attested in connection with witchcraft early in the eighteenth century. Another of Burns's sources must have been the Chapbooks which circulated over the south-west at this period, particularly the ever-popular broadly humorous sketches of Dougal Graham. To Dougal, Burns certainly owes *clinkumbell* as a nickname for a kirk-beadle, most likely *fligma-gairies*, and possibly also *bow-kail*, and *lallan*. *Fiere* in 'Auld Lang Syne' is from the vocabulary of the ballads.

Burns then is a skilful adapter of the poetic language of his predecessors, another follower in the long if intermittent tradition coming down from the Middle Ages, of which echoes can still be heard among our moderns who write in Scots. For if there is any one quality more than another which characterizes Scottish literature it is the recurrent theme, the repeated metaphor and image, the resumed standpoint, due not only to the tenacity of the native strain in spite, or perhaps because, of alien pressure but also in no small measure to the limits imposed on it by the use of Scots. But within the tradition Burns made his own contribution to the poetic vocabulary of Scots, of which his innumerable imitators have made good use ever since, as *agley*, *bethankit*, *blellum*, *burnewin*, *catch-the-plack*, *glib-gabbit*, *hogshouther*, *Johnny Ged*, *primsie*, *raible*, *redwatshod*, of which Carlyle said, 'in this one word, a full vision of horror and carnage, perhaps too frightfully accurate for Art', *run deil*, *skelvy*, *skinking*, *smytrie*, *snick-drawing*, *staumrel*, not necessarily all Burns's own invention but first recorded in his works.

When we come to consider the question of the language of the later Burns, especially the Burns of the songs, we are considerably helped by Burns's own explicit statements. To Thomson he was quite emphatic,[9]

> If you are for English verses, there is, on my part, an end of the matter. . . . These English verses gravel me to death. I have not that command of the language that I have of my native tongue.— In fact, I think my ideas are more barren in English than in Scotish.—I have been at 'Duncan Gray', to dress it in English, but all that I can do is deplorably stupid.—For instance—
> Song—Tune, Duncan Gray—Let not woman e'er complain.

And most readers would agree with him.

Burns's argument, constantly repeated to Thomson, is that in the music of the songs there is a pastoral simplicity, pathos or liveliness which should be matched with a similar simplicity in the words, which he associates with Scots. Even 'a sprinkling of the old Scotish' is better than nothing. In the event this turns out something like 'Ae Fond Kiss' on paper, but when one reflects that it is in the simpler type of diction that Scots and English vocabulary coincide, and that if one follows Burns's instructions in his glossary to ignore the anglicized

spelling and pronounce in the Scots manner, the poem is in effect a
Scots poem with one or two Englishisms, like 'groans', rather than the
other way round.

One must remember that Burns got his Scots orthography from
Ramsay—one of his less happy borrowings, since Ramsay's spelling is
haphazard, inconsistent and often so anglicized as to blur the distinction
in phonetic values between Scots and English, as for instance in
spellings like *light* for *licht*; *poor, moon, coost*, for *puir, mune, cuist*; *down*
for *doun*; *wrath* for *wraith*; *how* for *hoo*; *hours* for *oors*; *arm* for *airm*; etc;
-ed, more often than not, appears for *-it*, and *-ing* for the participle *-in*,
or as Burns would have it, *-an*, but the English form is preferable to
the Scots in the first verse of 'Ca' the yowes', to preserve the assonance
with *sang* and *amang* and reproduce the prolonged ringing echo of the
bird's song through the woods.

In his refashioning of older songs Burns is guided by the language
of the original and as many of his models were from the seventeenth
century, English as well as Scots, the language is naturally mixed in
varying degrees according to the prescription given above, with the
seasoning of old Scots *quantum sufficit*. If it were too thickly Scots to
his mind, then 'I will vamp up the old song and make it English enough
to be understood' he says to Thomson in regard to the song 'Sleep'st
thou or wauk'st thou'.[10]

But this is the exception with him rather than the rule. On one
occasion at least he did the opposite by trying to write down the anglicized courtly or cavalier song of the seventeenth-century poet,
Sir Robert Aytoun, 'I do confess thee sweet', with the usual involved
epigrammatic style but a good song for all that, to the popular level by
Scotticizing it. 'I do think I have improved the simplicity of the sentiments by giving them a Scots dress.' But here for once he misconstrued
his model and his customary good taste in language failed him so that
he comes second-best out of the comparison.

'Simplicity' was his motto, and in his long-protracted wranglings with
George Thomson over the text as well as the music of his songs he had
to tell him that he was apt to sacrifice simplicity for pathos, sentiment
and point. To Thomson's constant niggling for more English, he
answered bluntly 'I'll rather write a new song altogether than make
this English. The sprinkling of Scotch in it, while it is but a sprinkling,
gives it an air of rustic naïveté, which time will rather increase than
diminish.'[11] In general he rings the changes freely within this mixed
Anglo-Scots style, theme and mood being usually a determining
factor. The gay extravert comic song, the social or community song, is,

as one would expect, from its immediacy and concreteness, in Scots, like 'The Deil's awa wi' th' Exciseman', or 'Willie brewed a Peck o' Maut', or 'Willie Wastle', or 'Whistle an' I'll come to ye, my Lad', or 'Duncan Gray', or 'Contented wi' Little'.

The same colloquial dexterity of 'The Holy Fair' is reproduced in 'Tam Glen' and 'Last May a Braw Wooer', and to this he adds sprightly wit in 'Green grow the Rashes', 'There was a Lad', 'Whistle o'er the Lave o't', 'The Carle o' Kellyburn Braes'. All these are in good rich Scots. The 'pastoral simplicity' vein is worked in 'The Banks o' Doon', where the student of Burns's styles has the advantage of having three versions to compare, the first with the rather halting opening 'Sweet are the banks—the banks o' Doon'; the second trimmed in the direction of even greater simplicity with the starkness of the ballad in it and faint echoes of 'O waly, waly up the bank' and much the best version; and the third, the modern popular one, verbally spun out to suit a different tune from the original. It provides an object lesson in showing how Burns's taste was pretty unerring when he was left to himself, and it compares favourably too with the turgid English of 'To Mary in Heaven' where the poet is simply attitudinizing with the same general thought and imagery.

In this type of song, though it is more personal and reflective, good idiomatic Scots is still the medium, and universality is achieved by the simplicity, and this is true of many of his other great songs, 'John Anderson, my jo', 'My Luve's like a Red Red Rose', 'O a' the Airts', and 'Auld Lang Syne'. There is more English in the pensive melancholy or sentimental mood of 'Bonie Wee Thing', where the last verse wanders off into an Augustan conceit, or of 'O, wert thou in the Cauld Blast', and the graceful and courtly 'A Rosebud by my Early Walk'. On the other hand, 'It was a' for our Rightfu' King' for all its cavalier and Jacobite overtones is in Scots, suggesting an intensity and spontaneity of feeling which made the mother tongue inevitable, when the particular human situation is posed against the general political background. This ability to fix in the vivid concrete terms of ordinary experience a universal truth is of course Burns's strongest suit and the essential secret of his genius and popularity. We have already seen it in 'The Twa Dogs'. In his songs it appears splendidly in 'A Man's a Man'. It is indeed 'prose thoughts inverted into rhyme', as Burns himself said—the prose thoughts of Tom Paine's *Rights of Man*, but out of the English prose Burns has made an immortal song in plain Scots. As Snyder points out, out of 263 words in the whole poem, 240 are monosyllables. The relationship of Scots and English and the potentialities of the one as against the other in the hands of Burns could hardly be better illustrated.

'Scots wha hae', which was written about the same time, has the same background in the ferment of the French Revolution and one can hear echoes of 'La Marseillaise' in it. Here Burns is striking the attitude of the patriot, and doubtless it was intended as a kind of national anthem of a nation that may even yet find the moral courage to sing it. It is a rhetorical address to the whole people; it deals with the abstractions of liberty, nationalism and tyranny, it demands dignity and solemnity, and, at this metaphysical level, one would expect English instead of Scots. In the event Burns has compromised according to his usual formula. The grammar is English, the rhymes are Scots, the forms are mixed, *sae*, for instance, but *woe*, *foe*; the usage in the first two lines is not the idiomatic vernacular, as Sir James Murray remarked;[12] yet there can be no question of its success as a poem and of Burns's skill in wedding the two linguistic traditions. On a larger canvas the two traditions appear again side by side and partly fused in 'The Jolly Beggars'. The recitativo, the intimate homely detailed description, is in Scots, the songs of the soldier and his doxy who had served so long abroad are in English; the wit of the Merry Andrew's song is conveyed in the Scots of that sort in which Burns excelled; the sentimentality of 'A Highland Lad' is in the mixed style he normally favoured; the fiddler and the tinker, as 'gangrel bodies' of no fixed abode, sing in different degrees of Scots, conditioned partly by the tunes prescribed for them. The bard's song is similarly attuned to his literary trade, with snatches of older songs and allusions to Castalia and Helicon, but in the main in Scots. But when the particular gives way to the general, when the individuals unite in a chorus of social criticism and formulate their philosophy of life, the language, as has often enough been noticed, turns to Augustan English in a kind of secular hymn.

Burns, like so many Scottish writers before him, took his traditions as he found them and worked within them, chiselling and polishing till his best reaches almost to perfection, and in his own line no one has ever surpassed him. His sound linguistic schooling, which was essentially classical, mediated through the Augustans, made him realize the weaknesses of a broken-down language, such as eighteenth-century Scots had become, deficient in a prose tradition and limited in abstract vocabulary. Yet, through his predecessors in both written and oral literature, he knew what it would still do and he chose it for himself because it was his own heritage. It was sound instinct in him that made him go for simplicity, and marry the language of feeling with that of thought by conceiving both in their most concrete terms. It is this that makes his language so vivid and quotable. No one has ever wrung so much humour, passion and beauty out of monosyllables as Burns, even at times magic:

> The wan moon sets behind the white wave,
> And time is setting with me, Oh.

And in so doing he gave the old Scots tongue a new lease of life, a new dignity and a renewed worth which even today and even in spite of the Scots themselves it has not altogether lost.

Notes

1   In Chambers-Wallace, *Life and Works of Burns* (Edinburgh, 1896), I, p. 35.
2   J. De Lancey Ferguson, *Letters of Robert Burns* (Oxford, 1931), I, p. 109.
3   *Ibid.*, p. 111.
4   O. Ritter, *Quellenstudien zu Robert Burns 1773-1791* (Berlin, 1901), pp. 23-6.
5   *Letters*, I, p. 113.
6   Scott, in *Quarterly Review* (February 1809), p. 35.
7   *Burns Chronicle* (1925), p. 12.
8   Ritter, *passim.*
9   *Letters*, II, pp. 122, 268.
10 *Ibid.*
11 *Ibid.*, p. 205.
12 J. A. H. Murray, *Dialect of the Southern Counties of Scotland* (London, 1873), p. 71n.

Chapter 4

The Epistles*

Thomas Crawford

The eighteen months or so between the beginning of 1785 and May 1786 were a period of rapid development and achievement. They saw Robert's passionate spell of practical farming at Mossgiel; the birth of his first illegitimate child; the most dramatic incidents in the Armour affair; the courting of Highland Mary; a whole series of church squabbles in which the poet intervened with his pen; and the production not only of most of the pieces in the Kilmarnock volume but of some major works not printed until much later.

'Dear-bought Bess' was born to Elizabeth Paton, a servant in the Burns household, on 22 May 1785. For her Robert wrote 'A Poet's Welcome to his Love-begotten Daughter: The first Instance that entitled him to the Venerable Appellation of Father'[1]—a fine poem, full of pride, tenderness, and defiance of convention. 'To John Rankine: In Reply to an Announcement',[2] written shortly before this, had metaphorically announced Bess Paton's condition in two stanzas which ended on a characteristically jubilant note:

> But now a rumour's like to rise—
> A whaup's i' the nest.

The 'Epistle to John Rankine, enclosing some Poems',[3] the earliest of Burns's verse epistles, was also a response to the same affair. It is a light, confident, even impudent poem exhibiting many traits characteristic of the mature Burns. Rankine's personality is indicated by a few bold strokes only, so that the reader feels he has known this crude, hard-drinking old sinner all the years of his life; and in the third and fourth stanzas essentially the same method is employed as in 'Holy Willie's Prayer'. The trick consists in the apparent acceptance of the real or imputed ideas of those attacked, which here takes the form of a despairing, almost whining appeal to Rankine to spare Hypocrisy:[4]

> Hypocrisy, in mercy spare it!
> That holy robe, O, dinna tear it!
> Spare't for their sakes, wha aften wear it—
> The lads in black;

* Reprinted, with permission of the author, from his book *Burns: A Study of the Poems and Songs* (Oliver & Boyd, 2nd ed. 1965), pp. 82-104.

> But your curst wit, when it comes near it,
>   Rives 't aff their back.
>
> Think, wicked sinner, wha ye're skaithing:
> It's just the Blue-gown badge an' claithing
> O' saunts; tak that, ye lea'e them naething
>   To ken them by
> Frae onie unregenerate heathen,
>   Like you or I.

It is only in the seventh stanza that the main subject appears—an account of Burns's dealings with Elizabeth Paton in a comic allegory of guns and partridges and poaching. In the tenth, he swears that in revenge for having to make public confession before the Holy Willies, he'll make havoc next year on all the girls in sight:

> But, by my gun, o' guns the wale,
> An' by my pouther an' my hail,
> An' by my hen, an' by her tail,
>   I vow an' swear!
> The game shall pay, owre moor an' dale,
>   For this, niest year!

This is the humour of the lads of the village: rough, full of energy and pride in physical prowess, but not to be taken too seriously. It is an example of Burns making real poetry out of the commonest bawdy material.

The ideas and emotions out of which the best pieces in the Kilmarnock Edition were made can be traced in a series of poems less disciplined and more informal than his set pieces—the epistles to 'Davie', J. Lapraik, William Simpson, John Goldie and James Smith.

The first 'Epistle to Davie [David Sillar], a Brother Poet', written in January 1785,[5] is concerned with the contrast between riches and poverty which underlies 'Man was made to Mourn', as well as with another subject—the Rousseauistic glorification of 'the heart'.[6] Beginning with a firm and brisk impression of winter, the poem soon moves to those 'great-folk' who are well-housed and comfortable in winter. Burns feels, however, that it is very wrong of him to envy the rich—a sentiment that rather takes the edge off his criticism of their 'cursed pride'. In the second stanza he introduces one of his major preoccupations, the possibility of beggary, and decides—like many a member of the class of agricultural labourers into which the Burnses were always afraid of falling—that the prospect is less fearsome when treated philosophically:

> But Davie, lad, ne'er fash your head,
>   Tho' we hae little gear;
> We're fit to win our daily bread,
>   As lang's we're hale and fier:
> 'Mair spier na, nor fear na,'
>   Auld age ne'er mind a feg;
> The last o't, the warst o't,
>   Is only but to beg.

When utterly destitute, Burns and Sillar have nowhere to sleep except in kilns or deserted barns—

> Nae mair then, we'll care then,
>   Nae farther can we fa'.

He imagines Davie and himself enjoying an equality of perfect comradeship as 'commoners of air', taking pleasure in landscapes of 'sweeping vales' and 'foaming floods', complete with daisies and black-birds. In spring-time on the hillsides they will set words to traditional tunes, proud and free in their mendicancy like the beggars of W. B. Yeats:[7]

> It's no in titles nor in rank:
> It's no in wealth like Lon'on Bank,
>   To purchase peace and rest.
> It's no in making muckle, mair;
> It's no in books, it's no in lear,
>   To make us truly blest:
> If happiness hae not her seat
>   An' centre in the breast,
> We may be wise, or rich, or great,
>   But never can be blest!
> Nae treasures nor pleasures
>   Could make us happy lang;
> The heart ay's the part ay
>   That makes us right or wrang.

The Puritan 'inner light' has after many vicissitudes become with Burns the 'heart' of an eighteenth-century rustic Man of Feeling.

In the sixth stanza Burns comes back to the contrast with which he began, between the labouring poor and the idle rich. It is confidently asserted that men who 'drudge and drive thro' wet and dry' are just as happy as those who live in palaces and mansions:

> Think ye, are we less blest than they,
> Wha scarcely tent us in their way,
>   As hardly worth their while?
> Alas! how oft, in haughty mood,
>   God's creatures they oppress!
> Or else, neglecting a' that's guid,
>   They riot in excess!

Burns's solution of this class conflict, which fills him with such detestation of the aristocracy, is not a social one, but something personal and private—the cultivation of a contented state of mind, 'making the best of a bad job'. The epistle begins to deteriorate from this point. Surely these lines from the eighth stanza are as nauseating as any adjuration of 'the lads in black', and come perilously close to 'All is for the best in the best of all possible worlds':

> And, even should misfortunes come,
> I here wha sit hae met wi' some,
>   An's thankfu' for them yet,
> They gie the wit of age to youth;
>   They let us ken oursel;
> They make us see the naked truth,
>   The real guid and ill. . . .

In this eighth stanza Burns asserts that inner happiness (the positive Good of the poem) can be realized only in love and friendship—or as we would say today, in personal relationships—and in the ninth stanza he even depicts his feelings for Jean Armour as an escape from the woes of daily life:

> When heart-corroding care and grief
>   Deprive my soul of rest,
> Her dear idea brings relief
>   And solace to my breast.

If poetically the tenth stanza is not much superior to the ninth, yet intellectually it is one of the key passages in the epistle. One might paraphrase it, cockney-fashion, as 'It's bein' so tender as keeps me goin':

> All hail! ye tender feelings dear!
> The smile of love, the friendly tear,
>   The sympathetic glow!

Burns is in this poem taking himself seriously as a Man of Feeling having apparently forgotten the self-criticism of such moods as the following:[8]

> Beware a tongue that's smoothly hung,
> A heart that warmly seems to feel!
> That feeling heart but acts a part—
> 'Tis rakish art in Rob Mossgiel.

Yet the thought is one he returned to again and again, in various guises—that love is the only thing that makes life worth living for the poor. In slightly more robust form it is the ground and foundation of that well-known lyric 'Green grow the Rashes, O',[9] while the same idea (this time quite unashamedly equated with four-lettered words) is a recurrent theme of all the 'cloaciniad' verse in *The Merry Muses of Caledonia*:[10]

> And why shouldna poor folk mowe, mowe, mowe,
> And why shouldna poor folk mowe:
> The great folk hae siller, & houses & lands,
> Poor bodies hae naething but mowe.

Thus if the eighth, ninth and tenth stanzas of the 'Epistle to Davie' appear a trifle mawkish to modern readers, it is important to realize that they express but one variant—a refined and somewhat tenuous one, it is true—of a concept which would surely have met with the approval of D. H. Lawrence. In part, it is a gospel of 'Joy through Sex' that Burns is preaching here—not simply the sexual act itself (which receives its tributes in the *The Merry Muses*), but all the emotions and sentiments which grow out of its soil. The other 'positive' in the poem is friendship; and these two values of the heart are held to be sufficient to compensate for the exploitation of man by man. Was it because Burns knew in his heart of hearts that these 'positives' are not in themselves enough to offset the real ills of life that the poem remained an interesting but imperfect experiment clogged by abstract monstrosities of diction like 'sympathetic glow' and 'tenebrific scene'? Perhaps Burns flew to the pompous-sounding English words because he did not really believe what he was saying.[11]

The first 'Epistle to J. Lapraik, An Old Scottish Bard, April 1, 1785',[12] has none of these verbal infelicities. Written in the traditional 'Standard Habbie' measure, so eminently suited to poetic gossip and conversational topics, it is the very perfection of occasional verse. On Fasten-e'en, the evening before Lent, Burns had attended a traditional 'rockin' or small social gathering where women spun on the distaff or wove stockings while each member of the company sang a song in turn. One piece in particular pleased Burns—

> Thought I, 'Can this be Pope, or Steele,
> Or Beattie's wark?'
> They tald me 'twas an odd kind chiel
> About Muirkirk.

It was Lapraik's 'When I upon thy Bosom Lean', which happens to bear an extraordinary resemblance to a song published in Ruddiman's *Weekly Magazine* for 14 October 1773, under the *nom-de-plume* of 'Happy Husband': a circumstance which has led many editors to brand Lapraik as a plagiarist. But there is no evidence for this whatsoever; Lapraik himself may have been 'Happy Husband'. Burns longed to make the acquaintance of the man who could compose such a song and was, he felt, a kindred spirit. He sent him a verse epistle suggesting a meeting at Mauchline Races or Mauchline Fair—or, at the very least, that Lapraik should write him a few lines in reply.

The 'Epistle to J. Lapraik' is an important document because it is in some respects Burns's poetic manifesto, proclaiming the superiority of inspiration over the learned 'Jargon o' your Schools', and the relevance (to Burns at least) of the vernacular tradition:[13]

> Gie me ae spark o' Nature's fire,
> That's a' the learning I desire;
> Then, tho' I drudge thro' dub an' mire
>   At pleugh or cart,
> My Muse, tho' hamely in attire,
>   May touch the heart.
>
> O for a spunk o' Allan's glee,
> Or Fergusson's, the bauld an' slee,
> Or bright Lapraik's, my friend to be,
>   If I can hit it!
> That would be lear eneugh for me,
>   If I could get it.

Nevertheless, it should never be forgotten that this often-quoted statement expresses Burns in only one mood. In the very same poem in which the credo occurs, in a stanza already cited (stanza 4), he mentions the greatest English poet of the century, and finds it not in the least incongruous to praise Lapraik by saying he thought that Pope, or else Beattie—a Scotsman who usually wrote in English—had composed 'When I upon thy Bosom lean'. What he implies in this epistle is simply that creative imitation of vernacular verse is the way for him (indeed, it is perhaps only one of several possible ways), and that Scots poetry is a worthy kind in its own right, though not to the exclusion of others which might, for all we know, be superior to anything in the northern tongue. The famous condemnation of the classically educated pedants who go into college as 'stirks' and come out 'asses', and the claim that he himself has 'to learning nae pretence', but relies entirely on inspiration—

> Whene'er my Muse does on me glance,
> I jingle at her . . .

—all this is suspiciously like the disguise adopted in the prefaces to the Kilmarnock and Edinburgh Editions. But as a corrective to the self-portrait in these verses, one should remember the 'Elegy on the Death of Robert Ruisseaux',[14] where he appears as a voracious reader, pleased above all else when praised for his learning:

> Tho' he was bred to kintra-wark,
> And counted was baith wight and stark,
> Yet that was never Robin's mark
> To mak a man;
> But tell him, he was learned and clark,
> Ye roos'd him then!

This Robert, too, is something of a persona, ironically ridiculing his own pretensions to learning; but both pictures—the Child of Nature and the Eager Student—have their share of truth, for each reflects a characteristic mood.

The 'Epistle to J. Lapraik' contains one of the most thorough-going condemnations of money-grubbing and selfish calculation in the whole of Burns:

> Awa ye selfish, warly race,
> Wha think that havins, sense, an' grace,
> Ev'n love an' friendship, should give place
> To Catch-the-Plack!
> I dinna like to see your face,
> Nor hear your crack.

> But ye whom social pleasure charms,
> Whose hearts the tide of kindness warms,
> Who hold your being on the terms,
>   'Each aid the others,'
> Come to my bowl, come to my arms,
>   My friends, my brothers!

Exactly as in the first 'Epistle to Davie', money-economy and the values of humanity are irreconcilable opposites; but in this poem the antithesis is much more completely realized, without abstraction and without sentimentality. Those who chase after the yellow dirt subordinate everything—brains, reason and the generous feelings—to a frenzied pursuit of wealth. They live separate and alone; they abstain from consumption (and therefore from pleasure) in order to save. Real men are the direct contrary of such caricatures of humanity; they co-operate with one another. Individualism is the supreme evil, and mutual aid the greatest good[15]—surely a tremendous advance on the 'tender feelings' of the 'Epistle to Davie'.

Even in this epistle, with its frank and unqualified homage to Ramsay and Fergusson, Burns modulates into something which on the printed page is indistinguishable from Standard English. The change of diction takes place right at the climax of the poem, in the twenty-first stanza; but the reader does not feel that the transition to 'social pleasure' and the 'tide of kindness' is in the least discordant. When one considers the whole context of the poem, it is evident that Burns can scarcely have regarded the passage as essentially un-Scottish: rather, as spoken by a Scot it is related to the early vernacular of the stanzas beginning

> What's a' your jargon o' your Schools . . .

as, in music, one key is to another.

The 'Second Epistle to J. Lapraik'[16] contains, in the sixth and seventh stanzas, one of the most astonishingly spontaneous outbursts in the whole of Burns:

> Sae I gat paper in a blink,
> An' down gaed stumpie in the ink:
> Quoth I: 'Before I sleep a wink,
>   I vow I'll close it:
> An' if ye winna mak it clink,
>   By Jove, I'll prose it!'

> Sae I've begun to scrawl, but whether
> In rhyme, or prose, or baith thegither,
> Or some hotch-potch that's rightly neither,
> Let time mak proof;
> But I shall scribble down some blether
> Just clean aff-loof.

Here Burns transcends both Scots and English tradition in order to make a statement that is above all personal—one man speaking to another in his own individual voice, with little thought of models.

Written only three weeks after the first, in content the 'Second Epistle' strikes a completely new note. Fortune is still there in the background, but she is no longer all-powerful, as in 'Man was made to Mourn':

> Ne'er mind how Fortune waft an' warp;
> She's but a bitch.

Though ultimate beggary is still a possibility, the dancing lines are radiant with a light-hearted comedy that takes away all terror from the prospect. The rich are no longer an undifferentiated mass, but particularized as two separate groups, the town merchants, and the country landlords, whom Burns specifically terms 'feudal':

> Do ye envy the city gent,
> Behint a kist to lie an' sklent;
> Or purse-proud, big wi' cent. per cent.
> An' muckle wame,
> In some bit brugh to represent
> A bailie's name?

> Or is't the paughty feudal thane,
> Wi' ruffl'd sark an' glancing cane,
> Wha thinks himsel nae sheep-shank bane,
> But lordly stalks;
> While caps an' bonnets aff are taen,
> As by he walks?

Three weeks before, positive value had resided in sociability and co-operation; now (and this constitutes the innovation) it resides in a kind of individualism, which is however rather different from the individualism of calculating utilitarians soullessly planning their own advantage. The 'Second Epistle to Lapraik' presses the claims of the free man, glorying in 'wit an' sense', and, emancipated from the bonds of custom, turned adrift to fend for himself in a hostile Scotland. There is nothing to prevent this new and genuine individual from co-operating with others; he too is 'social'—but he is a person first, a friend and reveller second. Whatever is of worth in this kind of man would be destroyed if either the 'city gent' or the 'feudal thane' were according to nature; but, mercifully, it is the rich who are twisted and distorted, while men like Burns and Lapraik are after nature's stamp:

> Were this the charter of our state,
> 'On pain o' hell be rich an' great,'
> Damnation then would be our fate,
>   Beyond remead;
> But, thanks to heaven, that's no the gate
>   We learn our creed.

> For thus the royal mandate ran,
> When first the human race began:
> 'The social, friendly, honest man,
>   Whate'er he be,
> 'Tis he fulfils great Nature's plan,
>   And none but he.'

In the sixteenth and seventeenth stanzas the isolated Individual, uncircumscribed, free as air, who can yet join together with others in 'social glee', is identified with the archetypal figure of the Artist in a passage which makes amusing play with the doctrines of reincarnation. The poem ends with a hilarious vision of pie-in-the-sky for Lapraik and Burns, while all the moneyed classes are reduced to bestial shapes. Everything is bathed in a warm humorous glow—and yet the irreconcilable opposition between Art and Money, which was to take on almost tragic form in the nineteenth century, is already prefigured in the ending.

From the fourteenth stanza onwards, as he nears the end of the epistle, Burns once more modulates into Scots-English, without, however, leaving the vernacular completely behind; he retains the liberty to use words like 'remead', or Scots 'gate', or 'neivefu'. I cannot agree that the final stanzas are greatly inferior to most of the earlier ones—that is, if the magnificent sixth and seventh stanzas are left entirely out of consideration. One has only to look at the texture of the verse to realize that Burns's mastery of sound-patterns has not deserted him in Anglo-Scots:

Tho' here they scrape, an' squeeze, an' growl,
Their worthless neivefu' of a soul
May in some future carcase howl,
    The forest's fright;
Or in some day-detesting owl
    May shun the light.

We are entitled to condemn the poem's ending only if we are prepared to reject all the English poetry of the mid-eighteenth century. If Burns thought that the translation of himself and Lapraik

To reach their native, kindred skies,
And sing their pleasures, hopes an' joys,
    In some mild sphere

was the only possible artistic conclusion for the work, then he had no alternative but to employ Anglo-Scots; by itself, the vernacular did not have the resources to deal with such an abstract idea.

Like the first 'Epistle to Lapraik', the epistle 'To William Simpson of Ochiltree, May 1785',[17] contains some lines which suggest that Burns was dreaming of publication nearly a year before he circulated his proposals for the Kilmarnock Edition. Simpson had written in praise of Burns's verse, to which he replied:[18]

My senses wad be in a creel,
Should I but dare a hope to speel,
Wi' Allan, or wi' Gilbertfield,
    The braes o' fame;
Or Fergusson, the writer-chiel,
    A deathless name.

These lines exhibit, perhaps, the assumed modesty of a conventional disclaimer; one cannot reject the idea of becoming famous without at least having considered it as a possibility, and this in Burns's case surely implied a printed volume. As in the first 'Epistle to Lapraik' he is anxious to place himself in the vernacular tradition, which (he now claims) the upper classes have tried to strangle; for that is surely the implication of his statement that a tenth of what the Edinburgh gentry were accustomed to waste at cards would have been sufficient to keep Fergusson from destitution. Verse-writing in Scots has, for Burns, an essentially cathartic function—'It gies me ease', and is therefore a supremely natural activity. In the sixth, seventh, eighth and ninth stanzas, he relates his local patriotism to this general Lowland Scots tradition by stating his intention of making the rivers of Ayrshire as well known as Forth and Tay, Yarrow and Tweed, so often mentioned in vernacular poetry; but he enumerates the streams of Ayrshire in the wider context of the whole of Western culture, indeed of the whole known world, as revealed by geographical exploration. Irwin, Lugar, Ayr and Doon are part of a complex which includes 'Illissus, Tiber, Thames an' Seine', New Holland and the remotest seas:

> Or whare wild-meeting oceans boil
> Besouth Magellan.

In the tenth stanza the poem moves from a level which is both local and international to one which is national and patriotic, by way of allusion to William Wallace, who often triumphed over the English on 'Coila's plains an' fells'. At this point, in the eleventh stanza, there occurs one of the most vivid and startling images in the whole of Burns, presented by means of a compound adjective:

> Oft have our fearless fathers strode
> By Wallace' side,
> Still pressing onward, *red-wat-shod*,
> Or glorious dy'd!

The next development is a return to the locality in order to describe its natural scenery, as prelude to the introduction of something wider than either country or nation—Nature herself. The twelfth and thirteenth stanzas are as fine as any descriptive poetry written during the century:

> O, sweet are Coila's haughs an' woods,
> When lintwhites chant amang the buds,
> And jinkin hares, in amorous whids,
> Their loves enjoy;
> While thro' the braes the cushat croods
> With wailfu' cry!

> Ev'n winter bleak has charms to me,
> When winds rave thro' the naked tree;
> Or frosts on hills of Ochiltree
> Are hoary gray;
> Or blinding drifts wild-furious flee,
> Dark'ning the day!

The transition to Nature in general is made through the intermediary of the Man of Feeling. Nature has charms for 'feeling, pensive hearts', and a poet ought to wander by himself, letting his emotions well up within him till they issue forth in 'a heart-felt sang'. The isolated individual of the 'Second Epistle to Lapraik' is now viewed from another angle, in a mood which is far removed from even the joys of convivial drinking or friendly argument. Burns praises pensive pondering and the abjuration of rational thought, the sort of self-indulgent daydreaming condemned by Dr Johnson in the famous chapter on the dangerous prevalence of imagination in *Rasselas*.[19] In complete contrast to Johnson, Burns here considers such sensuous mind-wandering to be an essential part of the poetical character. Nature, contemplated in this way, has now become the antidote to Mammon, as Art fulfilled the same function in the 'Second Epistle to Lapraik':

> The warly race may drudge an' drive,
> Hog-shouther, jundie, stretch, an' strive;
> Let me fair Nature's face descrive,
>   And I, wi' pleasure,
> Shall let the busy, grumbling hive
>   Bum owre their treasure.

It is a fine stanza, with its images of jostling animals and buzzing hoarding bees—the real conclusion of the poem. The next two stanzas are simply an easy fade-out, while the Postscript, with its fable of the Auld and New Lichts, serves to heighten still further the informality of the piece.

Each of the epistles so far examined counterpoises some positive value to the mechanical utilitarianism of philistine hucksters and canting hypocrites. The epistle 'To John Goldie, August 1785',[20] which belongs rather with the ecclesiastical satires, sets the fellowship of the alehouse above that of the Church; a similar praise of alcohol is at the centre of the third epistle 'To J. Lapraik':[21]

> But let the kirk-folk ring their bells!
> Let's sing about our noble sel's:
> We'll cry nae jads frae heathen hills
>   To help or roose us,
> But browster wives an' whisky stills—
>   They are the Muses!

Though the second epistle 'To Davie'[22] is in some ways a disappointing performance—the second stanza in particular is almost as sickly sentimental and falsely rustic as the productions of the nineteenth-century kailyard school—it provides contemporary evidence of the tremendous energy expended by Burns (both in living and in writing) during his great creative period:

> For me, I'm on Parnassus' brink,
> Rivin the words to gar them clink;
> Whyles daez't wi' love, whyles daez't wi' drink
>   Wi' jads or Masons,
> An' whyles, but ay owre late I think,
>   Braw sober lessons.

In the following stanzas he holds fast once more to the convenient myth of the thoughtless, improvident 'Bardie clan' who are constitutionally incapable of behaving like ordinary mortals, and again (as at the end of that far more successful work, the 'Second Epistle to Lapraik') he sees in poetry the one sure buckler in a hostile world. Even in a bad poem the same preoccupations recur, as they do in the rather bathetic conclusion, with its hint of the beggar theme at the very end:

> Haud to the Muse, my dainty Davie:
> The warl' may play you monie a shavie,
> But for the Muse, she'll never leave ye,
>   Tho' e'er sae puir;
> Na, even tho' limpin wi' the spavie
>   Frae door to door!

The 'Epistle to James Smith'[23] is generally preferred to the other verse epistles. It is certainly a remarkable work, overflowing with effortless spontaneity and bubbling humour. Written a little earlier than April 1786, just before Burns had definitely decided to bring out an edition, it shows him once again in the role of the completely un-educated poet:

> Something cries, 'Hoolie!
> I red you, honest man, tak tent!
> Ye'll shaw your folly. . . .'

How can such a man as he possibly hope for immortality when so many literate poets have faded from remembrance after their brief day of glory? Surely it would be safer to eschew print altogether, and remain simply an unknown bard who rhymes for fun. In the twelfth stanza, the ills of life, inevitable suffering and death, even the cosy retirement

enjoyed by profiteers in their old age—all are viewed through a golden
haze of humour and well-being:

> This life, sae far's I understand,
> Is a' enchanted fairy-land,
> Where Pleasure is the magic-wand,
>> That, wielded right,
> Maks hours like minutes, hand in hand,
>> Dance by fu' light.

Not that he is utterly oblivious of Time's chariot. As with Marvell,
'To his Coy Mistress', the injunction is to

> . . . tear our Pleasures with rough strife,
> Thorough the Iron gates of life.

In an equally vigorous image, Burns puts it in his own way:

> Then top and maintop crowd the sail,
>> Heave Care o'er-side!
> And large, before Enjoyment's gale,
>> Let's tak the tide.

He wants nothing from life except the opportunity to make poetry:
the varied positives of the earlier epistles now give way to a single
positive, an idea which unites poetry and 'real, sterling wit'. The
worshippers of Mammon are now *identified* with the 'unco guid', the
main target of the ecclesiastical satires. Holly Willie and Cent.-per-Cent.
are fundamentally one and the same:

> O ye douce folk that live by rule,
> Grave, tideless-blooded, calm an' cool,
> Compar'd wi' you—O fool! fool! fool!
>> How much unlike!
> Your hearts are just a standing pool,
>> Your lives a dyke!

> Nae hair-brained, sentimental traces
> In your unletter'd, nameless faces!
> In *arioso* trills and graces
>> Ye never stray,
> But *gravissimo*, solemn basses
>> Ye hum away.

Ye are sae grave, nae doubt ye're wise;
Nae ferly tho' ye do despise
The hairum-scairum, ram-stam boys,
    The rattling squad:
I seen ye upward cast your eyes—
    Ye ken the road!

I suppose the recent equivalents of the 'rattling squad' are the young
'delinquents', beatniks, folkniks, Mods and Rockers, and all rebels with
or without a cause. Translated into these terms, the 'Epistle to James
Smith' states that the iconoclastic young (not the angry young men of
the middle classes, but those who make the street and coffee-bar their
rendez-vous) represent Life and Libido and the Horn of Plenty, while
the ordinary suburbanite worshipper of the god in the garage stands for
death, debility, and the crucifixion of essential humanity. It is an
opposition of this sort which lies at the heart of the 'Epistle to James
Smith', and indeed at the centre of Burns's own soul. On the one hand,
the peasantry's old, half-pagan lust for life, survivals of which take on
somewhat distorted shapes in twentieth-century dormitory towns; on
the other, puritanism, rationality, calculation and control. During
these two momentous years especially, Burns himself was one of the
'hairum-scairum, ram-stam boys'. But he was also the man who
preached Common-sense, whose favourite quotation was:[24]

                on reason build resolve,
    (That column of true majesty in man) . . .

This other side of Burns—Burns the Champion of Society, paying
his tribute to all the established virtues like any company-director,
executive or racing reporter after a spree—is exhibited in the last of the
early epistles, the 'Epistle to a Young Friend'[25] of May 1786, composed
at the very height of the Armour crisis, when he was also (so it would
seem) deeply involved with Mary Campbell. He advises his young
friend to keep to the path of conventional virtue:

The sacred lowe o' weel-plac'd love,
    Luxuriantly indulge it;
But never tempt th' illicit rove,
    Tho' naething should divulge it:
I waive the quantum o' the sin,
    The hazard of concealing;
But, och! it hardens a' within,
    And petrifies the feeling!

Amusingly enough, the young man is given a homily on the value of thrift—provided that he does not use his savings to lord it ostentatiously over others:

> To catch Dame Fortune's golden smile,
>   Assiduous wait upon her;
> And gather gear by ev'ry wile
>   That's justify'd by honour:
> Not for to hide it in a hedge,
>   Nor for a train-attendant;
> But for the glorious privilege
>   Of being independent.

This is indeed the morality of small farmers and petty traders! Established ethics, the maxims which his own father taught him, are of inestimable value in life; the only trouble with them is that they are so difficult to put into practice:

> And may ye better reck the rede,
>   Than ever did th' adviser!

Into this *pot-pourri* of all the bourgeois virtues—complete with

> An atheist-laugh's a poor exchange
>   For Deity offended!

—Burns intrudes the concept of personal honour, perhaps in the last resort derived from clan morality. Most significantly, he sets it side by side with the Calvinists' fear of Hell, so that the one doctrine appears as the negation of the other:

> The fear o' Hell's a hangman's whip
>   To haud the wretch in order;
> But where ye feel your honour grip,
>   Let that ay be your border. . . .

A good way of appreciating the variety of Burns's moods is to place the 'Epistle to James Smith' side-by-side with the 'Epistle to a Young Friend'. The latter is as much a fruit of experience as the former; it has taken some of its colouring from the remorseful mood of the fifth stanza of 'Despondency, an Ode':[26]

> O enviable early days,
> When dancing thoughtless pleasure's maze,
>   To care, to guilt unknown!

How ill exchang'd for riper times,
To feel the follies or the crimes
Of others, or my own!

The man who takes the tide before 'enjoyment's gale' is liable to find
that his fairyland turns into a desert because his actions have caused
suffering to others; as Burns remarks at the end of the second stanza of
the ode, the life of ordinary mortals striving for worldly success may
have its compensations after all:

You, bustling and justling,
    Forget each grief and pain;
I, listless yet restless,
    Find ev'ry prospect vain.

However, it would be wrong to represent this last position as final;
like the others, it is the reflexion of a mood. The self-dramatizations of
the epistles express a mind in motion, giving itself over at different
times to *conflicting* principles and feelings; they mirror that mind as it
grappled with a complex world. In order to body it forth, Burns had
to be, in himself, and not simply in play, both Calvinist and anti-
Calvinist, both fornicator and champion of chastity, both Jacobite and
Jacobin, both local and national, both British and European, both
anarchist and sober calculator, both philistine and anti-philistine. He had
to write in both Braid Scots and Scots-English and in a blend of the
two, being at one and the same time a man of the old homely Scotland
of village communities, a forerunner of the Scotland of capitalist
farmers employing wage-labour and the new agricultural implements,
and a poet who shared—even before he went to Edinburgh—something of the Anglo-Scottish culture of the capital. The occasional and
informal nature of the epistle was ideal for the expression of a plethora
of moods together with the transitions between them; consequently,
Burns's experiments with the genre contain much of his finest work.

Notes

1   *The Poems and Songs of Robert Burns*, ed. J. Kinsley (Oxford, 1968), no. 60.
    References here are to Kinsley's edition, but quotations are from *The Poetry
    of Robert Burns*, ed. W. E. Henley and T. F. Henderson, 4 vols (Edinburgh
    and London, 1896-7).
2   Kinsley, no. 49. Rankine was tenant of Adamhill, a farm near Lochlie.
3   Kinsley, no. 47.

4   There is an interesting ironical turn at the end of the sixth stanza: 'I'd better gaen an' sair't the King / At Bunker's Hill.' Burns, as we know from 'A Fragment: When Guilford Good' (Kinsley, no. 38), was opposed to the British foreign policy of his day. No course would have been more suicidal than enlistment for service in America, since it would have represented an ultimate in reckless despair; it would have meant risking his life, for spite or devilment, in a cause he knew to be wrong. Burns is, in this sixth stanza, expressing what has since become the ordinary working-class attitude to patriotism and soldiering—and not in Scotland only.

5   Kinsley, no. 51.

6   Rousseauism came to Burns through Henry Mackenzie, Shenstone, and the eighteenth-century cult of sentiment. The ideas behind his poem—and many other works of Burns—represent concepts common to both Rousseau and Anglo-Scottish sentimentalism.

7   Especially the 'Crazy Jane' and 'Old Tom' songs, in *Collected Poems* (London, 1950), pp. 290-307.

8   Kinsley, no. 43.

9   *Ibid.*, no. 45.

10   'When Princes & Prelates', in *Letters*, II, pp. 250-1.

11   When judged in terms of the kind of statement it is making, the 'Epistle to Davie' exhibits a fusion of English and Scottish influences; and the glorification of the 'heart' is based on ideas which, however popular they were in Edinburgh, came to Scotland from England and France. But considered as poetry, the work does not achieve a real synthesis of Scots and Scots-English. One reason for the failure is surely that this is the least conversational, the least 'familiar', of all the Burns epistles. On the whole, it lacks spontaneity—perhaps because of the form, which must have forced Burns to work hard at the piece. The metre is a modification of a traditional stanza, used by Montgomerie in *The Cherrie and The Slae* (1597), which was reprinted in Watson's *Choice Collection* (1706-11) and in Ramsay's *The Ever Green* (1724), and thus made familiar to the eighteenth century. Ramsay himself used it in works of his own composition, and Burns took it over from him, with certain modifications of his own.

12   Kinsley, no. 57.

13   The *general* part of this theoretical statement appears to be of English origin, though its particular application is Scottish. Cf. Sterne, *Tristram Shandy*, Bk III, ch. 12: 'Great Apollo! if thou art in a giving humour—give me,—I ask no more, but one stroke of native humour, with a single spark of thy own fire along with it—and send Mercury, with the rules and compasses, if he can be spared, with my compliments to—no matter.' Burns's Nature was, however, not Augustan Nature; it was quite a different concept from Boileau's, or Pope's or Shaftesbury's. To them, Nature was objective, and more or less equated with external reality; but to Burns, in this passage, Nature was subjective, the equivalent of 'genius' or 'originality'. (Cf. F. L. Beaty, 'Ae Spark o' Nature's fire', *English Language Notes*, I (1964), pp. 203-7.)

14   Kinsley, no. 141.

15   The positive values of the first 'Epistle to Lapraik' appear to be identical with those of Freemasonry, which was—significantly enough—at one and the same time a Scottish and a European movement.

16 Kinsley, no. 58.

17 *Ibid.*, no. 59.

18 Interestingly enough, Fergusson had made the same sort of statement before Burns, in his 'Answer to Mr. J. S's Epistle', stanza 5. The subject is his Muse:

> But she maun e'en be glad to jook,
> An' play *teet-bo* frae nook to nook,
> Or blush as gin she had the yook
> Upon her skin,
> Whan *Ramsay*, or whan *Pennicuik*
> Their lilts begin.

19 Chapter 44.

20 Kinsley, no. 63.

21 *Ibid.*, no. 67.

22 *Ibid.*, no. 101.

23 *Ibid.*, no. 79.

24 To [Mrs Maclehose], 19 Jan. 1788, and to other correspondents, in *Letters*, I, 166, and *passim*. The quotation is from Young's *Night Thoughts*, Night 1, ll. 30-1.

25 Kinsley, no. 105. In so far as there is any single source for the poem, it is probably Polonius's advice to Laertes in *Hamlet*, I, iii.

26 Kinsley, no. 94, stanza 5.

Chapter 5

The Satires: Underground Poetry

Alexander Scott

The unanimity of praise for the satires among modern Scottish critics of Burns is remarkable in a literary scene where controversy is more usual than consent. To David Daiches, 'The Holy Tulzie' is 'brilliant' and 'extraordinarily effective'; 'Holy Willie's Prayer' possesses 'cosmic irony' and 'perfect dramatic appropriateness'; 'The Holy Fair' is at once 'the finest of those [poems] in the Kilmarnock volume which show the full stature of Burns as a poet working in the Scots literary tradition' and a creation with 'revolutionary implications'; 'The Twa Dogs' is 'brisk, sharp-toned . . . with wit and point'; 'Address to the Deil' is 'effective' in that it 'blows up' the doctrine of original sin; 'The Ordination' is (again) 'effective', this time in 'the contrast between the form and the ostensible theme'; and 'Address of Beelzebub' is 'bitter and biting'.[1] To Thomas Crawford, 'The Holy Tulzie' shows 'developing still further the technique used in . . . the "Epistle to John Rankine"— the apparent assumption of the standards, beliefs and language of the opposite party'; 'Holy Willie's Prayer' is 'one of the finest satires of all time'; 'The Holy Fair' shows 'complete mastery of traditional poetic skills'; 'The Twa Dogs' has 'a pleasing manner'; 'The Ordination' is 'one of the finest and freshest things Burns ever did'; and 'Address of Beelzebub' is 'the most savage of all Burns's satires'.[2] To David Craig, despite his distrust of 'reductive criticism' and 'the reductive idiom and the poor man's defensive pose' in much eighteenth-century Scots satirical writing, 'Burns was in a wonderfully original and rich vein in the poems that may be called his satires'.[3]

All these works had been written before the publication in July 1786 of the Kilmarnock edition which created for Burns the national—and international—reputation he has enjoyed ever since. Yet references to the satires in the contemporary reviews are few and far between. The *Edinburgh Magazine* of October 1786, noting that 'some of his subjects are serious, but those of the humorous kind are the best', illustrates the point by quoting 'Address to the Deil' and excerpts from 'The Holy Fair', but none of the other satirical pieces is so much as mentioned by name; the *Monthly Review* (London) of December 1786 expresses the opinion that 'our author seems to be most in his element when in the sportive humorous strain', but neither discusses nor illustrates the work

which would exemplify that remark—perhaps because of a view that
'the poems of this cast . . . so much abound with provincial phrases and
allusions to local circumstances, that no extracts from them would be
sufficiently intelligible to our English readers'; the *Lounger* (Edinburgh)
of December 1786, where the reviewer was the novelist Henry
Mackenzie, mentions the 'Dialogue of the Dogs' [*sic*] among other
'lighter and more humorous poems' which demonstrate 'with what
uncommon penetration and sagacity this heaven-taught ploughman,
from his humble unlettered station, has looked upon men and manners',
but in defending Burns against the charge of 'irreligion' by remarking
that 'we shall not look upon his lighter muse as the enemy of religion
(of which in several places he expresses the justest sentiments) though
she has been somewhat unguarded in her ridicule of hypocrisy',
Mackenzie leaves the religious satires unrecorded by either title or
quotation; and the *English Review* (London) of February 1787, while
adducing 'Address to the Deil' and 'The Holy Fair' to exemplify its
view that 'the finest poems . . . are of the humorous and satirical kind,
and in these our author appears to be most at home', devotes most of
its space to the discussion of poems from which humour and satire are
entirely absent.

The temptation to berate those early critics of Burns for obtuseness,
however strong it may be, and however apparently justified in the
eyes of readers of his collected poems, does not survive reference to the
Kilmarnock edition. For of all the satires mentioned in the first paragraph above, only three, 'The Holy Fair', 'The Twa Dogs' and
'Address to the Deil', find a place in its pages. The others have
been suppressed, either by the poet himself, or by the poet following the views of his adviser, the lawyer Robert Aiken, 'Dear
Patron of my Virgin Muse'. When Burns made his first bow to the
public, he chose to do so with his strong right arm tied behind his
back.

If at first sight this seems to be extraordinary behaviour for a novice,
who might be expected to wish to make the maximum impact upon
his readers, the appearance is deceptive. Burns and his adviser had
sufficient reasons for deciding against the inclusion in the Kilmarnock
edition of those satires which are now among the most highly praised
of all his works. Most of them were certainly libellous—and, in the eyes
of some of those local readers in the west of Scotland for whom the
Kilmarnock edition was printed by subscription, they might have
appeared blasphemous at worst, and at best in extremely poor taste.

The clue to the situation lies in Burns's famous autobiographical letter to Dr Moore where, discussing the earliest of his satires, 'The Holy Tulzie', he writes:[4]

> The first of my poetic offspring that saw the light was a burlesque lamentation on a quarrel between two reverend Calvinists, both of them dramatis person in my Holy Fair.—I had an idea myself that the piece had some merit; but to prevent the worst, I gave a copy of it to a friend who was very fond of these things, and told him I could not guess who was the Author of it, but that I thought it pretty clever.—With a certain side of both clergy and laity it met with a roar of applause.

But there are always two sides (at least) to any Scottish reaction to works of art of a controversial kind, and how others among 'both clergy and laity' must have reacted to 'The Holy Fair' is indicated by their reception of its immediate successor, 'Holy Willie's Prayer'—'It alarmed the kirk-session so much that they held three successive meetings to look over their holy artillery, if any of it was pointed against profane Rhymers'.[5]

Both 'The Holy Tulzie' and 'Holy Willie's Prayer' were attacks on *local* personalities in the church—hence the caution, 'to prevent the worst', which led Burns to pretend ignorance of the authorship of the former when passing it out in manuscript. Rural Ayrshire in the late eighteenth century was still under a clerical discipline—or Calvinist dictatorship—whose restrictive power was all the greater for its basis in a public opinion which Henry Mackenzie, reflecting 'moderate' Edinburgh views, described as 'the ignorance and fanaticism of the lower class of the people in the country where these poems were written, a fanaticism of that pernicious sort which sets faith in opposition to good works'.[6] Moreover, at the time 'The Holy Tulzie' and 'Holy Willie's Prayer' were composed, early in 1785, Burns had placed himself in a highly vulnerable position *vis-à-vis* the kirk: 'Unluckily for me, my idle wanderings led me, on another side, point-blank within the reach of their heaviest metal.'[7] Less metaphorically, he was responsible for the pregnancy of Elizabeth Paton, the Burns family's domestic servant, who bore him a daughter on 22 May 1785, and consequently he would be required to appear on the church's stool of repentance, 'arrayed . . . in the black sackcloth gown of fornication',[8] for three successive Sundays. After that penance he would be regarded as having made his peace with the kirk, provided there were no other scandals appertaining to his person. But if his authorship of 'The Holy Tulzie' and 'Holy Willie's Prayer' had been avowed, or even acknowledged, the clerical authorities would have had every reason (in their own view) to continue to hold him under the ban of their baleful displeasure.

A year later, in the spring of 1786, when Burns was selecting poems for the Kilmarnock edition, he would have been in even worse trouble had all the facts of his sexual irregularities come to light, for at that time he had made himself a bigamist by contracting two irregular marriages, firstly with Jean Armour—who bore him twins on 3 September—and secondly (and secretly) with Mary Campbell. From the consequences of those follies he was rescued, through no merit of his own, by the sudden death of 'Highland Mary' in the autumn of that year. By then, however, the Kilmarnock edition had already been published, with most of the anti-clerical satires omitted.

Yet, ironically enough, the same system of clerical dictatorship which compelled Burns to deny the dignity of print to some of his liveliest poems would appear to have been responsible for their original composition. While the poet's Commonplace Book makes it plain that he had reached a 'moderate' view in religion, opposed to the narrow fundamentalist ('Auld Licht') principles of his local kirk-session, at least as early as 1784, it was not until 'the thorns were in his own flesh' and he found himself in peril of the kirk's censure as a result of his affair with Elizabeth Paton that he was stimulated into writing about the Calvinists of his own district in terms of the kind of attack which has traditionally been regarded as the best means of defence.

A notorious dispute about parish boundaries between two 'Auld Licht' ministers, 'hitherto sworn friends and associates', who 'lost all command of temper' when the matter was discussed at the Presbytery of Ayr, and 'abused each other . . . with a fiery violence of invective',[9] presented the poet with a golden opportunity for satire. The whole of 'The Holy Tulzie' is an extended metaphor, the nature of which is succinctly indicated by the poem's alternative title 'The Twa Herds', but the very orthodoxy of the time-hallowed images of the minister as shepherd and the congregation as his flock gives a keener edge to the mockery of the treatment, and the poet's adoption of the persona of an Auld Licht sympathizer, professing horror and dismay at the 'bitter, black outcast' between the two guardians of sanctity, sharpens the irony to a more penetrating point. Again, the presentation of the two pastors as actual—as well as metaphorical—Scottish shepherds, their business to protect the sheep 'frae the fox / Or worrying tykes', their practice to trap 'the Fulmart, Wil-cat, Brock and Tod' and 'sell their skin', deprives them of dignity and makes their blowing of 'gospel horns' and swinging of 'the Gospel-club' all the more ludicrous by the brilliantly daring association of the scriptural with the mundane— while the presentation of their flocks as real sheep ('the Brutes') puts beyond argument the propriety of patronage in the presentation of parish ministers, since it would appear that the only alternative is to 'get the Brutes the pouer themsels / To chuse their Herds'. Technically, too, the poet's command of the Habbie Simson stanza is already consummate, although this is only the third occasion he has employed it.

Despite those various virtues, however, the poem falls short of being a masterpiece. As Hilton Brown remarks, '[Burns] was always lazy . . . even in his best days many of his most promising openings peter out for lack of just that finish and pulling together which an extra ounce of effort would have supplied',[10] and he gives 'The Holy Tulzie' as an example of this fault. The poem ends too abruptly, as if the writer had suddenly run out of steam. But even before that point is reached, readers from other airts than eighteenth-century Ayrshire find themselves in difficulty and compelled to start grubbing in editorial notes. During the first fifty-four lines, no such grubbing is necessary, for even although we know nothing about the two protagonists, 'Moodie man and wordy Russell' as Burns punningly names them, their natures and their functions emerge so clearly from the verse that they quickly establish themselves in our minds as recognizable clerical types, as true to life now as then. But in the next thirty lines the poet lets loose an avalanche of ministers' names, all of them familiar enough to his original local audience, but now unknown to fame except for their appearance here and elsewhere in Burns's work, and none of them sufficiently delineated to achieve a living reality in the verse. From being a local poem which yet contains implications of wider significance, 'The Holy Tulzie' here becomes parochial, concerned with personalities of interest only to a limited circle of readers. Those very elements which gave the poem much of its notoriety among Burns's Ayrshire contemporaries decrease its appeal to the present day.

Some stanzas of 'Holy Willie's Prayer' suffer from the same disability. To say as much is not to deny a jot of the brilliance of Burns's parody of the style of 'the Scottish Presbyterian eloquence' with its incongruous combination of the Biblical and the broad, or the satirical skill of the presentation of his protagonist, the arch-hypocrite of Calvinist fanaticism, disguising yet revealing his lust and greed under 'a veil that is rent', a tattered screen of sanctified self-interest, and betraying himself out of his own all too awfully eloquent mouth. For the first sixty-six of the poem's one hundred and two lines, Holy

Willie is a prototype as well as a local personality, and given the slightest acquaintanceship on the reader's part with the doctrines of original sin and predestination, the theme of Christianity un-christianized is of universal—and ageless—relevance. Even the intro-duction, by name, of Willie's most hated 'enemy', Gavin Hamilton, requires no external explanation, for he too is not only individual but representative, a personality who enjoys the pleasures frowned upon by the kirk ('He drinks, and swears, and plays at cartes') while posses-sing such charm that he commits the even greater 'crime' of winning more regard than the community's religious leader ('Frae G—d's ain priest the people's hearts / He steals awa').

But then occur two stanzas in which Willie demands that the Lord should 'hear my earnest cry and prayer / Against that Presbytery of Ayr!' and describes 'that glib-tongu'd Aiken' who created such terror among the godly that even 'Auld wi' hingin lip gaed sneaking'. These lines are a good deal less than self-explanatory to readers unaware of what occurred when Gavin Hamilton appealed to the 'moderate' Presbytery of Ayr, against the adverse judgment on his alleged absence from public worship passed by the 'Auld Licht' kirk in the parish of Mauchline, and won his case thanks to the successful pleading of his lawyer and friend Robert Aiken. To 'the rustic inmates of the hamlet'[11] who constituted Burns's first audience, the affair was so recent, and the gossip concerning it so rife, that detailed description would have been otiose, but what was daylight to them is darkness to us unless we are given editorial assistance, for the parochial nature of the subject-matter defeats unaided comprehension.

Both 'The Holy Tulzie' and 'Holy Willie's Prayer' are concerned with specific local religious scandals, so notorious in the west country that, had the poems been printed, the characters who feature in them could not have failed to be recognized, even if their names had been omitted and replaced by asterisks. The risk of a libel action, or of clerical condemnation, or of both, was too great for that unconfessed bigamist among 'rakish rooks',[12] Robert Burns, to include them in the Kilmarnock edition—even although there can be little doubt, human nature being what it is, that those subjects of scandal and concern had created much of that local interest in the author which led to his first publication being so heavily subscribed by his neighbours. 'The Holy Tulzie' remained unpublished during the poet's lifetime, the first to appear in print being 'Holy Willie's Prayer', in an anonymous pam-phlet of 1789, when it was accompanied—appropriately—by 'quota-tions from the Presbyterian eloquence'.

This linking of Burns's late-eighteenth-century poem with a work published in 1694 as a result of the religious strife in seventeenth-century Scotland is significant, for although Professor James Kinsley indicates a more recent model for 'Holy Willie's Prayer' ('Burns may have taken a hint from Ramsay's "Last Speech of a Wretched Miser to his hoard"'[13]), it has much in common with Drummond of Hawthornden's late near-vernacular poem, 'A Character of the Anti-Covenanter, or Malignant',[14] first published among the posthumous poems in the 1711 edition of Drummond's works. Here Drummond, himself an 'anti-Covenanter, or Malignant' (or Cavalier), adopts the persona of a Covenanter in order to 'attack' the Cavalier view, in exact anticipation of the way in which Burns, himself a moderate (with the same dislike of Presbyterian extremism as the Cavaliers had possessed before him), adopts the persona of an Auld Licht in order to 'attack' the moderate standpoint, and in each poem the Calvinist fanatic who is the protagonist brings down the reader's condemnation upon himself while seeking to destroy the opposition.

'A Character of the Anti-Covenanter', 106 lines long—only four lines longer than 'Holy Willie's Prayer'—is written in octosyllabic couplets instead of the 'standard Habbie' of Burns, but its jaunty, irregular rhythms, its at least equally irregular rhymes, its brutal jocularity, its plain blunt energy—at the opposite pole of style from the stately and mellifluous decorum of Drummond's earlier verse, published during his lifetime—give it a force no less devastating, and no less remarkable for its counterpointing of the profound and the profane, than the later work. There is, however, one major difference between the two poems, for the speaker in Drummond is not identified by any nickname; he represents all extreme Calvinists rather than, like Holy Willie, a particular spokesman speaking for all. In the same way, the targets at which the earlier extremist fires his musket are not specific opponents like Gavin Hamilton and Robert Aiken, but each and every member of the 'malignant' party. It may be argued that Burns's particularity of characterization gives 'Holy Willie's Prayer' more point (although in fact Hamilton is as much a type as an individual, and Aiken is scarcely particularized at all, except as 'glib-tongu'd'), or it may be held that this very particularization narrows the range of Burns's attack, compared with Drummond's; but it is beyond dispute that the present-day reader of Drummond does not require to acquaint himself with seventeenth-century Scottish biography in order to gain full appreciation of his poem, as must be done with regard to the following century in respect of 'Holy Willie's Prayer'.

Unlike that dramatic lyric, Burns's next religious satire, 'The Holy Fair', which followed in the autumn of the same year, was considered 'safe' enough for inclusion in the Kilmarnock edition—although that safety was ensured only by a liberal substitution of asterisks for proper names whose owners would have regarded their appearance in print in such a context as being highly improper. A further measure of safety arises from the fact that 'The Holy Fair' is less personal than public, less concerned with the follies committed by particular individuals than with the festivities enjoyed by a whole community, for the poem belongs to a Scots tradition of 'come-to-the-fair' verse-comedy traceable to the medieval celebration of village life in 'Christ's Kirk on the Green' (which had been brought up to date earlier in the eighteenth century by Allan Ramsay, with the addition of extra cantos of his own).

Again, 'The Holy Fair' is not concerned with one specific, easily recognizable occurrence—an undignified row between two Calvinist ministers, or a legal battle between fundamentalist priest and liberal parishioner—but might derive from observation of any and every public communion held in the open air in the west of Scotland. The scene is in fact set in Burns's local parish of Mauchline, as we now know (from the manuscript), but the asterisks in the Kilmarnock edition give no clue to this, and there are no merely parochial descriptive details (except perhaps the mention of 'Racer Jess', the half-witted daughter of 'Poosie Nansie' Gibson, who kept a local tavern) which might give the game—and the name—away to readers not already in the know. Moreover, the references to the various preachers who waste the sweetness (or sourness) of their eloquence on the desert air—while 'the godly . . . gie the jars an' barrels / A lift that day' and 'the lads an' lasses . . . are cozie i' the neuk'—are of such a generalized kind that their actual identities, indicated in the printed text only by asterisks, matter little or nothing.

> Now a' the congregation o'er,
> Is silent expectation;
> For ****** speels the holy door,
> Wi' tidings o' s-lv-t--n:
> Should *Hornie*, as in ancient days,
> 'Mang sons o' G-- present him,
> The vera sight o' ******'s face,
> To's ain *het hame* had sent him
> Wi' fright that day.

Who cares, or needs to care, that scholarly research has revealed the minister there as 'Sawnie', otherwise Alexander Moodie (of 'The Holy Tulzie'), 'educated at Glasgow, ordained to Culross in 1759, and minister of Riccarton from 1762'?[15] What difference does it make to the reader's enjoyment to know that the asterisks in '***** opens out his cauld harangues' represent that grand old Caledonian cognomen, Smith? Yet Burns himself, publishing his volume while he poised precariously on the razor's edge dividing acknowledged fornication from unadmitted bigamy, was compelled to care, and the difference between asterisks and actuality was vital. He might risk revealing the truth in 'The Holy Fair', but not the whole truth. The real identities of his preaching protagonists remained 'underground'.

Of all the many poems in the 'Christ's Kirk' tradition, 'The Holy Fair' is the most masterly, in its command of verse technique, the idiomatic cut and thrust of its style, the combination of comedy and criticism in its action and characterization, and the cunning of its transitions between panoramic views of general activities and close-ups of individuals and particularities. Yet Hilton Brown, while finding the poem 'excellent as a descriptive piece', dismisses it as 'surely too crude for successful satire',[16] a view which seems eccentric—unless the critic is using 'crude' in the sexual sense, expressing disapproval of such scenes as the lover taking advantage of everyone else's eyes being fixed on the preacher, and engaging meantime in intimate caresses of his 'ain dear lass'. But this is surely to have overlooked the central theme of the poem, the triumphant survival of life-creating sexuality even under the dreary domination of the most repressive puritanism.

The satire on Calvinism in 'Address to the Deil' (written in the winter of 1785-6) is so indirect, and so devoid of specific local references, that it was included in the Kilmarnock edition almost as written. Almost, but not quite. In lines 61-6 the demands of decorum have led to the toning down of the tragic tale of how devilish witchcraft deprives the new bridegroom of his virility at the most vital of all moments; and in lines 85-90 'my bonie Jean, / My dearest part' is removed from the poem. The first of these departures from the manuscript is significant in showing how Burns, despite his contempt for convention, was the kind of rebel poet who is not above deciding, on occasion, that discretion is the better part of valour where the interests of publication are concerned—and even then he was not discreet enough for some, since the Rev. Hugh Blair advised that even the revised stanza 'had better be left out, as indecent'[17] from the Edinburgh edition of 1787.

Of the revision of lines 85-90 Kinsley takes the view that it was 'probably made just before going to press, to remove the allusion to Jean Armour, from whom he was estranged',[18] but this does much less than justice to the difficulty and danger of Burns's situation in June 1786, when he was secretly married not only to a pregnant Jean Armour but also to Mary Campbell (whose reputation was far from being impregnable). 'Estranged' from Jean Armour, Burns undoubtedly was, when her parents compelled her to acquiesce in the defacement of the 'marriage certificate' which the poet had given her and then packed her off to Paisley in the hope that she might contrive a more suitable match; but he did not languish after her for long. On the contrary, the speed with which he was off with the old love and on with the new, and his recklessness in giving the second girl the same kind of documentary evidence of his 'honourable intentions' as he had already presented to the first, put him in a position of vulnerability to the law—if his secrets were discovered—that would have weakened even the steeliest nerves. For Burns to have published a declaration of his regard for Jean ('A dancin, sweet, young, handsome queen / Wi' guileless heart') at a time when he was risking a charge of bigamy—against which he could have defended himself only by swearing that she had no claim upon him whatsoever—would have been an act of self-destruction too apparent for even the most impractical poet to ignore. As far as his published work was concerned, it was imperative that Jean be kept 'underground', consigned to oblivion, become a non-person. And so it happened, Burns replacing her person with 'the Soul of Love', an unconscious irony which was lost upon those of his original readers who had not already encountered the poem in manuscript. Even in its altered state, the 'Address' remains one of his most attractive works, a humorous mock-attack on the Great Enemy which reduces more orthodox assaults upon him to the status of superstitious nonsense, but the excised stanzas have a bite and a particularity lacking from their published counterparts.

The last of the religious satires composed before the Kilmarnock edition made Burns famous, 'The Ordination' (written early in 1786) was as parochial in origin as 'The Holy Tulzie' and 'Holy Willie's Prayer', and it suffered the same fate, exclusion. For all the asterisks with which the text is bespattered fail to conceal from even the most cursory reader that the scene is Kilmarnock and the occasion the presentation to the ministry of the Laigh Kirk there of a fundamentalist minister, the Rev. James Mackinlay, who owed his preferment to the favour of the patron, the Earl of Glencairn. Written to console the moderate party in their defeat, the poem uses the pastoral imagery of 'The Holy Tulzie' to present a ludicrously grotesque picture of Kilmarnock's Auld Licht congregation in the shape of a ram which has had only 'scanty' feeding while the Moderates held the field but which can now revel in rich repasts of '*gospel kail*' and '*runts o' grace*' provided by the fundamentalist Mackinlay. The work's daring juxtapositions of the sacred and the profane must have seemed blasphemous to contemporary readers of the evangelical persuasion, and the concluding episode, when Orthodoxy flogs Learning, Common Sense and Morality through the town as if they were rogues and vagabonds, possesses a brutal jocularity, equating 'righteousness' with sadistic revenge, which lays it open to the same charge. This is the only one of Burns's pre-Kilmarnock satires occasioned by a Moderate defeat rather than by an Evangelical upset, and the sharper bitterness of its tone may well reflect the rage felt by the poet's party, and by the author himself, at their discomfiture on a battleground where they had begun to believe that they were on the winning side.

But Burns did not leave 'The Ordination' unacknowledged and underground for very long. Although he omitted it from the Kilmarnock, he found it a place in the Edinburgh edition of 1787, and one can only speculate on the reasons which led him on that occasion to accept a risk which he had refused to take a year earlier, and which he still refused on behalf of 'The Holy Tulzie' and 'Holy Willie's Prayer'. Perhaps he had realized that irony remains unnoticed by persons without a sense of humour, and that a poem written in the style of a victory-song for the fundamentalists might well be interpreted as such by them and hence escape their strictures? Whatever the explanation, there is no doubt that Burns experienced some difficulty in finding sufficient previously unpublished poems for the Edinburgh edition to justify it in the eyes of readers who had already bought the earlier book—this accounts for his inclusion in the Edinburgh collection of 'Death and Dr Hornbook', a *jeu d'esprit* which has been greatly admired for its witty command of dialogue but which the poet himself had considered 'too trifling and prolix'[19] to publish in the Kilmarnock volume. He may have felt that, having 'got away' with 'The Holy Fair' in the Kilmarnock, where it had even been praised and quoted in the reviews, he might now take a chance on the publication of another religious satire, and chose 'The Ordination' as being less of a pointed personal attack on individuals than 'The Holy Tulzie' and 'Holy

Willie's Prayer'. The question must remain in doubt, but—given the necessity of finding some 'new poems' for the Edinburgh volume—the hypothesis seems not unreasonable.

In his religious satires, Burns is the artist-intellectual in rebellion against the obscurantism of local public opinion, and his allies are the men of education who favoured patronage (exercised by land-owning heritors) in the establishment of parish ministers, rather than election by the elders of individual kirks, as the uneducated majority preferred. In his social satires, however, Burns becomes the lower-class radical hostile to the gentry, and his allies are the same peasant masses—the crofters and small farmers—for whose fundamentalist religious opinions he had the highest contempt. 'The Twa Dogs' (early 1786), an eclogue consisting of canine comparisons between the virtues and vices of the rich and the poor, much to the latter's advantage, eschews all discussion of religion, and its implicit Biblical moral, that 'Satan still finds work for idle hands to do', in contrasting the idle aristocracy with the hard-working peasantry, avoids any scriptural association. This is perhaps 'natural' enough, in the sense that the dialogue is conducted between a pair of brute beasts to whom the spiritual aspects of existence might be expected to remain unknown, but in view of Burns's own religious alignment, the omission is also highly significant.

Radical as 'The Twa Dogs' is in its attack on the privileged, its inclusion in the Kilmarnock volume placed its unprivileged author in no danger of any kind of prosecution or persecution by authority. When social criticism emerges from the mouths—or muzzles—of dogs, it is bound to create the effect that their bark is worse than their bite. Moreover, Burns takes care to make exceptions to his general strictures on the gentry—'there's some exceptions, man an' woman'—and thereby provides the opportunity for any reader belonging to the upper classes to include himself among the exceptional few to whom the satire does not apply. Again, the introductory descriptions of the two canine characters have such charm as to make it well-nigh impossible to take offence at anything they say. Their dialogue is both racy and pointed, and Burns's success in giving his octosyllabic couplets the cadence of Scots vernacular speech is so remarkable as to be quite unremarked in the reading. Yet, at the same time, one can appreciate the doubt in Hilton Brown's mind when he commented that 'to talk of . . . "The Twa Dogs" . . . as "poetry" seems to strain a little the accepted meaning of words'[20] and preferred to consider the work's medium as being verse; for in capturing the tone of conversation Burns frequently strays so far from the poetical that passage after passage is no more than rhythmical rhyming prose, entirely devoid of imagery.

Different in every way, except its octosyllabic couplets, is 'Address of Beelzebub', also written in 1786, but never published in Burns's lifetime. Dated from 'Hell 1st June Anno Mundi 5790', and signed by Beelzebub, the poem is only too particular in the point of its attack, being directed to

> the R^t Honble JOHN, EARL OF BREADALBANE, President of the R^t Honble the HIGHLAND SOCIETY, which met, on the 23^d of May last, at the Shakespeare, Covent garden, to concert ways and means to frustrate the designs of FIVE HUNDRED HIGHLANDERS who, as the Society were informed by M^r McKenzie of Applecross, were so audacious as to attempt to escape from theire lawful lords and masters whose property they are by emigrating from the lands of M^r McDonald of Glengary to the wilds of CANADA, in search of that fantastic thing—LIBERTY.

The savage sarcasm of the poem's sixty-two lines makes it one of the most fiercely effective of Burns's works, a furious condemnation of aristocratic arrogance, which lashes authority with as stinging a whip as his lordship is pictured as using on 'the tatter'd gipseys' who are wives to those 'Poor, dunghill sons of dirt an' mire', his Highland tenants. For attempting to interfere with their freedom of choice, Breadalbane is not only doomed but also pre-eminently damned, fated to a special place in hell, 'The benmost newk, aside the ingle / At my right hand', and the brutality of the punishment to be inflicted by him upon the lower orders ('smash them! crush them a' to spails!') is evoked by Burns in a passage of such ferocious energy as to make eternal hell-fire seem no outrageous sentence when compared with the crime.

Yet the power in the land which permitted Breadalbane and his associates among the Scottish gentry to curtail the liberties of their tenants was also too great for a mere tenant-farmer such as Burns to risk defying it by publication, however violently he might denounce that power in manuscript. In a Scotland where political—and judicial—authority was concentrated in the 'happy few' who constituted the landed interest, and where that authority was well-nigh absolute (as Burns and other radicals were to discover to their cost when they dared to favour the French Revolution a few years later), the public defiance of a belted earl by an untitled nobody from the hilts of a plough might well have exposed the latter to a legal system for which the social hierarchy was still sacrosanct, and would certainly have placed him beyond the pale so far as any prospect of public employment was concerned. It is even a matter of doubt whether he could have continued as a tenant-farmer, for as a 'marked man', a radical who had published an attack on one of the greatest landlords in the country, he would have found most other landlords refusing to rent him a farm. Such were the perils daunting enough to force the freest spirit in eighteenth-century Scotland to confine 'Address of Beelzebub' to an underground existence.

Ironically, it seems to have been safer to satirize the monarch in far-off London than a mere magnate with a Scottish estate. When King George III's birthday was celebrated on 4 June 1786 with a Pindaric ode by the poet-laureate, Burns immediately retorted with 'A Dream', and inserted it into the copy for the Kilmarnock edition just before it went to press. Although his aristocratic acquaintance Mrs Dunlop informed him that the work was disliked by 'numbers at London'[21] and suggested that he amend it for the Edinburgh edition, Burns rejected her advice on the grounds that 'I set as little by kings, lords, clergy, critics etc. as all these respectable Gentry do by my bardship'.[22] This appears to be very bold, but in fact it is little more than bravado. For while some readers of 'A Dream' might take offence at its tone of impudent familiarity, addressing the king and his family as if they were near neighbours, the poem is innocent of any attack on the institution of monarchy. On the contrary, it protests the author's 'loyal, true affection' alongside its waggish depreciation of the flattery of courtiers and the pecadilloes of the royal princes. Its publication might be regarded as being in doubtful taste, but it could scarcely be denounced for advocating revolutionary principles of equality, since its democratic attitude remains implicit, as a matter of manner, and is never explicitly stated, and even stressed, as in the overt onslaught upon aristocracy in 'Address of Beelzebub'.

After the publication of the Kilmarnock edition in July 1786 and Burns's consequent departure from his native heath to become consecutively a literary lion in Edinburgh, a farmer in Dumfries-shire, and an exciseman in Dumfries, there was a marked decline in his satirical production, both in quantity and in quality. For this there would appear to have been two reasons—rootlessness and respectability. Burns the famous poet, elevated out of the ranks of the tenantry and commissioned as an officer in the Excise, and domiciled in a district different from that in which he had shared the trials and tribulations of the labouring life, was inevitably distanced from the people and the places, the pulpits and the politics, which had provided his radical attacks on religious orthodoxy and aristocratic privilege. Occasionally he attempted to hark back to his parochial past in Ayrshire, but 'A New Psalm for the Chapel of Kilmarnock' (25 April 1789), written in the mock-scriptural style of 'Holy Willie's Prayer', was innocuous enough —in its avoidance of personalities—for immediate publication in the London *Morning Star*, while 'The Kirk of Scotland's Garland' (autumn 1789), published as an anonymous broadsheet, is a repetitive catalogue of individual insults rather than a rounded poem. Well might the author ask himself, 'Poet Burns, Poet Burns, wi' your priest-skelping turns, / Why desert ye your auld native shire?' The short answer, financial necessity (''tis luxury in comparison of all my preceding life'[23]), had been expressed more poignantly by the poet a twelvemonth earlier, in his 'Extemporaneous Effusion on being appointed to the Excise'—

> Searching auld wives' barrels,
>   Ochon, the day!
> That clarty barm should stain my laurels;
>   But—what'll ye say?
> These muvin' things ca'd wives and weans
> Wad muve the very hearts o' stanes!

With the solitary exception of 'Tam o' Shanter'—his only excursion into narrative—the rest of the best of Burns is not satire but song.

Notes

1   David Daiches, *Robert Burns* (New York, 1950).
2   Thomas Crawford, *Burns* (Edinburgh and London, 1960).
3   David Craig, *Scottish Literature and the Scottish People 1680-1830* (London, 1961).
4   *Letters*, ed. J. De Lancey Ferguson (Oxford, 1931), I. p. 114.
5   *Ibid.*
6   The *Lounger*, December 1786.
7   *Letters*, I, p. 114.
8   R. H. Cromek, *Remains of Nithsdale and Galloway Song* (London, 1810), Appendix D.
9   J. G. Lockhart, *Burns* (Edinburgh, 1828), I, p. 85.
10 Hilton Brown, *There Was a Lad* (London, 1949), p. 202.
11 *Letters*, I, p. 70.
12 'O leave novels', *Poems and Songs*, ed. J. Kinsley (Oxford, 1968), no. 43.
13 Kinsley, Vol. III, p. 1048.
14 *The Poetical Works of William Drummond of Hawthornden*, ed. L. E. Kastner (S.T.S., 1913), Vol. II, pp. 218-21.

15   Kinsley, Vol. III, p. 1100.
16   Brown, *op. cit.*, p. 204.
17   *Burns Chronicle* (1932), p. 95.
18   Kinsley, Vol. III, p. 1132.
19   *Letters*, I, p. 25.
20   Brown, *op. cit.*, p. 186.
21   *Robert Burns and Mrs Dunlop: Correspondence*, ed. William Wallace (London, 1898), p. 11.
22   *Letters*, I, p. 86.
23   *Ibid.*, I, p. 192.

Chapter 6

Two Poets of the 1780s:
Burns and Cowper

John D. Baird

The juxtaposition of Burns and Cowper has been attempted before. Josiah Walker, in his *Miscellaneous Remarks on the Writings of Burns* (1811), offers a 'parallel' of the two poets (clearly modelled on Johnson's comparison of Dryden and Pope), and comes to the conclusion that 'from the whole of this estimate, it will probably appear that Burns excels Cowper in genius, less than he is excelled in taste'.[1] Walker may have been 'an ass', as De Lancey Ferguson calls him,[2] but the passage of time seems to have thrown little more light on the relationship. Indeed, Walker is rather more illuminating than the late George Sherburn, in his chapter on 'Cowper and Burns' in a standard literary textbook published in 1948.[3] Cowper and Burns, says Sherburn, are alike largely poets of domestic emotion, and they share that most dreaded of literary fates, they are transitional figures. When we have overcome our surprise at finding the very different domesticities of Mossgiel and Weston Underwood brought together under the same roof, we may well wonder whether it is the case, as Sherburn's chapter tacitly suggests, that Burns and Cowper are linked only by chronological accident and the most superficial resemblances of subject-matter, and cannot therefore be considered together fruitfully.

It is almost tempting to accept this view. Cowper and Burns could hardly have been more different, as men and as poets. Cowper belonged to a family distinguished in law and politics; he was educated at Westminster School with such distinguished contemporaries as Warren Hastings and George Colman the elder; trained, or given the opportunity to train himself in the law, with the promise of a parliamentary sinecure, Cowper at the age of thirty should have been standing on the brink of a respectable if not brilliant future as a man of affairs. Instead he plunged into despair, attempted suicide, and was removed to an asylum at St Albans where Dr Robert Cotton restored him to health and implanted in him the Evangelical religion which was to shape so much of his life.[4] Retirement at Huntingdon brought him into contact with the Unwin family; on Morley Unwin's death in

1767, Cowper accompanied his widow and daughter to Olney, where they might enjoy the ministrations of the Reverend John Newton, converted slave-trader. Cowper's second major breakdown, in 1773, left him with the conviction that he was cast away by God, condemned to annihilation (worse than eternal punishment), and under orders to destroy himself at the first opportunity—'*Actum est de te; periisti!*'[5] Recovery from this attack was slow, aided by a succession of pastimes: hares, gardening, drawing—and finally poetry, an art which the young William Cowper had cultivated in his days in the Temple, and to which he returned in the late 1770s, stimulated as much by public events as by private ones, as the titles of the period indicate. In 1780 the publication of *Thelyphthora*, a treatise in which his cousin Martin Madan advocated polygamy as a means of raising the moral tone of England, provided the stimulus for a longer poem in couplets, *Anti-Thelyphthora* (published anonymously in 1781); this in turn led to the composition of the eight so-called 'moral satires' which form the bulk of the volume published in 1782 as *Poems by William Cowper, of the Inner Temple, Esq.* This book caused little stir; the self-secluded poet's first popular success was *John Gilpin* (published anonymously late in 1782); he established himself as a leading author of the age only with *The Task* in 1785. Literary fame led to the renewal of many old ties and the formation of new friendships, but the modest recluse remained rooted in north Buckinghamshire, sipping his tea (or was it tar-water?) across the fireside from Mrs Unwin.

It is not necessary here to give a similar summary of Burns's career up to the establishment of his literary fame with the Kilmarnock volume of 1786 and the Edinburgh edition of the following year. The contrasts are obvious; in age, circumstances, education, religious background, social activities and dozens of particulars, they stand apart: the gentleman and the farmer. Nor did they essay, for the most part, the same kinds of poetry; in content and style they are remote from each other. At this point, we may be inclined to think, the case for comparing them should be dismissed.

Yet against these arguments must be weighed the fact that Burns and Cowper are contemporaries not only in the technical sense that they lived and wrote at the same time but also in the more significant sense that they became famous and popular at the same time. They seem to have shared an audience; the *Monthly Review*, for instance, lauded Cowper in March 1786, and Burns in December of the same year.[6] Each admired, though not without reservation, the work of the other, though they never met or communicated personally. Cowper wrote to

Samuel Rose, after reading the Edinburgh edition of 1787 through twice:[7]

> I think them on the whole a very extraordinary production. He is I believe the only poet these islands have produced in the lower rank of life since Shakespeare, (I should rather say since Prior,) who need not be indebted for any part of his praise to a charitable consideration of his origin, and the disadvantages under which he has laboured.

(He goes on, it is interesting to note, to wish that Burns would 'hereafter divest himself of barbarism, and content himself with writing pure English, in which he appears perfectly qualified to excel'.) And Burns, addressing Mrs Dunlop on Christmas Day 1793:[8]

> Now that I talk of Authors, how do you like Cowper? Is not the Task a glorious Poem? The Religion of The Task, bating a few scraps of Calvinistic Divinity, is the Religion of God & Nature; the Religion that exalts, that ennobles man.

Some twenty years later Wordsworth linked the two in a letter to R. P. Gillies: 'I assure you that, with the exception of Burns and Cowper, there is very little of recent verse, however much it may interest me, that sticks to my memory.'[9]

The fact that two so very different poets established themselves almost simultaneously as important and popular authors, authors in whom, as Wordsworth's remark indicates, interest remained high, is surely worthy of investigation. Since it would require a book, and a bulky one at that, to document adequately the shared cultural matrix of their work, the present essay can offer no more than indications and pointers, pursuing, it may be, indirections whereby others may find directions out.

It is one of the minor misfortunes of literary history that T. S. Eliot should have propounded his theory of the 'dissociation of sensibility' in an essay on the Metaphysical poets.[10] The result has been a tendency to think of this phenomenon as something primarily important to the seventeenth century, and to forget that Eliot is speaking of a change that runs from Herbert to Tennyson. Indeed, the pace and violence of literary change were considerably more marked at the end of the eighteenth century, and were more consciously felt, as anyone may see by comparing Dryden's comments on Donne with Wordsworth's account of his predecessors in the 1800 Preface to the *Lyrical Ballads*.[11]

The nature of the late-eighteenth-century shift in values is hard to define. For some hints as to the older way of looking at the question we may turn to Dr Johnson. On 15 August 1773 Johnson upheld in conversation with a number of Edinburgh literati that all forms of mental activity are essentially alike; some minds are more powerful than others, but they do not differ in kind.[12]

No sir; it is only, one man has more mind than another. He may direct it differently; he may, by accident, see the success of one kind of study, and take a desire to excel in it. I am persuaded that, had Sir Isaac Newton applied to poetry, he would have made a very fine epick poem. I could as easily apply to law as to tragick poetry.

Beside this should be set what follows the famous rejoinder to the question whether Pope was a poet: 'If Pope be not a poet, where is poetry to be found?'[13]

To circumscribe poetry by a definition will only shew the narrowness of the definer, though a definition which shall exclude Pope will not easily be made. Let us look round upon the present time, and back upon the past; let us enquire to whom the voice of mankind has decreed the wreath of poetry; let their productions be examined, and their claims stated, and the pretensions of Pope will be no more disputed.

Johnson's notion of a poet, therefore, is based on the distinction between artificer and artefact; there is a radical discontinuity between the maker and the made, for Newton might have written an epic instead of the *Principia* without being any the less the Sir Isaac Newton known to history. No personal data are relevant to the question of Pope's status as a poet; the matter will be resolved by comparing his *productions* with those of others to whom the title 'poet' has been applied. This account of poetry as craft, as a human activity no different in essentials from any other form of human creativity, has a long history.

Wordsworth's definition of a poet belongs to another world.[14]

He is a man speaking to men: a man, it is true, endowed with more lively sensibility, more enthusiasm and tenderness, who has a greater knowledge of human nature, and a more comprehensive soul, than are supposed to be common among mankind; a man pleased with his own passions and volitions, and who rejoices more than other men in the spirit of life that is in him; delighting to contemplate similar volitions and passions as manifested in the goings-on of the Universe, and habitually impelled to create them where he does not find them, . . . he has acquired a greater readiness and power in expressing what he thinks and feels, and especially those thoughts and feelings which, by his own choice, or from the structure of his own mind, arise in him without immediate external excitement.

Wordsworth's 'man speaking to men' has an unfortunate tendency to turn into a superman, but the intention is clear: a poet shares in and articulates in language the human condition, and his poetry has value in proportion as he is exceptionally endowed. Johnson's approach is thus rendered irrelevant; literary judgment has become a matter of psychology, not connoisseurship.

Johnson and Wordsworth do not, of course, represent the average literary thinking of the years 1780 to 1800. The quotations are offered as suggestive merely—poles which define the field in which Burns and Cowper appeared. Three points demand attention: the relation between the biographies of Burns and Cowper and their poetry; the disappearance of the notion of poetic kinds; and the attitudes of late-eighteenth-century readers towards poetry.

Burns and Cowper are the first important British poets of whom it can be said that the critical estimate of their works was from the first bound up with biographical controversy. Half a century before, Pope's personal character was fiercely attacked in his own lifetime, but his assailants did not believe they could make Alexander Pope any the less a great poet by showing that Mr Pope was a liar and a knave; that was left to Whitwell Elwin and the nineteenth century. But when we turn to Cowper and Burns, the situation has changed; readers are making less of a distinction between the life and the works.

It is well known that Cowper's posthumous fame was slightly clouded by squabbles between various shades of religious opinion;[15] it is not always recognized that biographical criticism began before his death. Anna Seward devotes much of her letter to Miss Scott of 27 May 1786 to a discussion of *The Task*. Cowper, she writes,

appears to me at once a fascinating, and great poet; as a descriptive one hardly excelled. Novel and original, even in landscape-painting, whose stores the luxuriant and exquisite Thomson seemed to have exhausted; but true poetic genius, looking at the objects of nature with its own eyes, rather than through the medium of remembered descriptions from the pen of others, will ever find her exhaustless.

She mentions a number of passages which have struck her as particularly fine, noting that she disapproves of a detected tone of acrimony, an 'envious grudging of well-earned praise'; the author seems to hate mankind, but lavishes tenderness on brutes. She continues:[16]

> You plead Cowper's constitutional melancholy in excuse for his misanthropy. That plea is often made for Johnson also; but if it is possible that melancholy can so narrow the mind, as to render a man of genius, like Mr. Cowper, the avowed foe of national gratitude, and of honour to the manes of such beings as Shakespeare and Handel, it then becomes a vice, against which every generous reader will bear the most renouncing testimony.

These remarks foreshadow many a later page of criticism, for the perennial topics of Cowper's perception of the natural world, and of the influence of his state of mind on his compositions are here adumbrated. In a later letter, Anna Seward brings the religious issue forward explicitly: to the Reverend R. Fellowes she pointed out signs in *The Task* of the 'bitter fanaticism' that deprived Cowper of his reason, noting besides that the poem owes none of its sublimity to the author's melancholia.[17] In these comments by 'the Swan of Lichfield' we find a new way of assessing poetry demonstrated; interest focuses on the interplay of critical and biographical observation.

Such a response to *The Task* is hardly surprising, for Cowper had put a great deal of himself into his masterpiece. Such a passage as the famous 'I was a stricken deer that left the herd'[18] owes much to the tradition of spiritual autobiography cultivated by the Evangelicals, and considered from that angle is unremarkable in content; yet it strikes a new note in English poetry (very different from Pope's presentation of himself in his poetry), and no doubt reinforced the movement towards the exploitation of poetry as a confessional mode.

Burns suffered from the start from being classifiable as a Poetical Ploughman, along with Mrs Yearsley the Poetical Milkwoman and the rest of that unhappy tribe—a designation inevitably leading to biographical inquiry. The more permanent biographical issue which has recurred in Burns criticism has been the relationship of moral evaluation of the poet's behaviour to an assessment of the poetry; put crudely, can a bad man write good poems? For a number of years now scholars breathing the liberated atmosphere of the twentieth century have been telling each other that Burns was not a bad man, so the heat has gone out of the debate, but it is still hardly possible to touch on the poet's life without adopting an apologetic tone. Force of habit, no doubt, since as early as 1788 James Maxwell, 'Poet in Paisley', launched his *Animadversions on Some Poets and Poetasters of the Present Age Especially R——T B——S*:[19]

> Of all British poets that yet have appear'd
> None e'er at things sacred so daringly sneer'd
> As he in the west, who but lately is sprung
> From behind the plough-tails, and from raking of dung.—
> A champion for Satan, none like him before,
> And his equal, pray God, we may never see more. . . .
> His jargon gives rakes and vile harlots delight,
> But all sober people abhor the vile sight.
> He makes of the scriptures a ribaldry joke;
> By him are the laws both of God and man broke.

Pointless to cite the classical doctrine that the author of indecent verses might yet be a worthy man.[20] To Mr Maxwell, as to many who followed him, the distinction is meaningless.

Interest in the biographical roots of a poet's work naturally leads to an emphasis on the uniqueness of the individual; attention is consequently directed more to content than to form, the more so if the poet is conceived as expresser rather than as maker. Inevitably this led to a weakening of the sense of a hierarchy of literary kinds, each offering a time-sanctioned union of subject-matter and form. *The Task* is a good example of this process; it is appreciably more desultory than *The Seasons*, the justification being that it is an expression of the mind of the poet, and is ordered in consequence on subjective principles.[21]

> The history of the following production is briefly this. A lady, fond of blank verse, demanded a poem of that kind from the author, and gave him the SOFA for a subject. He obeyed; and, having much leisure, connected another subject with it; and, pursuing the train of thought to which his situation and turn of mind led him, brought forth at length, instead of the trifle which he at first intended, a serious affair—a Volume.

The point was taken by Dr John Aikin (born 1747), who wrote in his comparison of *The Seasons* and *The Task*:[22]

> Between the poems no comparison can subsist; for while the Seasons is the completion of an extensive plan, necessarily com-

prising a great variety of topics, most of which would occur to every poetical mind occupied in the same design; the Task owes nothing to a preconceived argument, but is the extemporaneous product of the very singular mind and genius of the author. It had no model, and can have no parallel.

Burns, of course, found many of his 'kinds' in the Scots tradition, and it is probably fair to say that he was more conscious of a responsibility to match his subject-matter with the appropriate form than was Cowper—hence the odes and other 'serious' poems in a high-flown and lifeless 'pure English'. (Hence too, perhaps, Burns's preference in later years for the untrammelled medium of song.)

The fading sense of form as a determining element in composition opened the door to an altered perception of the nature of poems; in effect, long poems came to be regarded as anthologies of shorter passages—the development summed up by Poe half a century later when he claimed that a long poem is a contradiction in terms. The process is signalized by the disappearance of the old miscellanies in favour of *Elegant Extracts* and all those other anthologies of excerpts and short poems which flourished at the close of the eighteenth century. The increasing tendency to think in terms of poetry and emotion, rather than of poetry and thought, inevitably placed a premium on briefer poems—mood-length, one might say.

A passage in Jane Austen's *Persuasion* is helpful here. Anne Elliot is forced by circumstances to go with a group of companions for a walk which threatens to cause her distress.[23]

> Her *pleasure* in the walk must arise from the exercise and the day, from the view of the last smiles of the year upon the tawny leaves and withered hedges, and from repeating to herself some few of the thousand poetical descriptions extant of autumn, that season of peculiar and inexhaustible influence on the mind of taste and tenderness, that season which has drawn from every poet, worthy of being read, some attempt at description, or some lines of feeling.

And later, after she has heard a conversation which distresses her:

> Anne could not immediately fall into a quotation again. The sweet scenes of autumn were for a while put by—unless some tender sonnet, fraught with the apt analogy of the declining year, with declining happiness, and images of youth and hope, and spring, all gone together, blessed her memory.

These passages postdate our period, but they suggest how those whose literary taste was developed in the 1780s and 1790s regarded the relation between the poet and his subject ('that season which has drawn from every poet'), and how they believed poetry was to be used by its readers. 'Nay, mama, if he is not to be animated by Cowper!' says Marianne Dashwood, lamenting Edward Ferrars's painful lack of sensibility.[24] One cannot imagine one of Pope's original readers behaving like either of these young ladies. Poets and readers alike use poetry to cultivate the emotions, to generate appropriate sentiments. And 'sentiment' is a key word for our period; a 'sentiment' was a thought, a moral feeling, but it was also the form in which that thought or feeling found expression. Here, at least, form and content were at one; the moral utterances of Joseph Surface and Sir Peter Teazle's admiration can direct our attention to a kind of effect that both Cowper and Burns sought and achieved in their most popular poetry.

> Both derived the most ardent enjoyment from the sublime and beautiful spectacles of nature, and possessed a peculiar capacity of analysing their delight, by fixing at once on the minute and circumstantial appearances from which it sprung, and both had the power of portraying, the objects which had caused them:— Burns by a few daring and decisive strokes, and Cowper, by patient touches of more softness, delicacy, and grace.[25]

The essential truth of Josiah Walker's account of the two poets' treatment of external nature survives our impression that his critical vocabulary is outmoded—an impression strengthened a few lines further on, when he remarks that 'both felt the acutest sentiment of tenderness for the animal tribes'. Yet this very inappropriateness of terminology is indicative of the qualities of the writing he is describing. Thomson's *Seasons* succumbs readily to analysis based on the sublime and the beautiful; these concepts are clearly less appropriate to *The Task*, and still less so to the relevant passages in Burns.

It is in their treatment of nature, indeed, that Burns and Cowper may best be described as transitional poets, if we are to admit such a category at all. On the one hand, for obvious biographical reasons, neither favours the 'natural religion' familiar in the works of Addison and his contemporaries; on the other hand, a strong georgic strain runs through the work of both. Cowper's knowledge of agriculture was derived from observation, not participation, but he, like Burns, finds a high value in the relationship of human labour to the land, and in the third book of *The Task* he includes what has been identified as a 'garden georgic'—in his own sphere he lived up to the ideal.

More interesting is the treatment of specific natural objects by the two poets; what Walker had in mind when he spoke of 'animal tribes', though inanimate objects must also be considered.

In the mid-twentieth century, we are highly conscious of our kinship with animals; as 'naked apes' we tend to take 'Nature's social union' for granted. In the eighteenth century, the gulf between man and the brute creation was much more strongly felt. In the age of the RSPCA the Houyhnhnms are largely deprived of much of their original shock value, and Uncle Toby's sparing of the fly has lost much of its point since Schweitzer spared all the insects at Lambaréné.

It is significant, of course, that animals play a relatively large part in the poetry of both authors, who in this respect differ from most of their predecessors (I exclude from consideration such works as Gay's *Fables*). They exhibit, too, a more sympathetic interest in the nature of these animals, those they knew and observed in the course of their daily lives, than earlier poets; yet their treatment of these creatures is still basically emblematic. Significance lies not in the creature itself, nor in the details of its existence, still less in any reflection by the creature of a transcendent reality (contrast Wordsworth's 'The Green Linnet'), but in the relationship between observed phenomena and a moral principle apprehended by the poet.

To make this point clear, we may first look at Cowper's 'The Dog and the Water-Lily'. The incident on which the poem is founded is described in a letter to Lady Hesketh of 27 June 1788:[26]

> I must tell you a feat of my dog Beau. Walking by the river side, I observed some water-lilies floating at a little distance from the bank. They are a large white flower, with an orange-coloured eye, very beautiful. I had a desire to gather one, and, having your long cane in my hand, by the help of it endeavoured to bring one of them within my reach. But the attempt proved vain, and I walked forward. Beau had all the while observed me very attentively. Returning soon after toward the same place, I observed him plunge into the river, while I was about forty yards distant from him; and, when I had nearly reached the spot, he swam to land with a lily in his mouth, which he came and laid at my foot.

The first nine stanzas of the poem are essentially a versification of this account; the conclusion follows:[27]

> Charmed with the sight, 'The world', I cried,
>   'Shall hear of this thy deed:

> My dog shall mortify the pride
> Of man's superior breed:
>
> But chief myself I will enjoin,
> Awake at duty's call,
> To show a love as prompt as thine
> To Him who gives me all.'

The 'moral' is not inherent in the story, nor does Cowper wish to suggest that the relationship of a human soul to God is that of a spaniel to its master. The link between the final stanza and the rest of the poem is purely conceptual—the abstraction 'promptness of love is a good'—and the function of the dog's action, apart from its interest as an example of canine sagacity, is emblematic only.

A mountain daisy is not strictly speaking an animal, but Burns's address to one was so popular in his own day that it may properly be considered here. As David Daiches points out, Burns makes 'deliberate use of pathetic fallacy',[28] but this disappears when we approach the climax of the poem. In the last four stanzas, the downturned daisy sustains an emblematic role; it is relevant only as a specific victim of sudden and unsuspected ruin. The four hypothetical examples of the same fate are arranged in ascending order of calamity (assuming that Burns valued a simple Bard over an artless maid), but they are not otherwise connected, and they require the reader to bear in mind slightly different aspects of the daisy's past existence if they are to be individually effective—this is most noticeable in comparing the first and third. In essence, Burns's use of the daisy differs little from Catullus' treatment of an unidentified flower, which may have been a daisy:

> nec meum respectet, ut ante, amorem,
> qui illius culpa cecidit uelut prati
> ultimi flos, praetereunte postquam
> tactus aratro est.*

(XI, 21-4)

Burns's attitude to living animals is at first glance somewhat different. Critics have rightly praised the Mailie poems and 'The Auld Farmer's New-year-morning Salutation to his Auld Mare, Maggie', and the best known of all, 'To a Mouse', has been generously treated of late. Again, this poem was a favourite of Burns's contemporaries. Here Burns

---

* And let her not look to find my love, as before; my love, which by her fault has dropped, like a flower on the meadow's edge, when it has been touched by the plough passing by (Loeb translation).

seems to abandon the emblematic model. He keeps ploughman and mouse apart, neither humanizing the mouse nor animalizing the man; the similarities which are developed to unite them, justifying the phrase 'Nature's social union', are real on both sides, and not the arbitrary creation of the poet. Yet this is not the whole story. In the penultimate stanza mice and men are alike 'In proving *foresight* may be vain': but in the final stanza, with a noteworthy reversion to the singular, mouse and man are separated by the mental limitations of the mouse— showing that the mouse's proof of the principle can have only emblematic force—and at the end we share the experience of the poet alone:[29]

> Still, thou art blest, compar'd wi' *me*!
> The *present* only toucheth thee:
> But Och! I *backward* cast my e'e,
>   On prospects drear!
> An *forward*, tho' I canna *see*,
>   I *guess* an' *fear*!

Burns had his own reasons for anxiety, but that closing sentiment must have found a responsive echo in many contemporary hearts.

The decade of the 1780s was a troubled time; troubled by political dissension and incipient industrialization, troubled too in conscience, for the campaign against slavery was launched during these years.[30] Something of the carefree atmosphere of the earlier time was gone; the England of Tom Jones was a good deal further from existing than it had been in 1749. A domestic court had replaced the scenes so lovingly detailed by Lord Hervey; the Earl of Chatham, vigorous and outrageous to the end, was succeeded by the chilly reserve of Mr Pitt.

The watershed was the American War, never a cause which united the nation, and a fruitful source of later political stress. The ideas which had informed and sustained the Americans were now well known, their proponents widely admired as exemplars of a kind of virtue lost to the decayed mother country. On 1 January 1780 the *Mirror* had the Scottish censor Mr Umphraville remark on the francophile 'macaroni' MP Sir Bobby Button: 'Had the *American Congress* been composed of Bobby Buttons, would America ever have made such a stand against us?'[31] 'What had he to do to make Joshua his hero, when he had Washington of his own growth?' asked Mrs Barbauld at the end of the decade, on receiving a copy of Timothy Dwight's epic, *The Conquest of Canaan*.[32] There is ample evidence that many Britons in the 1780s saw themselves as citizens of the decaying nation foreseen by Burke in his 1777 *Letter to the Sheriffs of Bristol*:[33]

> ... the American war,—a war in my humble opinion productive
> of many mischiefs, of a kind which distinguish it from all others.
> Not only our policy is deranged, and our empire distracted, but
> our laws and our legislative spirit appear to have been totally per-
> verted by it. We have made war on our colonies, not by arms only,
> but by laws. As hostility and law are not very concordant ideas,
> every step we have taken in this business has been made by
> trampling on some maxim of justice or some capital principle of
> wise government. ...
>
> Nor is it the worst effect of this unnatural contention, that our
> *laws* are corrupted. Whilst *manners* remain entire, they will correct
> the vices of law, and soften it at length to their own temper. But
> we have to lament that in most of the late proceedings we see very
> few traces of that generosity, humanity, and dignity of mind,
> which formerly characterized this nation. War suspends the rules
> of moral obligation, and what is long suspended is in danger of
> being totally abrogated. Civil wars strike deepest of all into the
> manners of the people. They vitiate their politics; they corrupt
> their morals; they prevent even the natural taste and relish of
> equity and justice. By teaching us to consider our fellow-citizens
> in a hostile light, the whole body of our nation becomes gradually
> less dear to us. The very names of affection and kindred, which
> were the bond of charity whilst we agreed, become new incen-
> tives to hatred and rage when the communion of our country is
> dissolved. We may flatter ourselves that we shall not fall into this
> misfortune. But we have no charter of exemption, that I know of,
> from the ordinary frailties of our nature.

The struggle for parliamentary reform, the concern for the administration of India, the impeachment of Warren Hastings, and many other
political events of the 1780s can be seen as the attempts to cleanse and
heal the body politic of the wounds so eloquently predicted here.

The same concerns can be identified in the poets. The famous passage
in Book II of *The Task*, 'England, with all thy faults, I love thee still, /
My country!', offers the best-known statement of this theme in the
poem. Chatham and Wolfe are dead, their places have been taken by
'effeminates whose very looks / Reflect dishonour on the land I love'.
And later in the book, in 'The Time-Piece', which 'is intended to
strike the hour that gives notice of approaching judgment',[34] Cowper
identifies the root of this moral degeneration:

Now basket up the family of plagues
That waste our vitals; peculation, sale
Of honour, perjury, corruption, frauds
By forgery, by subterfuge of law,
By tricks and lies as numerous and as keen
As the necessities their authors feel;
Then cast them, closely bundled, every brat
At the right door. Profusion is its sire.

    . . .   .

    . . . [Profusion] unties the knot
Of union, and converts the sacred band
That holds mankind together to a scourge.
Profusion deluging a state with lusts
Of grossest nature and of worst effects,
Prepares it for its ruin: hardens, blinds,
And warps the consciences of public men
Till they can laugh at virtue; mock the fools
That trust them; and, in the end, disclose a face
That would have shocked credulity herself
Unmasked. . . .

(667-74; 685-95)

In its religious conception of the nature of the body politic, this passage harks back to the quotation from Burke; in its identification of self-indulgence at the expense of the community as the fundamental social peril, it points forward to the conclusion of 'The Cotter's Saturday Night':

> And O may Heaven their simple lives prevent
>   From *Luxury*'s contagion, weak and vile!
> Then howe'er *crowns* and *coronets* be rent,
>   A *virtuous Populace* may rise the while,
> And sand a wall of fire, around their much-lov'd ISLE.

(176-80)

Both poets are giving expression to a commonplace of the age. The *Monthly Review*, for example, remarked of Thomas Day's *Sandford and Merton* that physical hardiness might be unduly insisted upon, yet 'if it be an error, it lies, however, on the right side, in an age in which there is so general a bias toward luxurious effeminacy'.[35]

It is, indeed, in 'The Cotter's Saturday Night' that Burns appears most clearly as the spokesman of his age.[36] It embodies one of the central articles of faith of that time, that true virtue is manifested in the life of the husbandman; the rural *paterfamilias* stands forth as the pattern of moral excellence. If a few years later Joel Barlow could forget the heady wine of French revolutionary fervour to materialize a world of heroic virtues in the humble hasty-pudding, it is not surprising that Burns attempted to elevate the cotter's life he knew into a pregnant moral fable. The achievement stops short of success; description and comment are not wholly fused. However, they are not discrete elements, and we must resist at all costs the temptation to amputate tacitly the sections which displease us—a procedure lamentably reminiscent of those nineteenth-century disintegrators of Shakespeare, who closed their eyes to the dirty bits in the belief that they had been foisted in to satisfy the deplorable taste of the groundlings. In recognizing the different literary antecedents of description and comment we must not ignore their interdependence in the poem.

Take, for example, the notorious tenth stanza. Its exclamations and rhetorical questions are indeed ungrateful to the ear, yet the questions might be defended as a means of directing the reader's attention outward from the world of the poem into the 'real' world, which is where Burns wants his fable to be effective. The *substance* of the stanza is essential to the significance of the whole poem. Burns's underlying awareness that the cotter's way of life is threatened leads him through-out to stress the fragility of the happiness of the rustic family. 'Guile-less', 'artless', 'simple'—these are the epithets by which they are digni-fied; consequently they are most seriously menaced by a deceiver 'lost to love and truth', a villain who would with 'perjur'd arts' 'betray sweet *Jenny*'s unsuspecting youth'. A 'wild worthless *Rake*' of the Rob Mossgiel type would be bad enough, but his very wildness would make his nature plain and render him to that extent innocuous. The cold-blooded 'wretch' of the tenth stanza, an urban sophisticate like Valmont in *Les Liaisons Dangereuses*, poses an altogether more terrible threat.

This tenth stanza, then, echoes Cowper's belief that deceit in the service of self-indulgence is the fundamental assault that society must withstand. In this light, it is worth looking again at the vexed issue of Burns's 'sincerity' at this point. Was Burns sincere when he wrote this? (It is interesting to note that both Daiches and Crawford find forms of words to evade this question. Daiches writes: 'we do not have to know anything of the history of the poet's own relations with women to notice at once the absurd artificiality of the stanza in such a context'.[37] And Crawford: 'it is not our knowledge of the poet's life-history which makes us distrust his pose here, so much as the hysterical rhodomontade which runs through the stanza'.[38]) The answer is that of course Burns was sincere; if he were not, there could have been no poem. 'Love and truth' is precisely what 'The Cotter's Saturday Night' is all about. The cotter and his family, and Jenny's suitor, demonstrate love in their dealings with each other, and join in the contemplation of divine truth. Stanza 10 shows us, in terms of action, what the abandonment of these values entails.

The nature of that action is, admittedly, highly conventional, and on that ground censurable. Yet conventional though it be, the presence of such a scene reminds us that what distinguishes 'The Cotter's Saturday Night' from Fergusson's 'The Farmer's Ingle', Shenstone's 'The Schoolmistress', and Cowper's treatment of domestic interiors is the intensely dramatic nature of Burns's imagination. The evening activities that Fergusson describes are typical; his evening might be any evening, and his title insists on the place, not, like Burns's, the occasion. Cowper, in the well-known passage at the beginning of Book IV of *The Task*, slips easily from typical actions ('Now stir the fire, and close the shutters fast') to moral reflection and back again. Burns, on the other hand, is not presenting a typical Saturday night, although typical activities are described; this, as the episode of the arrival of Jenny's young man makes clear, is a specific Saturday night. Moral significance can be found in *particular* action—and in accepting this principle Burns perhaps testifies to the influence of the new art-form of the eighteenth century, the novel.

The sense that the poem presents a particular occasion contributes to the sense of contingency which pervades the work. The way of life exhibited to us in this 'slice' is frail and endangered, yet these 'manners' embody values essential to what Burke called 'the communion of the country'. Hence the persistent concern for the future: '*Anticipation* forward points the view', the parents' prayer in stanza 18, the conclusion. Again, this is in sharp contrast with 'The Farmer's Ingle'. Fergusson ends, not with a prayer for the survival of those values which define his native land, but with a benison:[39]

> May SCOTIA's simmers ay look gay and green,
>   Her yellow har'st frae scowry blasts decreed!
> May a' her tenants sit fu' snug and bien,
>   Frae the hard grip o' ails and poortith freed,
>   And a lang lasting train o' peaceful hours succeed.

Fergusson assumes the continued existence of the way of life he has described (hence perhaps his readiness to describe it in typical terms), and in the hope that its harsher aspects—to which he attaches no moral significance—may be mitigated, he prays for good weather. In Burns's poem, the stakes are altogether higher. The fate of the hardy sons of rural toil involves the fate of the nation.

Made implicitly in this essay is a point which now deserves explicit statement. Alluring though it may be to disregard those passages written by Burns the late-eighteenth-century sentimentalist as attempts to appeal to a sophisticated, effete, anglicized audience—the implication being that Burns was forced by circumstances to prostitute himself to an audience whose taste he did not share—we should be led to a fresh consideration of Burns's relationship to his time, in every aspect and in the widest cultural context. Isolating Burns merely diminishes him. 'Only connect.' No poet stands to gain more from the sympathetic application of Forster's precept than Robert Burns.

Notes

1 *Poems by Robert Burns* (Edinburgh, printed for the Trustees of the late James Morison, 1811), II, p. 355. The comparison is called a 'parallel', *ibid.*, p. 352.
2 *The Letters of Robert Burns*, ed. J. De Lancey Ferguson (Oxford, Clarendon Press, 1931) (hereafter *Letters*), II, p. 375.
3 *A Literary History of England*, ed. A. C. Baugh (New York, Appleton), pp. 1095-1108.
4 The standard authority on Cowper's early life is Charles Ryskamp, *William Cowper of the Inner Temple, Esq.* (Cambridge University Press, 1959).
5 *The Correspondence of William Cowper*, ed. Thomas Wright (London, Hodder, 1904) (hereafter *Correspondence*), I, p. 343.
6 *Monthly Review*, LXXIV, pp. 416-25; LXXV, pp. 439-48.
7 *Correspondence*, III, pp. 145-6 (letter of 24 July 1787).
8 *Letters*, II, p. 225.
9 Letter of 22 December 1814; *The Letters of William and Dorothy Wordsworth*, ed. E. de Selincourt, *The Middle Years* (Oxford, Clarendon Press, 1937), II, p. 615.
10 *Selected Essays* (London, Faber & Faber, 1958), pp. 286-8.
11 John Dryden, 'A Discourse Concerning the Original and Progress of Satire' (dedicated to Dorset), in *Of Dramatic Poesy and Other Critical Essays*, ed. George Watson (London, Dent, 1962), II, pp. 75-6; William Wordsworth, *Poetical Works*, ed. E. de Selincourt (Oxford, Clarendon Press, 1944), II, esp. pp. 385-92, 405-9.
12 James Boswell, *The Journal of a Tour of the Hebrides*, in *Boswell's Life of Johnson*, ed. G. B. Hill, rev. L. F. Powell, V (Oxford, Clarendon Press, 1950), p. 35.
13 *Lives of the Poets*, ed. G. B. Hill (Oxford, Clarendon Press, 1905), III, p. 251.
14 *Poetical Works*, II, p. 393.

15 Convenient summaries and documentation will be found in N. H. Russell, *A Bibliography of William Cowper to 1837* (Oxford, Clarendon Press, 1963), pp. 227-30, 241.

16 *Letters of Anna Seward Written between the Years 1784 and 1807* (Edinburgh, 1811), I, pp. 295-7.

17 *Ibid.*, V, pp. 327-8.

18 *The Task*, III ('The Garden'), p. 108, in *The Poems of William Cowper*, ed. J. C. Bailey (London, Methuen, 1905), p. 287. All references to Cowper's verse are to this edition, cited as *Poems*.

19 *Animadversions on Some Poets and Poetasters of the Present Age Especially R——T B——S and J——N L——K with a Contrast of Some of the Former Age* (Paisley, printed by J. Neilson and sold by the author, 1788). A vicious pamphlet by one of the 'unco' guid'.

20 Joshua Whatmough, *Poetic, Scientific and Other Forms of Discourse* (Berkeley and Los Angeles, University of California Press, 1956), p. 31.

21 *Poems*, p. 248. We need not accept this as the whole truth, but the language remains significant: 'pursuing the train of thought to which his situation and turn of mind led him . . .'.

22 Lucy Aikin, *Memoir of John Aikin M.D. with a Selection of His Miscellaneous Pieces, Biographical, Moral, and Critical* (London, Baldwin, Cradock & Joy, 1823), II, pp. 197-8.

23 *Persuasion*, ed. R. W. Chapman (London, Oxford University Press, 1965), pp. 84, 85.

24 *Sense and Sensibility*, ed. R. W. Chapman (London, Oxford University Press, 1967), p. 18.

25 Walker, *op. cit.*, p. 351.

26 *Correspondence*, III, p. 293.

27 *Poems*, p. 410.

28 David Daiches, *Robert Burns* (London, Deutsch, 1966), p. 154. 'To a Mountain Daisy' will be found in *The Poems and Songs of Robert Burns*, ed. James Kinsley (Oxford, Clarendon Press, 1968) (hereafter Kinsley), I, pp. 228-9.

29 Kinsley, I, p. 128.

30 Such an interpretation of the period is developed more fully by Asa Briggs in the first two chapters ('Economy and Society in the 1780s' and 'Politics and Government on the Eve of the French Revolution') of *The Age of Improvement, 1783-1867* (London, Longman, 1959).

31 The *Mirror*, No. 68 (written by Alexander Abercromby).

32 Anna Letitia Le Breton, *Memoir of Mrs. Barbauld, Including Letters and Notices of Her Family and Friends* (London, Bell, 1874), p. 57.

33 *A Letter to John Farr and John Harris, Esqrs., Sheriffs of the City of Bristol, on the Affairs of America* (1777), in *Writings and Speeches of Edmund Burke*, Beaconsfield ed. (Toronto, Morang, 1901), II, pp. 202-3.

34 To the Rev. John Newton, 13 December 1784; *Correspondence*, II, p. 282.

35 *Monthly Review*, LXXV (1786), pp. 363-4.

36 Kinsley, I, pp. 145-52.

37 Daiches, *op. cit.*, p. 146.

38 Thomas Crawford, *Burns: A Study of the Poems and Songs* (Edinburgh, Oliver & Boyd, 1965), p. 179.

39 *Poems on Various Subjects* (Perth, Morison, 1788), II, p. 59.

Chapter 7

The Music of the Heart*

James Kinsley

The union of poetry and music was associated more and more, as the century advanced, with the ideal of simplicity which had been realized in ancient lyric. James Thomson invoked ancient Greece as

> The sweet enforcer of the poet's strain;
> Thine was the meaning music of the heart.
> Not the vain trill, that, void of passion, runs
> In giddy mazes, tickling idle ears;
> But that deep-searching voice, and artful hand,
> To which respondent shakes the varied soul.

When Music was young in the ancient world, says Collins, the passions thronged round 'to hear her Shell'; but where is her 'native, simple Heart' now?

> Thy humblest Reed could more prevail,
> Had more of strength, diviner Rage,
> Than all which charms this laggard Age,
> Ev'n all at once together found,
> Caecilia's mingled World of Sound—
> O bid our vain Endeavours cease,
> Revive the just Designs of Greece,
> Return in all thy simple state!
> Confirm the Tales Her Sons relate!

Considering the contemporary achievement of Handel, says Professor Bronson, this passage 'betrays an abject flight from experience . . . Collins' failure to escape from the library'. But by the middle of the eighteenth century many men of sensibility were growing dissatisfied with the kind of music represented at its best by Handel; and the longing for primitive simplicity is an expression of changing feeling as well as what Bronson calls 'the cant of the Schools', 'sheer learned humbug'. The primitivism that is so widely diffused in mid-century thinking, and is (rather than any mere classical nostalgia) to be seen in

* Based on the Gregynog Lectures delivered at the University College of Wales at Aberystwyth in February 1963, and reprinted, with permission of the author, from *Renaissance And Modern Studies* (University of Nottingham), vol. VIII (1964), pp. 25-36.

Thomson and Collins here, is a symptom of this change in feeling as well as the academic *imprimatur* on a shift in taste.[1]

In *The Mirror and the Lamp* (1953) Professor Abrams, of Cornell, has traced the growth of the idea of poetry as 'expressive', and as having its origin in the utterance of primitive man. He shows how Giambattista Vico, for example, elaborated a theory of language—from Lucretius, Longinus and other classical sources—as developing from interjections 'articulated under the impetus of violent passions', and therefore (as the utterance of passion is naturally rhythmical and figurative) primordially poetry and song. Views of this kind are not uncommon in English criticism in the mid-eighteenth century (though not necessarily derived from Vico); but it is among the Scottish philosophers, with their strong primitivist interest, that they were most influentially expressed.[2]

The earliest of the Scottish writers is Thomas Blackwell, Professor of Greek at Marischal College, Aberdeen, from 1723 to 1748 and thereafter Principal. In 1735 Blackwell published an *Enquiry into the Life and Writings of Homer*, where he suggests that language originated in 'rude accidental Sounds' expressing primitive passion—such 'as Terror, Rage, or Want (which readily extort Sounds from Men)'—and elaborated into song. Adam Ferguson, Professor of Moral Philosophy at Edinburgh in the 1760s and 1770s, speaks of Homer as the bard of a society of noble savages:

> The simple passions . . . are the movements of his own mind . . .
> Simple and vehement in his conceptions and feelings, he knows no diversity of thought, or of style, to mislead or to exercise his judgment. He delivers the emotions of the heart in words suggested by the heart; for he knows no other.

These judgments are not merely historical. They lead to (and support) a general belief that the qualities of such a poetry as Homer's are the fundamental qualities of all poetry. So Beattie celebrates Homeric society as civilized, but not yet 'so high in the ascent towards politeness, as to have acquired a habit of disguising their thoughts and passions' in literary artifice. Homer's was the period at which

> the manners of men are most picturesque, and their adventures most romantic . . . when the appetites, unperverted by luxury, the powers unenervated by effeminacy, and the thoughts disengaged from artificial restraint. . . . Homer's simple manners may disgust a Terrason, or a Chesterfield; but will always please the universal

taste, because they are more picturesque in themselves, than any form of artificial manners can be, and more suitable to those ideas of human life which are most familiar to the human mind.

Beattie has 'no partiality' to the arguments of philosophers who recommend the manners of the heroic age, but he reiterates that in the poetry of such an age 'the undisguised energies of the human soul' are expressed.[3]

Hugh Blair, first Professor of Rhetoric and Belles-lettres at Edinburgh (1762-83), and arbiter of taste in that dogmatic city, took his proper share in the study and adulation of primitive society. He had also read John Brown and others on the union of poetry and music—and in a country where antiquarian and literary studies were flourishing, had read them with close attention. Man, says Blair with the innocent assurance of his trade,[4]

is both a Poet, and a Musician, by nature. The same impulse which prompted the enthusiastic Poetic Style, prompted a certain melody, or modulation of sound, suited to the emotions of Joy or Grief, of Admiration, Love, or Anger. There is a power in sound, which, partly from nature, partly from habit and association [here he follows Beattie], makes such pathetic impressions on the fancy, as delight even the most wild barbarians. Music and Poetry, therefore, had the same rise; they were prompted by the same occasions; they were united in song; and, as long as they continued united, they tended, without doubt, mutually to heighten and exalt each other's power.

Now Blair's literary fame rested—insecurely, as it has turned out—on his critique of James MacPherson's *Poems of Ossian*: presented to the polite world as the work of an ancient Gaelic bard and (like Beattie's Homer) a type of the noble savage; and translated by (if we believe David Hume) an ignoble savage, who should have been advised 'to travel among the Chickisaws or Cherokees, in order to tame him and civilize him'. Blair's *Dissertation* (1763) is 'as good as could possibly be written by a gentleman lecturing on a language he did not know, of a past he had not studied, of a poem on whose origin he was utterly mistaken'. It offers—as one expects—an extended comparison of Ossian with Homer, in which the Gaelic poet takes the prize for sentiment, gravity and pathos: no poet knew better how to seize and melt the heart. His is the art of expressing 'simple and natural emotions'; he[5] felt strongly himself; and the heart, when uttering its native language, never fails, by power sympathy, to affect the heart. . . .

He moves perpetually in the high region of the grand and the pathetic. . . . His poetry, more perhaps than that of any other writer, deserves to be styled, *The poetry of the heart*. It is a heart penetrated with noble sentiments, and with sublime and tender passions . . . a heart that is full, and pours itself forth. Ossian did not write, like modern poets, to please readers and critics. He sung from the love of poetry and song. . . . Ossian still has power . . . to command, to transport, to melt the heart; . . . his productions are the offspring of true and uncommon genius.

When Blair turns in his *Lectures* to illustrate his primitivist thesis on the union of poetry and music, he naturally draws less on the history of the ancient civilizations than on that of the Celts and Goths—and on the tradition of national balladry: rather as le Fèvre, Vauquelin de la Fresnaye, and Ronsard looked back from the sixteenth century to the Hebrew and Gallic bards and the troubadours for illustrations of musical 'effect'. As long as the two arts remained united, music enlivened and animated poetry; and poetry gave force and expression to music. 'The Music of that early period', says Blair romantically,

was beyond doubt, extremely simple; and must have consisted chiefly of such pathetic notes, as the voice could adapt to the words of the Song. Musical instruments [were intended] simply to accompany the voice, and to heighten the melody of Song. The Poet's strain was always heard; . . . the Bard sung his verses, and played upon his harp or lyre at the same time. In this state, the art of Music was, when it produced all those great effects, of which we read so much in ancient story. . . . When instrumental Music came to be studied as a separate art, divested of the Poet's Song, and formed into the artificial and intricate combinations of harmony, it lost all its ancient power of inflaming the hearers with strong emotions; and sunk into an art of mere amusement, among polished and luxurious nations.

So Blair elaborates John Brown's account of instrumental music which, 'ennobled by the principles of a complex and varied Harmony', worked free of poetry and 'went in Quest of . . . Discords, Resolutions, Fugues and Canons . . . to the neglect of Expression and true Pathos'. This is, of course, grotesquely oversimplified; and it shows an imperfect sympathy with both the music of the Elizabethans, who brought poetry and music together after medieval polyphony had driven them apart, and with the art of Purcell and Handel.[6]

But it is, like Collins's appeal for the recovery of passionate simplicity, an expression of something deeper and more potent than 'the cant of the Schools'. Implied here, and in all that Beattie and others have to say about simplicity and the primary appeal of the singing voice to the heart, is a concern for melody. Rameau, in his *Traité de l'harmonie* (1722), declares that harmonies can raise the passions; but he refers back to Zarlino's suggestion that among the ancients, who offer so many *exempla* of 'effect',

> 'harmony' often signified nothing more than simple melody and that all these effects arose more from an energetic discourse, whose force was intensified by their manner of reciting or singing it, and which can certainly not have enjoyed all the diversity which perfect harmony . . . has obtained for us today.

More important and (among the literati) more influential is Rousseau's discussion of melody and 'effect' in his *Lettre sur la musique* (1753) and in the Encyclopaedia. His exultation over the way his opera *Le Devin de Village* was received is a familiar illustration of the 'premise of feeling':

> From the first scene, which is really touching in its simplicity, I heard a murmur of surprise and applause. . . . Around me I heard a whispering of women who seemed to me as lovely as angels, and who said to one another under their breath: 'That is charming. That is delightful. There is not a note that does not speak straight to the heart.' The pleasure of affecting so many pleasant people moved even me to tears, which I could not restrain during the first duet, when I noticed that I was not the only one who wept. I . . . [was continuously devoured] by the desire to catch with my lips the delicious tears I had evoked. . . . I have never known so complete, so sweet, and so touching an enthusiasm pervade a whole theatre.

How, asks Rousseau in his *Lettre sur la musique française*, written about this time, does music produce great effects on the soul? It is not by multiplying harmonies, parts, instruments; for in such music the melody is lost in a succession of chords. The primary function of music is to carry sentiments, the agents of feeling, to the listener's heart, and everything in the piece must help to strengthen the main impression:

> The harmony must serve only to make it more energetic; the

accompaniment must embellish it without covering it up or dis-
figuring it; the bass, by a uniform and simple progression, must
somehow guide the singer and the listener without either's per-
ceiving it; . . . the entire ensemble must at one time convey only
one melody to the ear and only one idea to the mind.

The unity of a song lies in the melody, and it is the song that gives
beauty to the accompaniment. The accompaniment, conversely,
should correspond so closely to the song that it 'often seems to deter-
mine the action and to dictate to the actor the gesture which he is to
make', the music serving as interpreter. It is in melody that music
'conveys every sentiment to the heart and every picture to the mind';
it is in the air that the musician expresses 'all the imaginable characters
of words'. A similar ideal in accompanied song is set out by Gray's
correspondent Algarotti in his *Saggio sopra l'opera* (1755), translated
into English in 1768. Seventeenth-century Italian music, he says (with
the familiar backward glance of his time), knew her way to the human
heart; she 'had the secret of incorporating herself . . . with the meaning
of the words', and was 'to the last degree simple, yet affecting'. (The
self-sufficiency of melody in song was stressed also in mid-eighteenth-
century German criticism, and as late as the *Lieder* of Schubert melody
and accompaniment were held in equilibrium. It was in later Romantic
song, and opera, that vocal music became 'instrumentally conceived'
and whole operatic scenes were 'symphonically created'.)[7]
Criticism of complex harmonies—'Discords, Resolutions, Fugues
and Canons'—and emphasis on 'Expression and true Pathos' made
particularly good sense in Scotland, where the traditions of folk-song
and balladry were strong. Here as elsewhere in the eighteenth century,
of course, there was a growing sophistication in musical taste and
performance, in the cities and in the drawing-rooms of the great
houses. The Edinburgh Concert, established in 1728, flourished until
late in the century and offered a great variety of orchestral and vocal
music. By 1772 Robert Fergusson could lament, with enough truth to
make his poem worth the writing, that folk-songs were giving way to
continental music:

> Now foreign sonnets bear the gree,
> And crabbit queer variety
> Of sound fresh sprung frae *Italy*,
>   A bastard breed!
> Unlike that saft-tongu'd melody
>   Which now lies dead.

And Henry Mackenzie, Edinburgh lawyer and man of letters, looking back on the later eighteenth century in his native city, wrote of the changes he had seen 'in musical instruments as well as science':[8]

> the Guitar [the common instrument for beginners], the Lute (tho' rarely played on), and the Harp; the Virginals, the Spinette, the Pianoforte. In performance [from] singing plain Scots songs without accompaniment to singing Italian music accompanied, and now bravuras with loud accompaniments that 'rowze as with a rattling peal of thunder'.

But even in the great houses, and in high society in Edinburgh, sophisticated musical taste was weak and comparatively thin: the heart of Scottish music, as well in the drawing-room and concert hall as in the cottage, was the native tradition. In the highlands it was the clan piper, and not the household band of strings, that provided music at table—and this ancient custom, still not quite dead, has doubtless had a conservative influence on music in the north and west. In the lowlands, ballads and pastoral songs in the vernacular were the common possession and delight. Ramsay of Ochtertyre tells how, in the 1720s, 'persons of wit and fashion' were trying their hand at Scots songs; and he contrasts England, where 'a song in the dialect of Cumberland or Somersetshire could never have been generally acceptable ... because it was never spoken by people of fashion'. When the famous Italian *castrato* Tenducci came to Edinburgh in the 1770s and 'entered zealously' into the programming of the city Concert, he took special delight in singing the national airs, with appropriate 'tenderness and simplicity', before fashionable audiences (he excelled in 'I'll never leave thee' and 'The Braes of Bellendine', and Signora Corri in 'Will ye go to the Ewe-bughts, Marion'). Such songs had made their way to the concert hall through the informal family music parties of the aristocracy and gentry. Henry Mackenzie, his 'memory rushing in the songs of old', recalls the singing of traditional airs in the drawing-rooms of the Old Town:

> Some of these ring in my ears at this moment, and visit my sleeping or waking dreams. . . . The ladies of Edinburgh used to sing [them] without any accompaniment (indeed they scarce admitted of counterpoint, or any but a slight and delicate accompaniment) at tea or after supper, their position at table not being interrupted as now [c. 1825] by rising to the pianoforte. The youngest Miss Scott of Harden . . . sung some of these with the greatest expression

and effect. She was the reigning beauty of the time, and . . . a favorite with the then Duke of Hamilton. . . . Her *Lochaber no more* (of itself indeed a most tender and expressive song . . .) bro't tears into her own eyes, and seldom failed of the same effect on her audience.

The antiquary William Tytler, an accomplished flautist and a leading patron of the Edinburgh Concert for more than half a century, echoes Mackenzie's praise of the 'sensibility and feeling' with which Italian visitors sang Scottish songs. Yet he was a man of feeling enough to be moved to tears by the untutored song of a maid at her spinning-wheel, and to understand (with Mackenzie) that orchestration of any kind was foreign to the character of folk-song: the proper accompaniment of a Scots song is only 'a plain, thin, dropping bass, on the harpsichord or guitar', for 'those heartfelt touches which genius alone can express in our songs are lost in a noisy accompaniment of instruments'. The principle of melody as the vehicle of feeling, which was becoming so prominent in English and continental criticism, was being applied in the native song tradition of Scotland.[9]

The most striking feature of eighteenth-century Scottish culture, philosophy and historiography aside, is the cultivation of folk-song and traditional music. Scotland's passionate concern for her cultural heritage, deepened by her failure to retain political integrity,[10] was reflected in—and in turn nourished by—innumerable gatherings of poetry and airs. There were many collections of lyric poetry, from Allan Ramsay's *Tea-Table Miscellany* (1724) to David Herd's *Ancient and Modern Scottish Songs* (1776, 1791). There were more than thirty collections of Scots airs—some published in London—between Pearson's *Original Scots Tunes* brought out by Henry Playford in 1700-1 and Aird's *Airs*, published between 1782 and the end of the century and running to nearly 1,200 tunes. Many of these are collections of reels and country dances (the first book of strathspeys, made by Angus Cumming of Strathspey, came out in Edinburgh in 1780); or they are more varied collections, with settings for strings or the flute. The largest, Oswald's *Caledonian Pocket Companion*, was published in London, in twelve volumes, between 1743 and 1759, and contains more than 550 airs. There were upwards of twenty collections of songs with music, wholly or mainly Scots. Apparently the first Scottish secular song-books are *Orpheus Caledonius* (1725; a second edition, with a second volume, 1733) and Walsh's *Collection of Original Scotch Songs* (1731, 1734)—both published in London. The climax is reached in the great *Scots Musical Museum* of 600 songs, made by James Johnson and Robert Burns between 1787 and the end of the century, and—though with some touches of bathos—George Thomson's *Select Collection* (1793-1818), which includes nearly 100 songs by Burns in a more or less mangled state.

This energetic (if not always scrupulous) recovery and consolidation of Scottish song stands, of course, in a reciprocal relationship to the English antiquarian movement represented by men like Bishop Percy, Hurd and Ritson; to the Gaelic flummery of MacPherson in Scotland; and to the other Celtic revival associated with Edward Lhuyd, Evan Evans and the Morrises in Wales.[11] But although there were powerful patriotic and antiquarian impulses behind the harvesting of Scottish song, it was symptomatic also of an increasing dislike of artifice in both England and Scotland. 'The music of the most barbarous countries', wrote the antiquary Pinkerton in 1783,

> has had effects that not all the sublime pathos of Corelli, or animated strains of Handel, could produce. Have not the Welsh, Irish and Scotish tunes, greater influence over the most informed mind at this day than the best Italian concerto?

And indeed, as Dr Burney pointed out, the song-music of Thomas Arne—'so easy, natural and agreeable to the whole kingdom, that it had an effect upon our national taste'—has a marked Scottish strain. 'Many of his ballads . . . were professed imitations of the Scots style; but in his other songs he frequently dropped into it, perhaps without design.'[12]

Scottish music had been giving delight in England since the time of Dryden, and it had found a place in the English song-books before the native collections began to appear: in the first two volumes of *Wit and Mirth*, for instance, more than one tune in ten is named or can be reasonably identified as Scots. But by the middle of the eighteenth century, as the number of Scots song-books and music-books published in London underlines, northern music was making a strong appeal to an Augustan culture growing weary of 'Discords, Resolutions, Fugues, and Canons', and hungry for 'the meaning music of the heart'. Goldsmith criticized Handel for writing mimetic music that seldom expressed 'distinct passion', and said that 'the music of Mattei is dissonance to what I felt when our old dairy-maid sang me into tears with Johnny Armstrong's last Good-night, or The Cruelty of Barbara Allen.' By 1761 Percy was writing to Evan Evans:

The Scotch . . . are everywhere recommending the antiquities of their country to public notice, vindicating it's history, setting off it's poetry, and by constant attention to their grand national concern have prevailed so far as to have the [broken jargon] Dialect they speak to be considered as the most proper language for our pastoral poetry. Our most polite Ladies [affect to lisp out] warble Scottish Airs, and in the Senate itself whatever relates to the Scottish Nation is always mentioned with respect. [See the Eulogium on the Scottish Writers, &c., in Mr. Walpole's Noble Authors.]—Far from blaming this attention in the Scotch, I think it much to their credit.

It was from Scotland, in the last fifteen years of the century, that a new union of music and poetry came.[13]

In September 1785 Robert Burns, a young Ayrshire farmer who had nourished his literary talents on traditional Scottish poetry and English song collections, entered a long and important note in his Commonplace Book:

There is a certain irregularity in the old Scotch Songs, a redundancy of syllables with respect to that exactness of accent and measure that the English Poetry requires, but which glides in, most melodiously with the respective tunes to which they are set. For instance, the fine old Song of The Mill Mill O, to give it a plain prosaic reading it halts prodigiously out of measure; on the other hand, the Song set to the same tune in Bremner's collection of Scotch Songs which begins 'To Fanny fair could I impart &c.' it is most exact measure, and yet, let them both be sung before a real Critic, one above the biasses of prejudice, but a thorough Judge of Nature,—how flat and spiritless will the last appear, how trite, and tamely methodical, compared with the wild-warbling cadence, the heart-moving melody of the first. . . . There is a degree of wild irregularity in many of the compositions and Fragments which are daily sung to them by my compeers, the common people. . . . This has made me sometimes imagine that perhaps, it might be possible for a Scotch Poet, with a nice, judicious ear, to set compositions to many of our most favorite airs, particularly that class . . . independent of rhyme altogether.

There is a noble sublimity, a heart-melting tenderness in some of these ancient fragments, which show them to be the work of a masterly hand; and it has often given me many a heart ake to reflect that such glorious old Bards—Bards, who, very probably, owed all their talents to native genius . . . their very names are 'buried mongst the wreck of things which were'.

O ye illustrious Names unknown! who could feel so strongly and describe so well! the last, the meanest of the Muses train . . . a poor, rustic Bard unknown, pays this sympathetic pang to your memory.

Here already, in remote Kyle, Burns expresses the antiquarian interest, the patriotic pride, and the response to simplicity and passion, of which I have been speaking. He accepts, almost verbatim, Blair's criteria of poetic genius—'to feel strongly, and to describe naturally'. He has a sense, not blunted by metropolitan 'elegance', of the spontaneous character of folk-song; and he recognizes, hardly yet explicitly, the importance of traditional tunes. 'It might be possible for a Scotch Poet . . . to set compositions to many of our most favorite airs.'[14]

It is likely that Burns by now had read—as he certainly did later—Beattie's discussion of the conditions on which poetry and music could be truly united. Beattie's declaration that Scottish music had originated neither from 'the monks of Melrose' nor from the Continent, but among the native peasantry who 'actually felt the sentiments and affections whereof it is so very expressive'; his emphasis on the virtue of tender feeling in song; and his references to the 'wild irregularity' of ancient 'fragments'—these are echoed or reflected in Burns's note. But the crucial passage in Beattie is on the poetic interpretation of music in song. Traditionally music expresses 'all the imaginable characters of words', conveying every sentiment of the poet's to the responsive listener, 'incorporating herself with the meaning of the words' and so stamping permanent impressions on the heart. But Beattie declares that music 'never appears to the best advantage but with poetry *for its interpreter*':

It is in general true, that Poetry is the most immediate and most accurate interpreter of Music. Without this auxiliary, a piece of the best music, heard for the first time, might be said to mean something, but we should not be able to say what. It might incline the heart to sensibility; but poetry, or language, would be necessary to improve that sensibility into a real emotion, by fixing the fancy upon some definite and affecting ideas. . . . [In song] all uncertainty vanishes, the fancy is filled with determinate ideas, and determinate emotions take possession of the heart.

What is important here is the view of poetry as interpreter rather than as initiator; it is this principle that Burns was to apply, quite explicitly, in his songs.[15]

Notes

1 Thomson, *Liberty* (1738), II, 285-90; Collins, *The Passions* (1746); B. H. Bronson, 'The Pre-Romantic or Post-Augustan Mode', *English Literary History*, XX (1953), p. 20.

2 M. H. Abrams, *The Mirror and the Lamp* (1953), IV, p. 3, 'Primitive Language and Primitive Poetry', pp. 79-81. On the Scottish primitivists, see D. M. Foerster in the *Philological Quarterly*, XXIX (1950), pp. 307-23, and Gladys Bryson, *Man and Society: The Scottish Inquiry of the Eighteenth Century* (1945), ch. 4. Cf. Lois Whitney, 'English primitivistic theories of epic origins', *Modern Philology*, XXI (1924), pp. 337-8. On Scottish critical theory, see A. M. Kinghorn, 'Literary aesthetics and the sympathetic emotions', *Studies in Scottish Literature*, I (1963), pp. 35-47. For modern composers' criticism of the expressive theory of music, see D. Cooke, *The Language of Music* (1959), pp. 11ff.

3 Ferguson, *An Essay on the History of Civil Society* (1773), pp. 290-1; Beattie, *Essays on Poetry and Music, as they affect the Mind* (1778), II, pp. 55-9. (But cf. Burney, *Review of English Studies*, XV (1964), pp. 32-4.)

4 *Lectures on Rhetoric and Belles-Lettres* (1783), II, pp. 315-16.

5 Hume, *New Letters*, ed. R. Klibansky and E. C. Mossner (1954), p. 72; H. G. Graham, *Scottish Men of Letters in the Eighteenth Century* (1908), p. 126; *The Poems of Ossian*, 1894 edn, pp. 68-71, 134, 140. Cf. J. S. Smart, *James MacPherson* (1905); E. D. Snyder, *The Celtic Revival in English Literature* (1923).

6 Frances Yates, *The French Academies of the Sixteenth Century* (1947), pp. 43-4; Blair, *op. cit.*, II, 323-4.

7 Rameau, in Strunk, *Musical Quarterly*, XXXII (1946), pp. 572-5; Rousseau, *Confessions*, trans. J. M. Cohen (1953), p. 353 (bk. 8, 1752); Rousseau, *Lettre*, trans. in Strunk, *op. cit.*, pp. 641-3 (cf. p. 644, the accompaniment and vocal part should constitute 'a single air, and a single melody'); Algarotti, trans. *ibid.*, p. 670. On the relation of accompaniment and voice in Romantic music, see A. Einstein, *Music in the Romantic Era* (1947), p. 35.

8 On the Concert, see, e.g. Henry Mackenzie, *Anecdotes and Egotisms 1745-1831*, ed. H. W. Thompson (1927), pp. 75-8; Fergusson, 'Elegy on the Death of Scots Music', II, 49-54 (cf. Burns, 'The Cotter's Saturday Night', st. 13); Mackenzie, *op. cit.*, p. 80.

9 Ramsay of Ochtertyre, *Scotland and Scotsmen in the Eighteenth Century* (1888), I, pp. 19-20 and note; Mackenzie, *op. cit.*, pp. 76, 79-80; Tytler, Dissertation on Scots music, quoted in Ritson, *Scotish Songs* (1794), 1869, I, pp. 8-10.

10 Generalizations about the cultural effects of the Union of 1707 are, however, commonly over-simple and misleading. See, for comment, David Craig, *Scottish Literature and the Scottish People 1680-1830* (1961), pp. 12ff.

11 See Saunders Lewis, *A School of Welsh Augustans* (1924); Thomas Parry, *A History of Welsh Literature* (1955), ch. 10. Note Percy's defence of his 'reliques of antiquity', which have 'a pleasing simplicity, and many artless graces' 'to interest the heart' (*Reliques of Ancient English Poetry*, 1767, Preface).

12 Pinkerton, *Select Scotish Ballads* (1783), I, xxv; Burney, *A General History of Music* (1776-89), ed. Frank Mercer (1957), II, pp. 1004, 1015.

13 Goldsmith, *Essays*, XIX, 'Schools of Music', and quotation in Chappell, *The Roxburghe Ballads* (1879), III, ii, p. 433; *Correspondence of Thomas Percy and Evan Evans*, ed. Aneurin Lewis (1957), p. 2. Cf. the change in taste taking place at this time in Germany, both in instrumental music built round melody and in 'hundreds of song melodies . . . almost primitive in their bare harmony, their intentional lack of all artistic complication' (H. Leichtentritt, *Music, History, and Ideas* (1938), p. 163).

14 *Commonplace Book 1783-1785*, ed. J. C. Ewing and D. Cook (1938), pp. 37-9; Blair in *Poems of Ossian* (1894), p. 138. Cf. the epigraph to the Kilmarnock edition of Burns's *Poems* (1786):

> The Simple Bard, unbroke by rules of Art,
> He pours the wild effusions of the heart:
> And if inspir'd, 'tis Nature's pow'rs inspire;
> Her's all the melting thrill, and her's the kindling fire.

15 Beattie, *op. cit.*, II, pp. 111, 140, 162-5.

Chapter 8

Robert Burns and Jacobite Song

David Daiches

By the bye, it is singular enough that the Scotish Muses were all
Jacobites. I have paid more attention to every description of Scots
song than perhaps any body living has done, and I do not re-
collect one single stanza, or even the title of the most trifling Scots
air, which has the least panegyrical reference to the families of
Nassau or Brunswick; while there are hundreds satirizing them.
This may be thought no panegyric on the Scots Poets, but I mean
it as such. For myself, I would always take it as a compliment to
have it said, that my heart ran before my head. And surely the
gallant though unfortunate house of Stewart, the kings of our
fathers for so many heroic ages, is a theme much more interesting
than an obscure beef-witted insolent race of foreigners whom a
conjuncture of circumstances kickt up into power and consequence.

So Burns wrote in the interleaved copy of the *Scots Musical Museum*
which he prepared for Robert Riddell of Glenriddell. His involvement
with collecting, reworking, patching up, imitating and creating
Scottish folk-songs as a result of the work he so enthusiastically
undertook to do for James Johnson and George Thomson, editors
respectively of the *Scots Musical Museum* and *A Select Collection of
Original Scotish Airs*, had brought him to realize the central significance
of the Jacobite movement in Scottish folk-song and its importance in
providing and perpetuating a genuine folk emotion well into an age of
literary sophistication when such emotion could no longer be expected
to enter spontaneously into widely circulated popular song. Of course,
ever since the seventeenth century the political conflicts between
Cavaliers and Roundheads, or Royalists and Commonwealth men, or
Tories and Whigs—the different sides had different names as circumstances changed and the terms of the conflict also changed, but the
basic division remained—had produced ballads, satirical squibs and
partisan songs, and the Jacobite movement and its opponents inherited
this tradition and kept going, well into the eighteenth century, some of
the songs that first appeared in the reign of Charles I and in the years of
Charles II's wanderings. 'The King shall enjoy his own again', for
example, the first song in James Hogg's *Jacobite Relics of Scotland*
(Edinburgh, 1819), was, as Hogg's note puts it, 'invented at first to

support the declining cause of the royal martyr, Charles I; and served afterwards, with more success, to keep up the spirits of the cavaliers, and promote the restoration of his son'. It also was a favourite song of Bonnie Prince Charlie, and he sang it on the night of 28 June 1746 on the rough journey from South Uist to Skye, disguised as Flora Macdonald's maid, in order to cheer up Flora and his other companions. But though some old Cavalier songs persisted into the mid-eighteenth century as part of the repertoire of the Jacobite movement, the activities and personality of the Prince himself, and particularly the nostalgic glamour shed over the Jacobite cause and its leader after the cause had been finally lost at Culloden, produced a new kind of song, generally more personal in feeling and more lyrical in tone. The older satirical and mocking note did not, however, die out, but existed side by side with the new element. Burns, who was a great satirical poet before he became a great song-writer, relished both these aspects of Jacobite song, as his reworking equally of the lyrical 'Charlie he's my darling' and the satirical 'Johnie Cope' testifies.

His own feelings about the exiled House of Stuart were not wholly consistent, but in general his statement that his heart ran before his head in this matter sums up his position pretty well. He had moments of strong Jacobite feeling, especially when in convivial Jacobite company, or when moved by some particular historical association, and he was capable of violent outbursts against the House of Hanover, at least one of which got him into trouble. The contemptuous reference to the 'obscure beef-witted insolent race' in the note already quoted was meant only for a private eye, but the lines 'written in the window of an inn at Stirling on seeing the Royal Palace in ruins' (Kinsley, no. 166) were deliberately put in a public place:

> Here Stewarts once in triumph reign'd,
> And laws for Scotland's weal ordain'd;
> But now unroof'd their Palace stands,
> Their sceptre's fall'n to other hands;
> Fallen indeed, and to the earth,
> Whence grovelling reptiles take their birth.—
> The injur'd STEWART-line are gone,
> A Race outlandish fill their throne;
> An idiot race, to honor lost;
> Who know them best despise them most.—

This was written in August 1787, at the start of his Highland tour, after a convivial evening at Stirling with his travelling companion, the lively but irascible William Nicol, and some local people—a schoolmaster called Doig ('a queerish figure and something of a pedant', as Burns noted in his journal of the tour), Captain Forrester of Stirling Castle ('a merry, swearing kind of man with a dash of the Sodger') and 'a joyous, vacant fellow who sings a good song' called Bell. It was not a tactful set of verses for someone who was seeking a position in the Excise service, and he had to do a lot of explaining.

On other occasions he was more cautious. The previous May he had written to William Tytler of Woodhouselee, author of a two-volume defence of Mary Queen of Scots against the charges that had been brought against her by Robertson and Hume, enclosing some in-different verses complimenting Tytler on his defence of 'beauteous Stuart' and going on to talk of her descendant:

> Tho' something like moisture conglobes in my eye,
>   Let no man misdeem me disloyal;
> A poor, friendless wand'rer may well claim a sigh,
>   Still more if that Wand'rer were royal.
>
> My Fathers that *name* have rever'd on a throne,
>   My Fathers have died to right it;
> Those Fathers would spurn their degenerate Son
>   That NAME should he scoffingly slight it.
>
> Still in pray'rs for King G—— I most cordially join,
>   The Queen and the rest of the gentry:
> Be they wise, be they foolish, 'tis nothing of mine,
>   Their title's allow'd in the Country.
>
>   (Kinsley, no. 152; *Letters*, I, p. 88)

'Burn the above verses when you have read them,' he adjures his correspondent, 'as any little sense that is in them is rather heretical, . . .' Yet the sentiment expressed here was mild compared to what he produced the following August in Stirling, and, further, it was communicated privately to a single individual.

Were Burns's 'fathers' really Jacobites, as he claims in these verses? In the seventh stanza of his 'Address to Edinburgh' (Kinsley, no. 135), composed in December 1786, he had written:

> Haply *my Sires* have left their shed,
> And fac'd grim Danger's loudest roar,
>   Bold-following where your Fathers led!

He was more explicit when he visited John Ramsay of Ochtertyre in October 1787, as Ramsay recalled:[1]

> Burns, the poet, told me here in the year 1787, that the Ayrshire clergy were in general as rank Socinians as himself. That poor man's principles were abundantly motley—he being a Jacobite, an Arminian, and a Socinian. The first, he said, was owing to his grandfather having been plundered and driven out in the year 1715, when gardener to Earl Marischall at Inverury [George Keith, tenth Earl Marischal, was a noted Jacobite: he commanded the Jacobite cavalry at the Battle of Sheriffmuir]; the second, to his great-grandfather, by the mother, having been shot at Airds Moss while with the Covenanters.

It was from Ramsay of Ochtertyre that Burns heard about the venerable Mrs Bruce of Clackmannan, with the result that he visited her. Dr James M'Kittrick Adair, who was travelling with Burns during this stage of his tour, later gave Dr Currie an account of what happened:[2]

> A visit to Mrs. Bruce, of Clackmannan, a lady above ninety, the lineal descendant of that race which gave the Scottish throne its brightest ornament, interested his feelings more powerfully [than the scenery]. This venerable dame, with characteristic dignity, informed me, on my observing that I believed she was descended from the family of Robert Bruce, that Robert Bruce was sprung from her family. Though almost deprived of speech by a paralytic affliction, she preserved her hospitality and urbanity. She was in possession of the hero's helmet and two handed sword, with which she conferred on Burns and myself the honour of Knighthood, remarking, that she had a better right to confer that title than *some people*. . . . You will of course conclude that the old lady's political tenets were as Jacobitical as the poet's, a conformity which contributed not a little to the cordiality of our reception and entertainment.—She gave as her first toast after dinner, *Awa' Uncos*, or away with strangers—Who these strangers were you will readily understand. Mrs. A. corrects me by saying it should be *Hooi*, or *Hoohi uncos*, a sound used by shepherds to direct their dogs to drive away their sheep!

The most detailed statement of his ancestral Jacobitism that Burns made is found in a letter he wrote in December 1789 to Lady Winifred Maxwell Constable, daughter of the Earl of Nithsdale who had suffered forfeiture for his part in the '45. He wrote:

Though my Fathers had not illustrious Honors and vast Properties to hazard in the contest; though they left their humble cottages only to add so many units more to the unnoted croud that followed their Leaders; yet, what they could they did, and what they had they lost: with unshaken firmness and unconcealed Political Attachments, they shook hands with Ruin for what they esteemed the cause of their King and their Country.

(*Letters*, I, p. 376)

In the long autobiographical letter to Dr John Moore, written in August 1787, Burns wrote: 'My Fathers rented land of the noble Kieths of Marshal, and had the honor to share their fate' (*Letters*, I, p. 105). He goes on to say that the ruin of his 'fathers' resulting from their association with the Jacobite cause 'threw my father on the world at large', thus clearly implying that William Burnes left his native Kincardineshire as a result of Jacobite activity. But there is no suggestion that William Burnes was a Jacobite, and indeed it is hard to conceive of that man of worthy Presbyterian piety as having any relationship with Jacobitism; it is even impossible to prove that *his* father, the poet's grandfather, really played the role in the '15 that Burns believed, or chose to believe, he did. The only thing we can be certain about is that William Burnes left his native district of Scotland in 1748, when he was twenty-seven years old, to settle eventually in Ayrshire, and he seems to have been forced to leave home because the rebellion of 1745-6 had ruined his father's schemes for farming on a larger scale and forced him into bankruptcy.

In his later years Burns, while never losing interest in Jacobite song, came under the influence of the ideas of the French Revolution, and paradoxically added a passionate political egalitarianism to his feelings of sympathy for the Stuart kings and their absolutist claims. (The paradox of being both Jacobin and Jacobite becomes less bewildering when we realize that one aspect of Jacobitism was an expression of frustrated Scottish national feeling, and that Scotsmen of all shades of the political spectrum could be drawn to that special variety of Scottish Nationalist Jacobitism which has a long and fascinating history. Further, there was a kind of cultural Jacobitism, a Scottish Cavalier tradition, almost, of lively song and music, persisting among Scottish Episcopalians of the north-east, who were Jacobites almost to a man. Burns met Bishop Skinner, primate of the Episcopal Church of Scotland, in Aberdeen in September 1787 and talked with him about his father, John Skinner, author of the rollicking song 'Tullochgorum'

which Burns greatly admired. The Skinners were interesting repre-
sentatives of the Jacobite culture in north-eastern Scotland associated
with the Scottish Episcopal Church. Burns entered into correspondence
with the older Skinner in October 1787 and requested his help in
collecting songs for Johnson's *Scots Musical Museum*.)

In November 1788 Burns wrote his longest and most carefully
reasoned statement of his attitude towards the Stuarts. This was in a
letter to the *Edinburgh Evening Courant* protesting against the offensive
language about the Stuarts used by the officiating minister when he
had gone 'last Wednesday to my parish church, most cordially to join
in grateful acknowledgments to the Author of all Good, for the
consequent blessings of the Glorious Revolution'. He professes his
adherence to the view that regards that event as the fount of 'our
liberties religious and civil' and pays tribute to 'the present Royal
Family, the ruling features of whose administration have ever been,
mildness to the subject, and tenderness of his rights'. But he pleads for a
historical understanding of the behaviour of the Stuarts. ' "The
bloody and tyrannical house of Stuart" may be said with propriety and
justice, when compared with the present Royal Family, and the liberal
sentiments of our days. But is there no allowance to be made for the
manners of the times? Were the royal contemporaries of the Stuarts
more mildly attentive to the rights of man?' The nub of his argument
is in the next paragraph:

> The simple state of the case, Mr. Printer, seems to me to be this—
> At that period the science of government—the true relation
> between King and subject, like other sciences, was but just in its
> infancy, emerging from the dark ages of ignorance and barbarism.
> The Stuarts only contended for prerogatives which they knew
> their predecessors enjoyed, and which they saw their contem-
> poraries enjoying; but these prerogatives were inimical to the
> happiness of a nation and the rights of subjects. In this contest
> between Prince and People, the consequence of that light of
> science which had lately dawned over Europe, the Monarch of
> France, for example, was victorious over the struggling liberties
> of the subject: With us, luckily, the Monarch failed, and his un-
> warrantable pretensions fell a sacrifice to our rights and happiness.
> Whether it was owing to the wisdom of leading individuals, or to
> the justlings of party, I cannot pretend to determine; . . .

The Stuarts have been condemned and laughed at for the folly
and impracticability of their attempts, in 1715 and 1745. That they

failed, I bless my God most fervently; but cannot join in the ridicule against them.—Who does not know that the abilities or
defects of leaders and commanders are often hidden until put to
the touchstone of exigence; and that there is a caprice of fortune,
an omnipotence in particular accidents, and conjunctures of
circumstances, which exalt us as heroes, or brand us as madmen,
just as they are for or against us?

(*Letters*, I, pp. 269-71)

Burns's Jacobitism here is chastened almost to the point of extinction.
He accepts the Glorious Revolution enthusiastically, but tries to
exonerate the House of Stuart by pleading the historical relativity of
political judgments, and defends the instigators of the '15 and the '45
on the grounds that anything *might* have happened and they are therefore not be be blamed for having made the attempts. It is a humane
and sensible argument, but shows no awareness of the deeper reasons
for the reverberation of Jacobite sentiment in Scottish folk-song. Of
course, in this letter Burns was trying to put himself right with
officialdom while at the same time protesting against the brutal anti-
Jacobitism still prevalent in certain quarters. And perhaps he also
wanted to free himself publicly to engage with Jacobite song without
hesitation or compunction. For it is in his engagement with Jacobite
song that he reveals his real understanding of the significance of
Jacobitism in the popular imagination.

Burns's interest in collecting and restoring Scottish songs, and in
writing new words to traditional Scottish airs, was bound up with his
interest in Scottish places and his determination to familiarize himself
with localities and with local traditions associated with popular songs
and airs. He had begun as the poet of his own part of Ayrshire, but the
success of the Kilmarnock volume stimulated his ambition to be a
national rather than just a regional Scottish poet, and he undertook
journeys for the precise purpose of visiting places all over Scotland
that were famed in folk tradition. He wrote to George Thomson in
January 1793:

I am such an enthusiast, that in the course of my several peregrina-
tions through Scotland, I made a pilgrimage to the individual spot
from which the song took its rise.—Lochaber, & the braes of
Ballenden, excepted, so far as the locality, either from the title of
the air, or the tenor of the Song, could be ascertained, I have paid
my devotions at the particular shrine of every Scots Muse.

(*Letters*, II, p. 148)

Many of the places, and many of the airs associated with places, had Jacobite associations, and Burns follows on at once with a suggestion about Jacobite songs.

> I do not doubt but you might make a very valuable Collection of Jacobite songs, but would it give no offence? In the mean time, don't you think but some of them, particularly 'The Sow's tail to Geordie', as an *Air*, with other words, might be well worth its place in your Collection of lively Songs?

'The Sow's Tail to Geordie' was one of the more scurrilous of the Jacobite songs directed against George I (the 'sow' was his mistress, Lady Darlington), but it went to a flowing reel tune that was popular throughout the century and was printed both in Alexander McGlashan's *Scots Measures*, 1781, and James Aird's *Selection of Scotch, English, Irish, and Foreign Airs*, 1782. Both Burns and Thomson liked the air, but Thomson would never have dared to print the original words, and even Burns did not suggest this. Instead, he eventually wrote for Thomson his own words to the air, which he sent to Thomson on 19 November 1794. So instead of

> It's Geordie's now come hereabout,
> O wae light on his sulky snout!
> A pawky sow has found him out,
> And turn'd her tail to Geordie.
>
> The sow's tail is till him yet,
> The sow's birse will kill him yet,
> The sow's tail is till him yet,
> The sow's tail to Geordie!
>
> (*Jacobite Relics*, Song LV)

we get an innocuous love-dialogue:

> *He*
>
> O Philly, happy be that day
>   When roving through the gather'd hay,
> My youthfu' heart was stown away,
>   And by thy charms, my Philly.
>
> *She*
>
> O Willy, ay I bless the grove
>   Where first I own'd my maiden love,
> While thou did pledge the Powers above
>   To be my ain dear Willy.
>
> (Kinsley, no. 468)

This is far from being one of Burns's best love songs, but it is an interesting example of his determination to preserve an admired Jacobite tune by writing inoffensive words to it.

More important, however, are the songs Burns wrote or adapted which are directly Jacobite in subject: there are about thirty of these in all—the 'about' indicating that in a few cases the Jacobite element is dubious or a matter of subjective interpretation; almost any song in which a woman laments her dead or departed Highland lover can be said to have Jacobite overtones. The first of these, 'My Harry was a Gallant gay' (Kinsley, no. 164), written some time after August 1787, is not specifically Jacobite in the version we find as no. 209 in the *Scots Musical Museum* (*SMM*), III (1790). The text here, unsigned, simply presents a woman sighing for the return of her Highland lover. It is set to the tune which *SMM* calls 'Highlander's Lament' but which was also known as 'The Highland Watch's Farewell to Ireland'. (The Black Watch was in Ireland from 1749 to 1756.) 'The oldest title I ever heard to this air, was *The Highland Watch's farewell to Ireland*', wrote Burns in the interleaved *SMM*. 'The chorus I pickt up from an old woman in Dunblane; the rest of the song is mine.' The version in the Hastie MS., however, gives several extra stanzas directly linking the song to the '45:

> Strong was my Harry's arm in war
> Unmatch'd in a' Culloden plain
> Now vengeance marks him as her prey
> I'll never see him back again.

And the final chorus runs:

> And oh! for him back again,
> The Auld Stewarts back again
> I wad gie a' my fathers lan'
> To see them safely back again.

The transcript in the Hastie MS. is in an unidentified hand, and Kinsley notes:

Unless Burns's note in his copy of *SMM* is misleading, and the transcript represents his 'original', it is probably an anonymous attempt at making his song more specifically Jacobite. Johnson had copies made of some of the songs Burns sent him, but there is no instance of such substantial revision done after a song came in.

The spelling out of the Jacobite implications was therefore probably not done by Burns, but the fact remains that they were there in the beginning for the spelling out.

Burns's next Jacobite song was prompted by a quite specific Jacobite occasion. This is the 'Scots Ballad', set to the air 'Mary weep no more for me', and beginning

> My heart is wae and unco wae,
>   To think upon the raging sea,
> That roars between her gardens green
>   And th' bonie lass of Albanie.

(Kinsley, no. 188)

The lass of Albanie was Charlotte, Bonnie Prince Charlie's daughter by his mistress Clementina Walkinshaw. After a lifetime of estrangement the Prince sent for her in July 1784 to join him in Florence. He had her legitimized and given the title Duchess of Albany, a title which she formally assumed in December 1787. Charlotte arrived in October, and the old Prince, lonely and broken down, made much of her: on St Andrew's Day 1784 he gave a banquet for her and invested her with the Green Ribbon of the Order of the Thistle. He seems to have thought of her as his heir, for he proposed to have medals struck for her, the design for one of which shows a storm-tossed ship approaching the English coast flying a flag bearing the Stuart arms and the motto *Pendet salus spe exigua et extrema*. Charles died at Rome at the end of January 1788 and Charlotte died in October of the following year. Burns's song was probably written soon after news reached Scotland of Charlotte's having assumed the title of Duchess of Albany. As Charles died little more than a year later, and the song appears to have been written before his death, it seems likely that the date of composition was at the end of 1787 or the beginning of 1788. Its Jacobite tone is uncompromising:

> Alas the day, and woe the day,
>   A false Usurper wan the gree,
> That now commands the towers and lands,
>   The royal right of Albanie.
>
> We'll daily pray, we'll nightly pray,
>   On bended knees most ferventlie,
> That the time may come, with pipe and drum,
>   We'll welcome home fair Albanie.

It was never published in Burns's lifetime, and according to Chambers it was turned down by Allan Cunningham when he was preparing his edition of 1834 on the grounds that 'George IV and the Duke of York were too recently deceased, and their brother William IV then occupied the throne'. It was first printed in volume VI of *Bentley's Miscellany*, 1843.

Burns must have been in a Jacobite mood at this time, perhaps brought on by the combination of news about the Duchess of Albany and Prince Charles's birthday on 31 December 1787. He wrote to James Steuart on 26 December (*Letters*, I, p. 148) talking about the approaching birthday and transcribing the second and third stanzas of the poem he had sent to William Tytler the previous May. According to Dr Currie, 'it appears that on the 31st day of December he attended a meeting to celebrate the birth-day of the lineal descendant of the Scottish race of Kings, Prince Charles-Edward'. Currie adds that nobody present was disloyal to the reigning monarch or hoped or wished for a Stuart restoration, 'but over their sparkling wine, they indulged the generous feelings which the recollection of fallen great-ness is calculated to inspire; . . . On this occasion our bard took upon himself the office of poet-laureate, and produced an ode, . . .' (Currie, I, p. 187). The ode, 'A Birth-day Ode. December 31st 1787' (Kinsley, no. 189), is in the Pindaric manner, and much of it is rightly described by Currie as 'a kind of rant'. Burns calls on 'Perdition, baleful child of Night' to rise and avenge the injured Stuarts by leading th' unmuzzled hounds of Hell . . . Full on the base, usurping crew, / The tools of Faction and the Nation's curse'. The preposterous rhetoric suggests that Burns was trying to work himself up into a mood of passion that did not correspond to his real feelings.

He did much better in songs. In *SMM*, II, p. 1788, No. 187, 'O'er the water to Charlie', is not attributed to Burns, but William Stenhouse, in his *Illustrations of the Lyric Poetry and Music of Scotland* (1839), originally compiled to accompany *SMM* and drawing on Burns MSS. of songs printed in *SMM*, says that it was 'revised and improved by Burns'. Burns had already used the lively Jacobite air 'Over the Water to Charlie' (which he knew as 'Shawnboy') in his Masonic poem, 'The Sons of old Killie', but here he uses it for a reworking of a Jacobite song which may have existed in several versions: two with the same phrase in the chorus appeared in a surreptitiously printed Jacobite song book, *The True Loyalist*, in 1779; Hogg prints Burns's version with an extra stanza in his second series of *Jacobite Relics* (1821), no. XXXVII. It may be that all Burns had to work on was the phrase 'over the water to

Charlie', which appears to have become traditional in Jacobite poetry and song: Alasdair Mac Mhaighster Alasdair (Alexander Macdonald) uses it in the opening of his 'Brosnachadh do na Gaidheil' ('An Incitement for the Gaels'):[3]

> O togamaid oirnn thar uisge 's thar tuinn,
>   O falbhmaid thairis gu Teàrlach!
>
> O, let us go over the sea and the waves,
>   O let us cross over to Charlie!

Burns's poem is in the purest folk tradition, and captures with complete success the personal and 'occasional' nature of much Jacobite folk-song. It opens

> Come boat me o'er, come row me o'er,
>   Come boat me o'er to Charlie;
> I'll gie John Ross anither bawbee
>   To boat me o'er to Charlie.

> *Chorus*
> We'll o'er the water, we'll o'er the sea,
>   We'll o'er the water to Charlie;
> Come weal, come woe, we'll gather and go,
>   And live or die wi' Charlie.

This song is followed in *SMM* by 'Up and warn a' Willie', which is not there attributed to Burns. In the interleaved *SMM* Burns wrote:

This edition of the song I got from Tom Niel of facetious fame in Edin[r]. The expression *Up and warn a' Willie* alludes to the *crantara* or warning of a highland clan to arms. Not understanding this, the Lowlanders in the West, and South, say, *Up and waur them a'*, &c.

It seems fairly certain that Burns made some alterations to the song he got from Niel which was itself an expansion (there is a version with many differences and one stanza less than the *SMM* version, printed in *The Charmer* (1752), signed 'B. G.'). The song was one of several satiric accounts of the Battle of Sheriffmuir, 1715. A better known one with a similar theme is by Murdoch McLennan and is found in David Herd's *Scots Songs* (1776), I, pp. 104ff. and opens:

> There's some say that we wan,
>   Some say that they wan,
> Some say that nane wan at a' man;

> But one thing I'm sure,
> That at Sheriff-muir,
> A battle there was, which I sa', man;
> *And we ran, and they ran, and they ran, and we ran,*
> *and we ran, and they ran awa' man.*

The *SMM* version has similar lines:

> Now if ye spier wha wan the day,
> I've tell'd you what I saw, Willie,
> We baith did fight and baith did beat
> And baith did rin awa, Willie.

Very different is the formal English poem of which Burns sent the first stanza to Robert Cleghorn on 31 March 1788, set to Cleghorn's favourite air, the Irish reel tune 'Captain O'Kane'. This stanza is a formal lament in rather stiff neo-classic English, beginning 'The small birds rejoice in the green leaves returning'. Cleghorn liked the lines and wrote Burns on 27 April: 'I wish you would send me a verse or two more; and if you have no objection, I would have it in the Jacobite stile. Suppose it should be sung after the fatal field of Culloden by the unfortunate Charles' (Currie, II, p. 144). Burns took Cleghorn's advice and added a second stanza in which the Prince defends his attempt 'a King and a Father to place on his throne' and concludes:

> But 'tis not my sufferings, thus wretched, forlorn,
> My brave, gallant friends, 'tis your ruin I mourn;
> Your faith proved so loyal in hot, bloody trial,
> Alas, can I make it no sweeter return!

(Kinsley, no. 220)

The song appeared, attributed to Burns, in Thomson's *Scotish Airs*, 1799, where the tune is marked 'andantino espressivo'. As a reel, the air, in 6/8 time, would go at a lively pace, but Burns discovered early that in slowing down a reel tune in a minor key he could bring out a plaintiveness that the faster pace obscured. (Perhaps the best-known example of this is his setting of 'Ye banks and braes o' bonie Doon' to the slowed-down reel tune, 'The Caledonian Hunt's Delight'.)

The version of 'Johnie Cope' (Kinsley, no. 297) which appeared unsigned in *SMM*, III (1790) (no. 234), was first attributed to Burns by Dick on the strength of Burns's own description, 'Mr. Burns's old words', in the Law MS. (a list of the contents of volume III of *SMM* in Burns's own hand). We know that Burns used this phrase to indicate old songs that he had reworked. This prolonged sneer at General Cope after his ignominious defeat at the Battle of Prestonpans is pretty rough-and-ready stuff, but it swings along effectively enough to the traditional air to which this and similar anti-Cope songs were set. Burns came to dislike the tune, and referred in a letter to Thomson in April 1795 to 'a squalidity, an absence of elegance, in the sentiment & expression of that air'. His dislike, as he admitted, probably came from association with the words he wrote and suggests that he was not especially satisfied with them.

'Carl an' the king come' (*SMM*, 1790, not attributed to Burns; Kinsley, no. 299), set to the popular tune of that name, is a lively little song anticipating celebrations on the restoration of a Stuart king, pure folk in feeling. Stenhouse says that Burns wrote only the second stanza; Ritson (*Scotish Songs* (1794), II, no. 47) quotes another stanza in the same rhythm and with the same refrain. Burns's precise part in the *SMM* song remains doubtful. (*SMM* prints on the same page as this song, Allan Ramsay's song to the same tune from his *Gentle Shepherd*, 'Peggy, now the King's come'; so there was clearly a version before Ramsay.) Also in the 1790 volume of *SMM* is 'Awa whigs awa' (Kinsley, no. 303), which the Law MS. describes as 'Mr. Burns's old words'. Burns evidently reworked an old song, a fragment of which is preserved in David Herd's MSS.:[4]

> And when they came by Georgie Mills
> They licked a' the mouter,
> The bannocks lay about there
> Like bandoliers and powder.
>
> > Awa, Whigs, awa!
> > Awa, Whigs, awa!
> > Ye're but a pack o' lazy loons,
> > Ye'll do nae good ava.

Burns keeps this chorus, but substitutes 'traitor loons' for 'lazy loons' and turns his four stanzas into a Scottish nationalist attack on the Whigs:

> Our thrissles flourish'd fresh and fair,
>   And bonie bloom'd our roses;
> But Whigs cam like a frost in June,
>   And wither'd a' our posies.
>
> (*Chorus*) Awa whigs &c.

This interestingly shows Burns picking up the Scottish nationalist aspects of the Jacobite movement, aspects which were very important in the development of Jacobite folk-song (and which Scott understood clearly in *Redgauntlet*).

'The White Cockade' (Kinsley, no. 306) is also in *SMM* (1790) (no. 272), and is described in the Law MS. as 'Mr. Burns's old words'. Again, the original is in Herd's MSS. (ed. Hecht, p. 124), but here it is 'the lad wi' the Highland plaidy' and not 'the boy wi' the White Cockade' (as in Burns) whom the speaker is determined to follow. The white cockade was, of course, as Burns explained in the interleaved *SMM*, worn by the Jacobite army in 1745. Burns thus took a traditional song about a girl determined to follow her Highland lover, set it to an air already known to him as a Jacobite air, a reel tune called 'The White Cockade' but also known as 'The Ranting Highlandman', and gave it clear Jacobite associations without changing its main theme or its folk character. (This is the air to which 'A Highland lad my love was born', in 'The Jolly Beggars', is now generally sung, though in fact Burns set it to a different tune.)

Continuing with volume III of *SMM*, we come to no. 282, 'The Battle of Sherra-moor', 'Written for this Work by Robt. Burns' (Kinsley, no. 308). Burns has here reworked a ballad by the Rev. John Barclay of Muthill entitled 'A Dialogue between Will Lickladle and Tom Cleancogue' written to the rather thumping air, 'Cameronian Rant'. Burns retains and indeed strengthens the lively dramatic quality of a ballad-dialogue and the song contains some of his most vigorous writing. The pervasive tone is humorously ironic, the irony arising from the fact (so common in songs about the battle) that neither side knew which had won. No. 292 in the same volume of *SMM* is 'Killiecrankie' (Kinsley, no. 313), said by Stenhouse to be Burns's stanzas to an old chorus. It is a short ballad-dialogue, with question and answer, and the answer is given by one of General Mackay's men, who opposed Claverhouse at the Battle of Killiecrankie and who survived only because 'Clavers gat a clankie, O' to die in the moment of victory. The tune, 'Killiecrankie', seems to have been composed soon after the battle.

The first Jacobite song in *SMM*, IV (1792), is 'Frae the friends and Land I love' (no. 302; Kinsley, no. 341), not attributed to Burns, who wrote in the interleaved *SMM* 'I added the four last lines by way of giving a turn to the theme of the poem, such as it is'. The air, 'Carron side', is described in the *Caledonian Pocket Companion* as 'a plaintive air', and the verses have a rhetorical plaintiveness which Burns tried to stiffen with his concluding four lines:

> Till Revenge, wi' laurelled head,
>   Bring our Banished hame again;
> And ilk loyal, bonie lad
>   Cross the seas and win his ain.

Yet the song remains an unsuccessful hybrid.

No. 15 in *SMM*, IV (1792), is 'There'll never be peace till Jamie comes hame' (Kinsley, no. 326). Burns sent the song to Alexander Cunningham in a letter of 11 March 1792 with this comment: 'You must know a beautiful Jacobite Air. There'll never be peace till Jamie comes hame.—When Political combustion ceases to be object of Princes & Patriots, it then, you know, becomes the lawful prey of Historians and Poets.' This is Burns's clearest statement of the literary appeal of Jacobitism after it had become a *lost* cause. In the interleaved *SMM* Burns noted, 'This tune is sometimes called *There's few gude fellows when Willie's awa*'; but I have never been able to meet with anything else of the song than the title'. Though *SMM* does not attribute the song to Burns, it is thus demonstrably his, written in an interesting mixture of English rhetorical and Scottish ballad style:

> By yon castle wa' at the close of the day,
> I heard a man sing tho' his head it was grey;
> And as he was singing the tears down came,
> There'll never be peace till Jamie comes hame.

More purely in the folk tradition is 'Bonie laddie, Highland laddie' (*SMM* (1792), no. 332, not attributed to Burns; Kinsley, no. 353) set to the very lively dance tune 'The Old Highland Laddie'. It gives a brief but vivid picture of the Duke of Cumberland in Hell. Equally in the folk tradition, though in a different way, is *SMM* (1792), no. 359, 'O Kenmure's on and awa, Willie' (Kinsley, no. 364). Viscount Kenmure was a leader of the 1715 Jacobite rising; he surrendered at Preston and was subsequently executed. The song is in the simplest and purest ballad style:

> O Kenmure's on and awa, Willie,
>   O Kenmure's on and awa;
> And Kenmure's Lord's the bravest Lord
>   That ever Galloway saw.

SMM does not attribute it to Burns, but Stenhouse says that 'Burns transmitted the ballad of Johnson in his own handwriting, with the melody to which it is adapted', and the holograph draft now at Alloway shows that Burns revised it for *SMM*. Kinsley (III, p. 1397) believes that 'it is possible . . . that Burns wrote the song', but it sounds too much like a genuine folk response to 1715 and shows no awareness of Kenmure's execution. It is more likely that Burns worked with a genuine older folk-song. The air is not traceable before its appearance in *SMM*.

Whether 'Ye Jacobites by name' (*SMM*, IV, no. 371, not attributed to Burns; Kinsley, no. 371) is a pro- or anti-Jacobite song depends on how it is read. Burns's part in this 'pithy ironical satire couched in equivocal terms which may be read by either Whig or Tory' (Dick) is dubious. No. 378 in the same *SMM* volume and again not attributed to Burns is 'Such a parcel of rogues in a nation' (Kinsley, no. 375), a nationalist anti-Union song. The Gray MS. attributes the words to Burns, but the refrain was certainly traditional. The sentiments expressed are the traditional anti-Union ones, as voiced by the critics of the Union in 1707:

> O would, or I had seen the day
>   That treason thus could fell us,
> My auld grey head had lien in clay,
>   Wi' Bruce and loyal Wallace!
> But pith & power, till my last hour,
>   I'll make this declaration;
> We're bought & sold for English gold,
>   Such a parcel of rogues in a nation.

SMM, V (1796), appeared after Burns's death, but contains songs he had sent Johnson. The first of these is no. 401, signed B, 'The lovely lass o' Inverness' (Kinsley, no. 554). The Hastie MS. has a holograph note by Burns simply calling these stanzas 'the old words of this song', and Burns in fact may have had no hand in it. It is a simple folk piece, dealing with a girl who weeps for her father and brothers slain at 'Drumossie moor' (i.e. Culloden). Kinsley finds 'the purity and finish' of the second and final stanzas evidence of Burns's hand, but the lines are in the purest folk idiom:

> Their winding-sheet the bludy clay,
>   Their graves are growing green to see;
> And by them lies the dearest lad
>   That ever blest a woman's e'e!
> Now wae to thee, thou cruel lord,
>   A bludy man I trow thou be;
> For many a heart thou has made sair
>   That ne'er did wrang to thine or thee!

It may be that, like some of Scott's ballads, these lines are in a purer folk idiom than any actual folk poetry can be seen to be, and this may reflect Burns's genius.

'Charlie he's my darling', succinctly described by Kinsley as 'Burns's lyric reduction of a long romantic street ballad', is no. 428 of *SMM*, V (Kinsley, no. 562). Around the lively chorus Burns has built a poem which deftly weaves together a number of different folk themes— Bonnie Prince Charlie as the romantic 'young Chevalier', the high-lander as lover, the milkmaids' real or pretended fear of the descent of 'Charlie and his men' from the mountains. The rollicking chorus— 'An' Charlie he's my darling, my darling, my darling . . .'—binds the song together, and it needs binding, for the opening stanza

> 'Twas on a Monday morning,
>   Right early in the year,
> That Charlie cam to our town,
>   The young Chevalier—

comes from a different folk tradition from the final one:

> Its up yon hethery mountain,
>   And down yon scroggy glen,
> We daur na gang a milking
>   For Charlie and his men.

The air is not known before its appearance in *SMM* and may have been collected by Burns. Another reduction to a lyric poem in the folk style of an earlier and longer work is 'Highland laddie' (*SMM* (1796), no. 648; not attributed to Burns; Kinsley, no. 578), which is an abridg-ment of 'The Highland Lad and the Highland Lass' published in *A Collection of Loyal Songs*, 1750. Burns contributed the first eight lines only. The song is about a girl specifically mentioned as Lowland in love with a Highland laddie who is adjured in the final stanza to procure renown for himself 'and for your lawful king his crown'. This kind of Jacobite song is important as indicating the sentimental bridging of Highland and Lowland feeling, so opposed in so many respects before the final Jacobite defeat, which developed after the movement had become purely nostalgic. (Needless to say, the Jacobite poetry of the Gaelic poets, much more immediately and directly involved with the movement, does not show any feeling of this kind. It is on the whole a professional, craftsmanlike poetry, both tougher and more deeply committed than Jacobite poetry in Scots.)

We can pass over 'Bannocks o' bear-meal', a fragment of folk-song about Highland loyalty to Charlie, since Kinsley is surely right in saying that 'it is unlikely that [Burns] did more than gather it from oral tradition' (III, p. 1512). But *SMM* (1796), no. 197 (not attributed to Burns; Kinsley, no. 589), 'It was a' for our rightfu' king', is demonstrably largely by Burns (in spite of Hogg's attribution of it to Captain Ogilvie of Inverquharity and Scott's ignorance of Burns's authorship). It is a lyrical reconstruction of a chap-book ballad 'Mally Stewart'. (Anyone who wants to see how marvellously Burns reworked the poem can find 'Mally Stewart' in Henley and Henderson, III, pp. 435-6, and make the comparison himself.) It is the finest of Burns's Jacobite lyrics and one of the finest of all his songs, set to a simple and thoroughly effective seventeenth-century ballad air. Here the themes of love, patriotism, Jacobitism and exile are woven together into a seamless whole. Burns picked up the repetition of the words 'my dear' from 'Mally Stewart', but uses it with infinitely greater skill:

> It was a' for our rightfu' king
>> We left fair Scotland's strand;
> It was a' for our rightfu' king,
>> We e'er saw Irish land, my dear,
>> We e'er saw Irish land.

Burns moves from the note of loyalty to a moving linking of patriotism and love and exile and a memorable rendering of the theme of the lost cause:

> Now a' is done than men can do,
>> And a' is done in vain:
> My love and Native Land fareweel,
>> For I maun cross the main, my dear,
>> For I maun cross the main.

The third stanza provides the pivot on which the whole poem turns:

> He turn'd him right and round about,
>> Upon the Irish shore,
> And gae his bridle-reins a shake,
>> With, Adieu for evermore, my dear,
>> And adieu for evermore.

We are held by this romantic figure of the horseman bidding an eternal farewell to his love, and in the last two verses the poem turns into a personal love elegy:

The soger frae the wars returns,
  The sailor frae the main,
But I hae parted frae my Love,
  Never to meet again, my dear,
  Never to meet again.

When day is gane, and night is come,
  And a' folk bound to sleep;
I think on him that's far awa,
  The lee-lang night and weep, my dear,
  The lee-lang night and weep.

Here Burns has given Jacobite feeling a new dimension, anchoring it firmly in personal elegy, but an elegy linked to a sense of the flinty reality of historical fact. It was the folk tradition that linked love lyrics to the Bonnie Prince Charlie theme, but Burns has here given this link a wholly new significance.

After this, 'The Highland widow's lament' (*SMM* (1796), no. 498, not attributed to Burns; Kinsley, no. 590) and 'The German lairdie' (Kinsley, no. 605) seem anti-climax. The former is ascribed to Burns on the evidence of the Hastie MS., but it was probably merely transmitted by him: it is a rather tinny lament by a woman whose husband fell at Culloden. The latter is a fragmentary piece with a nonsense chorus, attacking the Whigs and their 'Revolution principles', and appears to be an abridgment of an anti-Whig ballad of twelve stanzas, 'What now has ta'en the Whigs', which can be found in *Jacobite Relics* (1819), pp. 146-7. Even these undistinguished pieces, however, remind us that Burns was able to respond to and to capture a great number of the variety of moods evoked in Scottish breasts by the Jacobite movement, and that in creating, rewriting, altering and collecting Jacobite songs he gave Jacobite song in Scotland a new lease of life.

Notes

1 *Scotland and Scotsmen in the Eighteenth Century* (Edinburgh, 1888), II, p. 544.
2 *The Works of Robert Burns with an Account of his Life* . . . (Liverpool, 1800), I, pp.171-2.
3 *Highland Songs of the Forty-Five*, ed. J. L. Campbell (Edinburgh, 1933), no. XIII.
4 *Songs from David Herd's Manuscripts*, ed. Hans Hecht (Edinburgh, 1904), p. 181.

Chapter 9

Robert Burns, Writer of Songs

Cedric Thorpe Davie

I

The real nature of Burns's songs remains widely misunderstood. It is true that mid-twentieth-century writers such as Crawford, Daiches and Fitzhugh have done their best to give the songs something more like their due than their predecessors did but, for one reason or another, critical appraisement of the songs as integrated works of art still leaves a great deal to be desired. There is an implicit assumption in much literary criticism that the music of Burns's songs is a minor factor which must be recognized by the critic, but with reluctance.

In fact, the songs are the result of the fusion of two elements from different arts. In the best examples this fusion is complete, and the elements are inseparable without vital injury to one or both. But for the tunes, the words would never have come into existence, and it is absurd to regard the latter as poetry to be read or spoken aloud.

Those who have written of Burns's songs as if their tunes did not exist, or did not matter, or (worst of all) were an unnecessary and frivolous encumbrance, merely expose their own inadequacy. It is sad to find Robert Louis Stevenson, in his *Familiar Studies of Men and Books*, regarding the songs as marking a degeneration of the poet's powers, when he writes, 'during the remainder of his life, Burns rarely found courage for any more sustained effort than a song'. There is an arrogance in this attitude, with its implication that musical considerations are beneath the dignity of a man of letters, which ill befits a great practitioner of one art when writing of another.

The scholar, the research worker, and the merely curious may nowadays feel impelled to consult the works of Cromek, Stenhouse, Sharpe, Laing, Farquhar Graham and other early commentators on the songs of Burns; but the practical needs of most lovers of the poet's works are to a great extent met if they confine their attention to two more modern writers, Dick and Kinsley.[1] There is little concerning the provenance of the songs that has not been discovered and set forth by these two scholars; and it is a tribute to the quality of Dick's work that Kinsley, writing half a century later, should so seldom have to correct him or differ from him. Kinsley's principal and most important value lies rather in the additional facts that he has unearthed. He and Dick between them provide us with a critical summary of all that went before them, which, combined with the original research of each, presents a formidable body of detailed material for the study of this important branch of the poet's work. Other modern writers have done a valuable service to later generations of Burns-lovers by bringing together and digesting much of what was done by their predecessors in the field, but they add little to what can be found by a diligent search of the works of earlier writers, and their work on the songs can only be useful as a supplement to that of Dick and Kinsley.

An invaluable source of information on Scottish *airs* is John Glen's *Early Scottish Melodies*, published as long ago as 1900. Glen, of course, is dealing with the musical origin of the songs only, and with the whole of *The Scots Musical Museum* (*SMM*), not only with Burns's enormous contribution to that invaluable source-book.

Dick and Kinsley are not beyond criticism. Dick prefaces each of his works with an extended essay; both are full of erudition and each is a monument to the author's patent devotion to his subject, but it is a weakness that this very devotion sometimes leads the author to an unwillingness to see wrong in his hero. Dick overplays his hand when, in seeking to destroy the absurd myth that Burns was totally unmusical, he exaggerates qualities and accomplishments which the poet possessed to a limited degree only. (The myth, of course, arose because Burns's earliest biographers did nothing to contradict the ludicrously wrong judgment of the schoolmaster John Murdoch, who found that the boy Burns had an ear that was 'remarkably dull'.) The final paragraph of *Notes*, bringing together all the arguments in favour of Burns's exceptional musical gifts, claims for him a 'phenomenal' appreciation of melody which, considering the variable quality of the melodies which stimulated him to song-writing, is surely an exaggeration. It cites as a merit the poet's ability to compose an admittedly worthless tune; and it rather undermines its own argument by pointing out that the poet spent *hours* in learning the 'swing' and 'cadence' of the melodies, and in 'forming an impression of their import', surely matters which would have revealed themselves more quickly had the poet's appreciation really been as phenomenal as Dick claims.

In addition to this, Dick occasionally makes statements which reveal his own limitations as a musician, as when he refers to 'John Dowland's madrigal compositions' (which are non-existent), or states that Thomas Campion 'is now forgotten and known only to the student'; or when he refers to the tune of no. 43, 'O leave novels, ye Mauchline belles', as 'evidently a pipe-tune', when its compass far exceeds that of the pipes. Again, without adducing any evidence, in an endeavour to explain the enormous compass of some of the tunes, he says (p. 379) that 'it is necessary to know that the *falsetto* voice was much used among the peasantry'.[2]

Dick is not alone in falling into the familiar trap of seeing thematic connections between tunes in what are in fact no more than resemblances between tiny melodic clichés. The most questionable of these so-called affinities is that which Dick (rather uncritically supported by Kinsley) alleges to exist between the marvellous melody of no. 589, 'It was a' for our rightfu' king', and the humdrum English tune 'The Bailiff's daughter of Islington'. The first phrase of each, to be sure, is strung from the same commonplace series of notes from the general stock of melody; but the vital and really significant *difference* between the two, namely, the unusual and beautiful irregular phrasing of the Scottish melody as compared with the run-of-the-mill twice-four of the English one, evidently failed to reach Dick, whose ear, it may be inferred, was better at appreciating passing detail than larger structural subtlety. Conversely, there are some genuine melodic family ties which neither Dick nor Kinsley mentions. One which should be noticed is the tune no. 588, 'Loggan (or Laggan) Burn', which really is a close relative of no. 392, 'The lea-rig', and there are others.

In spite of such relatively unimportant flaws, it cannot be gainsaid that the enormous pains which Dick took to ensure a clean text, his wide knowledge of source-material and his ant-like industry, all combined with his enthusiasm and total devotion to produce two books of great value, which remain after more than half a century indispensable to everyone with an interest in the subject.

In printing the melodies, Dick has adopted the very sensible principle of giving them in keys adapted to the actual capacity of the human voice. I can find no merit in the reproduction of the air in keys which from the point of view of a singer are awkward or even absurd, merely on the ground that these were the keys selected by, let us say, the musical editor of *SMM*; still less the original keys of tunes from collections such as Oswald's *Caledonian Pocket Companion* (*CPC*), which were set not for singing but for playing on the violin. Dick also very sensibly rationalizes all the underlaying of words by means of the consistent use of one of the accepted methods of musical notation, with slurs joining two or more notes which are to be sung to a single syllable. In *SMM* this is done in a haphazard manner, owing to the laziness of the musical editor; as for the violin books, the slurs printed against the notes of the melodies have a totally different meaning. To reproduce these slavishly in a modern edition is surely to take textual faithfulness to unwarranted extremes.

It may appear captious to find fault with Kinsley's monumental edition, for he has laid us all under an obligation for the additional light which he has shed on countless details. Nevertheless, there is just ground for complaint at the number of inaccuracies in the music of his text. I have found nearly sixty misprints and mistakes of musical notation, not counting the myriad wrong or omitted slurs; many of these come as the result of Kinsley's copying into his text misprints, inaccuracies and inconsistencies already to be found in his sources. This seems to me to be carrying faithfulness too far; but a considerable number, including some of the worst, have no such dubious authority.

Strangely, and rather inconsistently, Kinsley does in fact sometimes make corrections of his sources, such as the time-signature of no. 391, which he has properly changed to 6/8 from the faulty 9/8 in *SMM*. Even these, few in number as they are, are not always happy; the attempt in no. 430 to amend the tune of *SMM* 9 to fit these words is an example of the inexpert carrying out of a justifiable intention.

Kinsley's strict reproduction of his sources is open to another criticism, that it sometimes leads to an absurd incompatibility of words and tune. This is particularly the case where he has chosen to print an original fiddle tune in preference to a modified vocal version of the kind that abounds in *SMM*. I have not made an examination of every example in detail, but a few cases are sufficient to illustrate the point. In no. 163, Kinsley has transcribed the air in *CPC* inaccurately, and has omitted some of the bowing-slurs; those slurs which he does print are therefore meaningless as directions either to a fiddler or to a singer. The *appoggiatura* in bars 12 and 20 are also wrongly transcribed, and we find both kinds of mistranscription occurring elsewhere in Kinsley, as in no. 209.

In no. 171, again, Kinsley copies all the bowing-marks (which are of no value or meaning to a singer, and may even mislead him), but not all of them accurately. He also cuts the tune, as is necessary if it is to fit the words, but in a clumsy way which makes singing the air both difficult and ungainly. Thus, the version given is neither a faithful reproduction of the original from which Burns worked, nor a reasonable accommodation of the tune to the words such as is given in Dick.

That literal transcription of an original, irrespective of glaring errors, can reach a height of absurdity is shown in the two songs no. 381 ('Up wi' the carls of Dysart') and no. 492 ('Fy let us a' to Kirkcudbright'), both of which Burns set to tunes in triple time; each was wrongly printed in the source used by Kinsley, with faulty barring indicative of duple time, and each has been so reprinted by the editor. (Dick corrects the former, but not the latter.) Again, Kinsley's exact reproduction of his sources, faults and all, sometimes gives us tunes in keys having a *tessitura* which only a freak voice could manage; a case in point is no. 228 ('O were I on Parnassus hill'). Kinsley gives the air in a fiddle version taken from *CPC*, no doubt on the grounds that it was here that Burns first found it; but as printed by Kinsley the music text contains five inaccuracies of notation, two of which are in the original; this version is totally unsingable, yet a vocal adaptation is given in *SMM*, presumably approved by Burns and printed along with the first publication of his verses.

Finally, Kinsley has perpetuated countless errors and misprints of underlaying which the carelessness, laziness or ignorance of musical editors like Stephen Clarke allowed to pass.[3] It is much to be regretted that Kinsley did not submit his music-copy to a minimum of realistic technical editing on the lines adopted by Dick, whose musical text is almost totally scholarly, and is practically free of misprints. There would have been the additional advantage that no tune would have been given in a version to which the words cannot be sung, as in the case cited above, and in others like no. 138, 'Again rejoicing Nature sees'.

Kinsley, while clearly acknowledging his (and our) debt to Dick, chides him from time to time, usually with justification; but once or twice he slips, as when, having described Dick's reference to a pipe-tune (see above) as 'nonsense', he continues with the equally nonsensical statement that 'the bagpipe has one octave'; nor are things made better by Kinsley's subsequently printing an actual pipe-tune whose compass exceeds the octave.

What is surprising is that the commentators attempt very few aesthetic judgments upon the tunes, either in themselves or in their relation to the words which Burns supplied for them. It is true that Dick and Kinsley occasionally, in passing, touch upon the merits of some particular melody. In such cases, Kinsley is usually concerned with the matching of verbal and musical climax, or with the correspondence of cadence to rhyme, matters verging on the technical rather than the aesthetic. Occasionally he goes further, as in his well-justified praise of no. 444, 'Wilt thou be my Dearie?'.

This diffidence, if such it be, is particularly hard to account for in

Dick's case, considering his boundless enthusiasm for the musical aspect of Burns's work, and it perhaps reinforces the impression which Dick creates, that this very enthusiasm tended to blunt his critical faculty. With Kinsley the case is rather different, and one might suppose the paucity of aesthetic criticism to be due to a desire to achieve objectivity, were it not that Kinsley is free with aesthetic judgments on the words, both of songs and poems. See, for instances taken at random, his commentaries on no. 81 ('To a Louse') and no. 558 ('Tam Lin').

Whatever the explanation of the tendency of commentators to avoid qualitative judgments of the songs in their complete form of words plus music, it seems to me that their absence leaves a serious gap in the general assessment of Burns's stature as a creative artist. Every line that the poet wrote has undergone scrutiny over and over again, and very many of them have formed the subject of more or less valuable criticism of some aspect of his work; but it is surely yet another indication of the under-estimation of the songs *as words intended to be sung*, and of lack of appreciation of their true nature as attempts at the wedding of the two arts, that there is such a shortage of equally close attention to the music, and to the welfare of the marriages.

II

Study of the songs as a whole suggests the formulation of a number of broad truths, which may be set down as follows:

(1) Something like one-fifth of all Burns's songs consist of fine words beautifully matched to worthy melodies, and these include most of the songs which are most widely known and loved; but a truly lovely air did not in every case draw highly inspired words from the poet: and conversely, some of the finest words were intended by Burns to be allied to tunes which most people would regard as indifferent. Such partial successes account for about a further tenth of the total. At the bottom of the scale there is a residue of some thirty songs where neither words nor melody is of much worth, or in which the fitting of words to tune is awkward or worse.

(2) Songs included in *SMM* are in general superior to those in Thomson, a fact which applies with particular force to songs especially written for one or the other. Of the former, Burns gave most of his best to the volumes issued during his lifetime; the songs published in

volumes V and VI after his death show a lower proportion of the poet's best work.

(3) Songs written in the vernacular are in general superior to those entirely in English, despite a small number of spectacular exceptions.

(4) Everyone concerned, *Burns included*, seems to have accepted that it might be proper to publish a song to a tune other than that which was originally in the poet's mind.

(5) Burns's avowed indifference to the more sophisticated aspects of the art of music blinded him to certain facts concerning the form in which his songs were published, and in particular prevented him from realizing (*a*) that the harmonizations in *SMM* were at best undistinguished and at worst barely competent, and (*b*) that the 'symphonies and accompaniments' in Thomson's grandiose scheme were at best quaint and at worst ludicrously inept, amounting in sum to a harsh comment upon Thomson's absurd assumption that the foremost European composers of the day were necessarily the most suitable agents of his laudable purpose.[4]

Before we consider each of these propositions in some detail, it will be useful to compare Burns's contribution to *SMM* and Thomson on a statistical basis. It is not so easy as one might suppose, as to the numbers appearing in each. I have thought it right to ascribe to the poet all songs in which he is proved to have had even the slightest hand, on the straightforward ground that he must have been quite satisfied with those parts of older or traditional poems which he left untouched, or else he would have made more extensive alterations and additions. I have taken no notice of songs which Kinsley relegates to his Appendix.

On this criterion it appears to me that *SMM* contains 213 songs by Burns, that is, just over one-third of the total. In the case of Thomson, it is more difficult to reach a firm figure. Those who are acquainted with Hopkinson's essay on Thomson's publications[5] will be aware that they constitute a bibliographer's nightmare, owing to Thomson's habit of withdrawing sheets or making substitutions even within so-called single volumes or parts.[6] It is therefore with some reserve that I give the figure of 114 as the total of Burns's contribution to Thomson, which actually contains substantially more songs than the 325 which is the number supposed to be contained in the six volumes issued between 1793 and 1841, even allowing for duplications in certain issues. (The number is further increased if we take into account the octavo edition brought out in 1822-5.)

In theory, something like 34 songs in *SMM* are to be found also in Thomson, but Thomson did so much gratuitous tinkering with Burns's work that in fact very few of the verses or melodies are identical in the two publications, and some differ very considerably. This figure refers to Burns's words only, and takes no account of differences in the airs; but it may be as well to complete the statistical account by noting that whereas in *SMM* only 9 songs are printed with music differing from that which the poet had in mind when writing them, the total of such tunes, mostly unauthorized, in Thomson is not less than 43, and almost certainly is more.

III

Aesthetic criticism applied to the arts remains, despite the rather half-hearted efforts of generations of moral philosophers, very much a matter of individual taste. This is not to suggest that one man's opinion of the value of the work of Picasso or Purcell is as good as another's, for such is manifestly not the case; but when a number of individuals have made themselves familiar with a large part of the output of a creative artist, and with the techniques that lie behind it, it is impossible to deny that their differing reactions to specific examples of that output are equally valid, and that they reflect the subjective preferences and prejudices of the reader, the viewer or the listener.

For this reason I do not expect every lover of Burns's songs to agree with all the judgments and criticisms which follow; they are my own judgments and criticisms, and they do not seek to invalidate the views of others who have considered the matter seriously.

I take it that everyone will agree that the quality of a complete work of art in the form of a song must be judged from three standpoints: the quality of the verse as such, the quality of the tune as such, and the success with which the one matches, enhances and sets off the other, giving the feeling that the whole is greater than the sum of its two parts. Making judgments on these criteria can be a tricky business, particularly with regard to the quality of the words. As many a heavenly song by Schubert demonstrates, verses of manifestly less than first-rate quality can sometimes form the basis of a union with music resulting in a complete work of art that defies adverse criticism. Some would go further, and maintain that verse which is in itself truly of the finest quality can only be harmed by being allied to another art.

This is not the occasion to go deeply into the arguments, nor need we be too concerned with them in so far as they relate to Burns's songs, if only for the reason that Burns wrote his verses for the specific purpose of making the music known, whereas the majority of the poets whose work was subsequently set to music by such composers as Schubert had no such idea in mind.

The habit of writing the words *to the music* instead of the other way round seems to have been a peculiarly British one. In England it goes back to d'Urfey's *Pills to Purge Melancholy* and beyond, while in Scotland Ramsay composed *The Gentle Shepherd* at just about the same time as John Gay in London was applying the method systematically in *The Beggar's Opera*. Ramsay had already begun publication of his *Tea-Table Miscellany*, in which he and others under his influence produced a large amount of mostly indifferent verse, designed to be sung to well-known folk-tunes. He thereby, in a sense, removed the tunes from the sphere of 'folk-art', founded what may be called 'national song' as distinct from 'folk song', and laid down the principles upon which collections like Thomson were later to be built. These principles, in a word, sought to lift Scottish folk-song out of the allegedly vulgar lower-class surroundings in which it had flourished, and to make it respectable and fit for the more refined ears of the middle and upper classes; and especially, as Thomson was forever insisting, for 'the ladies'. There is no doubt that Ramsay's songs were taken as models by Burns, who in his turn was emulated by such minor poets as Tannahill, and by a host of versifiers whose works the curious may sample in that couthy anthology, *Whistle Binkie*. Thomas Moore, though a poet of far smaller stature, performed for many Irish melodies a task analogous to that of Burns in Scotland.

The technique involved in writing successfully to pre-existing music raises unique problems for the poet and for the critic, and it is a remarkable fact that Burns, who on several occasions was at pains to stress his ignorance of the higher branches of musical art, and who wrote in 1785, 'I am not scholar enough to prick down my tune properly', succeeded so often in perfectly fusing the two arts.[7] This is not in itself proof of Burns's 'musicality' (though Dick seems to think otherwise), and we shall have to turn to that subject in a moment; but it *is* proof of the subtlety of his ear for the music of words or of melody, and of his skill in matching verbal and musical stress, in following the rise and fall of inflexion, and in paralleling rhyme with its corresponding musical feature, cadence.[8]

In the great majority of Burns's songs there is little or nothing of this technical aspect of his art at which one can cavil, even where the chosen tune is not a particularly inspired one. Sometimes, it is true, there is an irritating tendency to fit the *metre* of the verse to the tune, rather than its real rhythm. This usually results in an unpleasant stress upon weak syllables and unimportant words, as can be seen in no. 408, 'Blythe hae I been on yon hill', a poem not very remarkable in itself, but hardly deserving the metrical bumps on the words 'on', 'as' (twice), 'is', 'if' and 'in', all of them consequent upon a thoughtless, rather than an inept, subservience to the powerful regular *ictus* of the tune 'The Quaker's Wife'. That there should be fewer than a score of real misfits in a total of more than 350 songs is a tribute to the poet's instinctive perception of the qualities, particularly the rhythmic qualities, of his chosen tunes, and to his acquired craftsmanship.

A few of these misfits deserve a passing glance, if only to indicate how the attention of even the greatest genius may wander for a moment. For those with sufficient curiosity to see whether they agree with these strictures, the note gives the numbers in Kinsley; it should be remembered that Burns was to some extent at the mercy of his musical editor when it came to publication of the music print, and some of the faults may well lie at the door of Clarke or Thomson.[9]

No. 29, 'The sun he is sunk in the west', is a strange case of the forcing of a five-line stanza to the notes of what is essentially a four-phrase tune. The odd result is a sudden doubling of pace of delivery in the third and fourth lines of each stanza, and a return to the original pace at the fifth line. This is a unique instance so far as Burns's own composition is concerned, and it is a strange fact that the song in *SMM* entitled 'Go from my window', which Dick and Kinsley think is probably not by Burns, though in the same metre (divided into six lines), and set to the same air, does not give the listener the same feeling of dissatisfaction.

No. 175, 'Streams that glide in orient plains', and no. 176, 'Loud blaw the frosty breezes', are two attempts to set words to a Highland air for which Burns eventually found a satisfactory though undistinguished solution in no. 509, 'O wat ye wha that lo'es me'. It is a lovely tune, but one suspects that Burns was foxed by its irregular phrase-structure of five plus four bars. No. 175 is a truly dismal affair, and no. 176 is not much better.

No. 208, 'Musing on the roaring ocean', apart from being representative of the poet at his unhappiest as a word-spinner, is an acute case of false accentuation, and the feeble attempt to cope with the melodic oddity of the sixth and seventh bars is adversely commented on by Kinsley in terms of unwarranted gentleness.

No. 387, 'Will ye go to the Indies, my Mary', is another sad case of a poem poor in itself, totally unsuited to the chosen tune, and technically a bad fit. Thomson, in one of his few moments of critical awareness, said of it, 'This is a very poor song.' Nevertheless he published it.

Having discussed some of Burns's few really bad failures as a songwriter, let me now move to the other extreme. I find no fewer than seventy-three songs which come under the heading of 'Good poem, good tune, good match'. At the very head of the list, it seems to me, are the following:

no. 8	usually known as 'Corn Rigs'
no. 84b	'I once was a maid'
no. 216	'Rattlin, roarin Willie'
no. 227	'Of a' the airts'
no. 257	'Flow gently, sweet Afton'
no. 287	'Ay waukin, oh'
no. 326	'There'll never be peace till Jamie comes hame'
no. 328b	'Ye banks and braes o' bonie Doon'
no. 345	'O meikle thinks my Luve o' my beauty'
no. 357	'Bonie wee thing'
no. 386	'The deil's awa wi' th' Exciseman'
no. 456	'Ca' the yowes to the knowes'
no. 524	'Oh wert thou in the cauld blast'

Here we have a baker's dozen of perfect works of art, able to stand comparison with the best that Schubert could do, if we accept that the criterion of perfection is a complete integration of all the elements that go to make up such masterpieces. It is true that there have been those who have found the words of no. 84b, and even of nos 8, 216 and 386, not to their liking; it is perhaps not surprising that the cautious Thomson, ever mindful of the welfare of the fair sex, did not publish the last two, omitted no. 84b from his edition of 'The Jolly Beggars', and preferred Ramsay's words to those of Burns in the case of no. 8. I hope, however, that we have left that sort of prudishness behind us,[10] and can recognize the work of genius without allowing the hair-shirt to interfere with our judgment.

It will not pass unnoticed that my prize-list includes nine (ten if we include 'Bonie wee thing') of the best-known and best-loved of all the songs; and this, it seems to me, is a tribute not only to public discrimination but even more to that quality of universality in the greatest artists which ensures that the fifth and sixth symphonies of Beethoven, Shakespeare's *A Midsummer-Night's Dream*, Botticelli's *Birth of Venus* and St Paul's Cathedral will delight untold numbers of generation after generation of that humanity for which artists are the spokesmen. As will be seen later, the tally of those songs by Burns which can be classed as second only to the exclusive top list shows an equally prolific number of public favourites; few of the most widely popular songs, interestingly enough, appear in the lower categories, and those usually when set to airs other than those intended by the poet.

No. 8, 'Corn Rigs', bears all the signs of that youthful relish and virtuosity that one finds in Mendelssohn's early work, such as his *Octet for Strings*. No doubt at all that the quatrain which was 'All the words that ever I could meet in this air' fired the poet's young blood and inspired this torrent of felicitously expressed young passion; I dare to guess that it was written quickly and required little revision. The brilliantly original air, which despite its swift movement is eminently singable on account of its modest (but not restricted) range, and its infectious rhythm, is perfectly matched to the words, with never a doubtful stress (unless those 'haes' in the last stanza offend the hypersensitive), and with every half-close and full-close exactly adapted to the progress of the sense. A triumph of a song which makes the sixty-year-old feel, not that he wishes he were twenty again but that he *is* twenty, without in any way lessening the pleasure which the genuine twenty-year-old can take in it.

No. 84b, the second song in 'The Jolly Beggars' or 'Love and Liberty', is surely the most completely satisfying of all the songs in that revealing masterpiece. The progress of the argument of the poem, as much as the felicitous language in which it is couched and the brilliant variation of the basic idea in each successive stanza-ending, combines with the wonderful tune in so complete a way as to make one feel that they were all one single conception. Even in this list of what I regard as the pearls of Burns's output, I can think that only two, or at most three, could be claimed to surpass it.

No. 216, 'Rattlin, roarin Willie', surely needs no praise at this date. Its gentle, intensely human humour, with a touch of pathos lurking in the background, places it among the very best of a certain type of lyric in the composition of which Burns was unsurpassed; its quality of being almost a function of that brilliant three-times-three tune places it in a special category.[11] This song, and no. 386, as well as others in the genre only a little less superb, illustrate a side of the poet as endearing to many people as that gentler insight which is shown in the next two songs on my list, nos 227 and 257.

These two simple love-songs, the one couched in Scots and the other in English, melt the heart by the very language in which perfectly commonplace ideas are conveyed, but only when they are delivered in melody. Spoken aloud, they differ little from a million personal lyrics inspired by the amorous feelings which are at once the delight and the despair of the normal young man. Sung to their lovely tunes they are transformed, perfect witnesses to the truth of Burns's statement that inspiration came to him though a process of mulling over the air in his mind, and gradually allowing his thoughts to form. Even among the plethora of good strathspey tunes that are a feature of Scottish music, 'Miss admiral Gordon's strathspey', the air of no. 227, is outstandingly beautiful, with its series of three half-cadences[12] followed by a full close in each half, giving a remarkable sense of continuity. As for the tune of 'Sweet Afton' (who was the genius who wrote it?), it is incomparable in its beauty and delicacy; it is a strange comment on human unpredictability that this pearl among melodies should so often be sacrificed in favour of the weak-kneed effusion of the Victorian hack-composer Alexander Hume.

No. 287, 'Ay waulkin, oh', so seldom sung in the slow triple rhythm that is its air's most characteristic feature, has a strange haunting individuality, a restiveness if you like, which in a way that is impossible to define conjures up the peculiar distortions of thought that go with, and often are the cause of, insomnia; I find much in the allusive words that does not appear on the surface. This song is a prime example of the fusion of poem and melody into a form that is immeasurably greater than either separately, as can be proved by the simplest experiment.

No. 326, 'There'll never be peace till Jamie comes hame', is as little-known as no. 328b, 'Ye banks and braes o' bonie Doon', is famous. Maybe there is a certain artificiality and over-romantic quality about the poem, but it is a touching one to the listener who can use his imagination, and it is fitted to a melody of such sheer beauty as defies words to describe it.

The controversy that has continued for more than a century as to the relative merits of the two versions of 'Ye banks and braes' is born of the futility of considering the words without reference to the tune. A preference for the earlier version, which has been expressed by many of the most eminent commentators, ignores the whole question of the poet's intention that his verses should be *sung*. It may be regrettable that the tune of the first version is so feeble, with its tendency to sit down for a rest at each alternate bar, but it is an inescapable fact, which puts out of court any claim to superiority over the second version. Maybe

many of the words in the second version *are* superfluous to the require-
ments of strict verbal economy. What of it? This is poetry, not a lesson
in nature-study. Thomas Crawford has it right when he says that
when the poem is *sung* 'to the melody forever associated with it . . . it
becomes a beautifully poignant expression of love's melancholy'. It
may be added that the air is a wonderful example of the almost mes-
meric quality that can emerge from the use of the pentatonic scale.

There is perhaps a paradox in no. 345, which is better known under
the title 'My tocher's the Jewel', if one reads into the poem (as is
possible) a sardonic note; for in that case its beautiful air would seem
scarcely appropriate to the sentiment of the words. But if, as I believe,
the characteristic of the poem is the mournful one of a girl truly in love
with a man who does not return her affection, all slips into place, and
the melancholy tune is heard as its perfect musical expression. Doubtless the melody is related to 'The muckin' o' Geordie's byre', as Burns
said, but it is a distant relationship, and I would have thought that the
tune 'Adieu Dundee' was at least as close. Whatever the ancestry of the
three tunes, each has developed such an individuality as to make it a
matter of little importance.

No. 357, 'Bonie wee thing', when read aloud, may strike one as the
kind of poem that has caused ill-wishers to accuse Burns of the couthi-
ness of a frequenter of the kailyard. Sung to its exquisite air, what has
been described as bathos and sentimentality are found to be pathos and
tender sentiment, and the finished song shows up as a classic example
of the subtle chemistry that transforms words and music into an
entirely new compound.

I take it that nowadays nobody would want to sing the earlier words
of no. 185, 'Ca' the yowes', in preference to the version (no. 456)
written some seven years later and eventually printed by Thomson in
1815. So far as the main stanzas are concerned, neither set of words will
emerge from critical scrutiny as being poetry of a very high order; but
the exquisite recurring chorus transforms them, and when it is allied
to their unique modal tune the result is an emotive pastoral love-song
which has survived more bad 'arranging' and abuse by incompetent
musical editors than any other song of Burns. It seems to me not to
matter very much whether the eleventh note is sharpened or not, but
there is at least one valid (if not compelling) reason for supposing that
those who insist on the natural note are wrong, and that it stands un-
sharpened in *SMM* (where it accompanies the older words) owing to
an understandable oversight on the part of Stephen Clarke when noting
it down.

The last song in my list of matchless masterpieces, no. 524, 'Oh wert thou in the cauld blast', was written when the poet's days were numbered, and is in fact his last song of importance. Can it be that the romantic circumstances surrounding its composition (whether or not they have any basis in fact) affect one's capacity to view this song with detachment? Precisely the same question can be asked about the composition of J. S. Bach's last work, the chorale prelude 'Vor deinen Thron tret' ich', which the old master is said to have dictated on his death-bed when too weak and blind to write for himself. Does it matter very much? Who can say for sure what emotional considerations contribute to our critical judgments? However it may be, I find this to be the crowning glory of Burns's career as a song-writer. Not only is it couched in the most exquisite and carefully polished language but also it expresses the kind of thoughts which the younger Burns so often seemed to throw off in moments of spontaneous inspiration, but with that maturity and experience which are the main advantages (some would say the only ones) held by the middle-aged over the young. The melody of Burns's choice, a strathspey tune entitled 'Lenox love to Blantyre' (a name so poetical and mellifluous as to annihilate any desire to understand its meaning), is gorgeous—no other word will suffice. That it is inordinately difficult to sing well is a pity, because this led Thomson and others to put the words to all sorts of indifferent and unsuitable tunes; but it can be done, and the experience of hearing it is, to the listener attuned to Burns's magic, an unforgettable one.

I have neither space nor inclination to comment on all the other songs, sixty in number, which I rank high among the poet's output. For those who are interested, their Kinsley numbers are given in a note.[13] A few remarks on some of them, however, may add something to the estimate I am trying to make of Burns's achievement in an art in which he was not only supreme, but unapproached.

No. 43, 'O leave novels, ye Mauchline belles', is a piece of youthful virtuosity whose spirit, dash and ironic humour deserve to be much more widely recognized. Like no. 524 it has a splendid tune that is very difficult to sing well, which no doubt accounts for its being so seldom heard.

Of the eight songs in no. 84, 'The Jolly Beggars', six are included in my preferred list, and one of these has been dealt with above as being in the top class; the remaining two are disappointments, and will be discussed later.

No. 218, 'The winter it is past', has one of the loveliest of all the airs;

but its English words do not represent the poet at his happiest, containing as they do some strained metaphors and some infelicitously expressed clichés. Had the whole poem lived up to the merit of its first stanza, it might have qualified for the highest rank.

The troubled history of no. 240, 'Auld lang syne', is set forth at length in Dick and Kinsley, and need not be gone into here. I mention it, firstly because it is such a pleasure to draw attention to one of the few instances in which Thomson scores over *SMM*, and secondly because it does not seem to be generally recognized that the 'old' and 'new' melodies both come from the same stable, and indeed probably have a common ancestor. Although the differences as now seen are considerable, there is a correspondence between the two tunes in several vital matters: the melodic openings of the first, second and fourth phrases are almost identical; indeed, in the case of the second phrase the likeness is carried more than halfway through. Even more important is the identity of the unusual half-cadences with their subdominant implication (see note 12).

No. 361, 'I hae a wife o' my ain', is yet another instance of the type of melody in three-times-three time to which attention has been drawn. This tune is a little weaker than some of those mentioned in note 11, because of its tendency to halt at alternate bars. Burns's perfect matching of this characteristic in his words in this instance works to the detriment of the whole, giving the poem a slightly breathless quality which I find uncomfortable.

No. 364, 'O Kenmure's on and awa, Willie', is notable for the outstanding vigour of its rhythm. It comes as no surprise that this air has become popular as a bagpipe tune for marching, and that it has been adopted for an enchanting little Gaelic song entitled 'Am balachan ban'.

No. 392, 'When o'er the hill the eastern star', is another song which just misses inclusion in the most-preferred list. As in the case of 'The winter is past', this can be attributed to the failure of its second, and still more its third, stanza to live up to the sheer delight of the first.

The complex history of the magnificent no. 425, 'Scots, wha hae wi' Wallace bled', and the almost unbelievable tale of Thomson's tampering with both words and music, may be read elsewhere (see above, pp. 25ff.). It deserves notice because there does seem to be substance in the claim that public pressure forced Thomson to return to Burns's original intention, and if this is so it is another point in favour of the proposition that, in the last resort, public taste can be relied on. It can be set against the continuing (but I hope dwindling) popularity of inferior tunes like Hume's 'Flow gently, sweet Afton' and dismal gutter-scrapings such as 'Bonny Mary of Argyle'.

No. 444, 'Wilt thou be my Dearie?', draws from Kinsley one of his few detailed and fairly extensive critical judgments, a penetrating and, rightly, very favourable one. The melodic contours of the air are not in themselves particularly remarkable, but its phrase-structure most certainly is, consisting as it does of three bars plus thrice two bars, with the added subtlety that the first and third bars of the first phrase and the second bars of the third and fourth phrases are for all practical purposes identical. Add to this the unifying factor that the final bar-and-a-half of the first phrase is restated at the end of the final phrase, and you have a rhythmically taut and subtle whole such as would have delighted Haydn, that master of the irregular melodic sentence. With consummate skill, Burns precisely matches this unusual scheme in the structure and rhyme of his delightful verses; the success with which he does so makes it the more strange that some other instances of melodic irregularity seem to have caused him difficulty, and to have brought forth unsatisfactory verses; this is notably true of nos 175 and 176, already mentioned.

No. 457, 'Sae flaxen were her ringlets', is another piece of rhythmic and structural virtuosity whose sheer momentum conceals the fact that the verbal imagery is sometimes commonplace. This is an eminently singable tune, and I wish that the song were better known.

Yet another instance of technical virtuosity is no. 461, 'But lately seen in gladsome green'. Dick and Kinsley, in poking fun at Burns's conviction that this was an East Indian air, both claim a resemblance to the air of 'Chevy Chase'. This is true so far as a few chance notes of melody are concerned, but the structure and cadences are so different as to rule out any question of real kinship.

No. 484, 'Does haughty Gaul invasion threat?', is an occasional piece which might be said to be a lampoon of a certain type of patriotic versifying, and a brilliant one at that, were it not that in its own right it is so magnificently superior to all its kind. The air belongs to the 'British Grenadiers' school, and is quite as fine a piece of work. Nowadays, of course, it can only be presented with a good deal of tongue-in-cheek humour as a period-piece, but provided that there is no attempt to make a fool of it, a robust performance can be a very enjoyable experience.

No. 574, 'I'll aye ca' in by yon town', is a delicious piece of lightly etched amorous writing; both it and the superbly comical no. 585,

'The auld man's mare's dead', a kind of potted horse-doctor's manual, must be regarded as near the top of the list.

This is true also of the heart-rending no. 589, 'It was a' for our rightfu' king', which has been one of my greatest personal favourites ever since I first knew it. This incomparable melody with its cadence-diversion and two-bar extension at the close is the one which has been likened to 'The bailiff's daughter of Islington' on such inadequate grounds. Looking at it again, and singing it over to myself for the thousandth time, I find it hard to think of a good reason for excluding it from my list of the poet's finest creations.

It is time now to consider two groups of songs whose relative failure is cause for regret—I mean those where a good tune has failed to inspire the poet to write words worthy of it, and those where the poet's instinct for quality in an air has failed him, despite which he has produced a noteworthy set of verses. In the former class there is a score or so of songs, and in the latter about a dozen.

Not surprisingly, the first of these classes[14] includes a high proportion of songs specifically written for 'the egregious George Thomson's'[15] *Select Collection of Scotish Airs*. When one recalls Thomson's priggish distaste for the Scottish vernacular, his prurience, his arrogant meddling with the words and music submitted to him by all his contributors, and his absurd assumption that any words would go to any tune provided only that the number of syllables was correct, it is more than astonishing that the independent and outspoken Burns should so seldom have protested, and so often have meekly fallen in with Thomson's wishes. True, he sometimes rebelled at some of Thomson's suggestions: there is his famous and revealing remark that 'these English verses gravel me to death': there is the outburst of fury quoted by Kinsley[16] from a letter to Thomson (*Letters*, II, p. 203), and so on. Nevertheless, Burns continued to send songs to Thomson, voluntarily or at the latter's request, knowing that in the last resort he had no control over the form in which they would be presented. Why? May there not be something in the fact that Burns actually saw only six of the songs in print in Thomson's pretentious edition, in the first half-volume of twenty-five songs by various writers published in 1793, which was all that appeared before his death? It is true that even in those six undistinguished examples of Burns's work we find Thomson already tampering with the words, and altering one air of Burns's selection; true also that a great deal of correspondence was going on between the two men about songs which were not to see publication for a good many years. Nevertheless, had Burns lived long enough, the actual impact of seeing what a mess Thomson had made of his work might well have driven him to louder and more effective protest. We can only speculate about what went on in Burns's mind, remembering that his enthusiasm for perpetuating the Scottish airs and widening the circle of those acquainted with them may have dimmed his judgment to the extent that he accepted, *faute de mieux*, many things which he did not like.

The songs in which good tunes are accompanied by poor words include only one popular favourite, no. 388, 'She is a winsome wee thing', and in truth most of them are unlikely often to be sung over except by the curious. One possible exception, which one would like to hear occasionally, is no. 317, 'Sensibility how charming', a song found in *SMM* but not published by Thomson. The words certainly do Burns no credit, but the melody is so engaging that one might be induced to overlook their lack of inspiration.

I cannot believe that Burns ever wrote a worse set of verses than no. 9, 'From thee, Eliza, I must go', a youthful effusion which would have been much better lost; this is a pity, for his chosen air is an attractive one. One may be forgiven if the name 'Eliza' loses some of its appeal as a result of this lapse; but it must be remembered that not only Homer, but also Beethoven and Shakespeare, nodded from time to time.

Perhaps I spoke too soon about Eliza; Young Peggy, who blooms our boniest lass in no. 65,[17] runs her very close; so also do the lass of Ballochmyle (no. 89), my Highland lassie (no. 107), the lass of Albanie (no. 188), Lesley (no. 408) and Phillis (no. 421). Each of these ladies is allied to a tune worth remembering, yet each manages somehow to divert our attention from it by her own insipidity. As for Anna (no. 192), Isabella (no. 207), Clarinda (no. 217), my Bonie Bell (no. 379), Nancy (no. 431) and Chloris (no. 462), they do not even have the satisfaction of being coupled to airs which might have been memorable in spite of their cloying presence; for they belong to that residue of Burns's songs in which it is hard to find any merit whatever. There is a round dozen of these, and the less said about them the better.[18]

Yet another dozen of the songs provide their own puzzle,[19] for here we have airs which on the face of it have little merit. Yet they must have meant something to Burns, for they drew from him such lyrics as make us wish they were more of a pleasure to sing or to hear. No. 30, 'Mary Morison', no. 213, 'A rosebud by my early walk', no. 337, 'Ae fond kiss', and no. 242, 'Go fetch tae me a pint o' wine', are four songs of immense popularity; yet in each case the public instinct has rejected Burns's choice of air, and rightly so. These are songs for which, fortunately, happy alternatives have been found, exceptions to the rule that Burns knew best, and that to reject his choice is to diminish his stature.

Which brings me to the problem of the two weak members of the group of songs in 'The Jolly Beggars'. As we have seen, this work, which almost unanimous opinion now ranks among the greatest of Burns's achievements, contains a total of eight songs, of which six are to be counted among the poet's finest, one of the six being included in my short list of the thirteen greatest of all. What then are we to make of his choice of the feeble 'Auld Sir Symon' as the air for 'Sir Wisdom's a fool when he's fou'? It may do well for the bawdy 'I'll tell you a tale of a wife' in *The Merry Muses of Caledonia*, where the listener is not much concerned with the tune so long as he can fasten on the lewd lines. Even more upsetting is the vapid and spindle-shanked English tune which the poet has prescribed for his finale, 'See the smoking bowl before us', for this is one of the most superb things that ever came from his pen, a proclamation of his faith and of his philosophy which may have shocked the conservative of his day, but which stands firm after nearly two centuries in company with his finest creations. I have never heard a performance of the work in which the finale was actually sung to this feeble air, but I cannot imagine that to hear it twelve times through (as would be necessary) could do other than bore the listener just at the moment when he should be exhilarated. This tune gives the singers no chance to build cumulatively to that splendid affirmation in the final verse and chorus.

It is this instance above all that makes one wonder about the reliability of Burns's instinct; *could* he have reached the poetic and rhetorical heights of 'See the smoking bowl before us' if he had really had that ineffectual ditty ringing in his ears? I doubt it, and I think that it may have set him off on his first verse, after which purely poetic expression must have taken over, and the tune was forgotten. However that may be, I think that any editor or arranger who wishes to present 'The Jolly Beggars' with traditional music has got to solve this problem by finding good substitutes for the Merry-Andrew tune and the final air. It has been done, successfully I believe.[20]

That one-fifth of Burns's songs should be real successes, some of them outstandingly so, as integrated and unified products, puts him on a level with most great creative artists. Schubert in his 600 songs did not achieve such a proportion, and a disinterested assessment of the lyric output of any of the great poets or composers would usually lead to a similar conclusion. The slightly smaller number of demonstrably partial successes and total failures subtracted from the remainder, we are left with about 200 run-of-the-mill songs neither particularly successful nor notably the reverse. They contain much that pleases and little that offends. They are best regarded as the base of the pyramid whose apex is 'Oh wert thou in the cauld blast'.

IV

From what has been discussed, it should now be easy to accept my second and third propositions, and it will be found that statistical analysis backs up that which instinct tells us (see above, p. 163). That *SMM* should contain a higher proportion of Burns's most successful songs than does Thomson need not surprise us, for the whole of volumes II, III and IV of the former, as well as a goodly proportion of volumes V and VI (published after the poet's death), are the result of the enthusiasm with which he threw himself into Johnson's project, to the extent that he completely altered the original plan of making it an international collection, and became for all practical purposes its editor after it had taken its new direction. We must remember that it was a labour of love, wholly without thought of financial reward, and likely therefore to stimulate Burns often to give of his very best.

With Thomson the case is different. Burns had no part in the direction, editing or production of *A Select Collection of Original Scotish Airs*, and while it is true that many of his offerings to Thomson were spontaneously given, many more were written at Thomson's specific request, and therefore were more likely to be self-consciously worked out. Moreover, it cannot have been long before Burns became aware that he was not to have the last word even as to the form and detail of his own work, and in Burns's letters to Thomson we find several indications of the irritation and frustration which some of Thomson's impertinent proposals for change of wording or of air induced. That Thomson so often proceeded in his own way despite the poet's protests can only have made matters worse, and the whole frame of mind within which Burns did his work for Thomson must have progressively deteriorated, even though the poet may not have been conscious of the fact.

Of 213 songs by Burns in *SMM*, 52 come under my heading of 'good words well matched by good music'. In Thomson, the proportion is

19 out of a total of 114. Moreover, of those in Thomson, only 8 are unique to his edition,[21] the remaining 11 appearing also in *SMM*, usually in more definitive forms. Thomson, in fact, despite his expressed distaste for the alleged vulgarity of *SMM*, did not object to duplicating some of the songs that had already appeared there. There is no suggestion of piracy—on the contrary, it is clear that Burns, so far from objecting, encouraged the idea. For example, we find Burns, in a letter to Thomson dated November 1794 (*Letters*, II, p. 270), suggesting that he include no. 328b, which had appeared in *SMM* two years earlier. Thomson did so, but not until 1798, in the second batch of twenty-five songs making up his first 'volume'. Similarly in the same year Burns writes to Thomson (*Letters*, II, p. 250) offering two songs (nos 425 and 444), but saying that if Thomson does not want them 'I will give them to Johnson's Museum'. Thomson subsequently printed both, but not till three years after no. 444 had appeared in *SMM*. And so on; it would be tedious to draw attention to further instances.

On the other hand, it does seem that something nearer piracy occurred when Johnson, looking round for material with which to complete the final volume of *SMM* (which appeared in 1803), reprinted songs (e.g. nos 4 and 503) which had already appeared in Thomson. One wonders if this had anything to do with popularity manifested after publication by Thomson. On the face of it, this would seem to be a possibility in the case of, for example, 'Last May a braw wooer'.

With regard to *SMM* itself, there can scarcely be any dispute that those particular volumes over which Burns exercised such personal and far-reaching control contain the largest number of his best work for the publication. When Burns began to take an interest in *SMM*, volume I was nearly ready for publication. Apart from its containing a certain amount of material that is English or Irish (in conformity with Johnson's original plan), it naturally includes little of Burns's work—only Kinsley's nos 45, 65 and 99 appear. Volumes II, III and IV have respectively thirty-five, forty-seven and fifty-eight songs from Burns, including thirty-eight in my 'top fifth'. By the time volume V appeared, Burns was dead; but he had prepared most of the material, which includes forty-seven of his own productions, of which nine are first-class. Finally, there are twenty-six of Burns's songs in the last volume, published seven years after his death. At least fourteen of these (nos 591-604) were probably written towards the end of Burns's life specifically for *SMM*, and Johnson no doubt kept them by him, together with some earlier ones which for one reason or another had not previously appeared. In addition, there are one or two taken from

Thomson, as mentioned above. Of all these, only six qualify as of the first class.[22]

In the six volumes of *SMM*, only nine songs appear with airs other than those originally intended by Burns, for the reason that their airs had already appeared with words by other poets; of these, four are in volume VI and therefore did not have the poet's approval of the change. Contrast this with Thomson who, usually for arbitrary reasons, published forty-three songs with 'wrong' tunes, as against seventy-one with the ones prescribed by Burns, and without any such justification as can be credited to Johnson (or, in some cases, to the poet himself in his capacity as editor).

There we have it; a mere counting of titles shows an average higher quality in *SMM* than in Thomson, a disparity which becomes much bigger if we discount the titles common to both.

As for the question of vernacular versus English, the principal exceptions to the general rule that Burns was not at his best when writing in a tongue which he did not naturally speak are five in number: no. 43, 'O leave novels, ye Mauchline belles'; no. 84b, 'I once was a maid'; no. 84h, 'See the smoking bowl before us'; no. 218, 'The winter it is past'; and no. 257, 'Flow gently, sweet Afton'; and it may be noted that in three of these, a few vernacular words or pronunciations necessary for rhyme have been admitted. The remaining English verses, much fewer in number than those in Scots, are a pretty poor lot as poetry; there are relatively many more in Thomson than in *SMM*, as can be readily understood when one bears in mind Thomson's prejudices in this matter, but *SMM* is by no means free of specimens, some poor, others wretched. It is significant that in my list of the residual songs in which it is difficult to find anything to praise, there are exactly twice as many sets of verses in English as in Scots.

It is worth noting that despite Burns's occasional revealing outbursts on the subject of English poems, he willingly co-operated with Thomson, not only by writing some English verses at the latter's request and offering others voluntarily, but in searching out poems by English writers to fit some of the Scottish melodies which Thomson wished to include. For instance, on 19 November 1794 he writes to Thomson, 'Since yesterday's penmanship I have framed a couple of English Stanzas, by way of an English song to "Roy's Wife" ' (*Letters*, II, p. 277). The song in question was 'Can you leave me thus, my Katy'. A few months later he offers Thomson 'Long, long the night' for the tune of 'Ay waukin o' with the question, 'How do you like the foregoing? . . . as to English verses for Craigieburn, you have them in

Ritson's "English Selection" . . . by Sir Walter Raleigh, beginning "Wrong not, sweet mistress of my heart" ' (*Letters*, II, pp. 293-4). Some time earlier he gives Thomson a note of several poems in English from Ramsay's *Tea-Table Miscellany* and other sources, which he had found in 'turning over some volumes of English Songs' (*Letters*, II, p. 208). But the same letter contains the following significant sentence: 'You must not, my dear Sir, expect all your English songs to have superlative merit: 'tis enough if they are passable' (p. 207). This, coupled with the poet's remark quoted above, 'These English verses gravel me to death', surely explains the inferior standard of most of Burns's songs in English.

The controversial question of 'alternative airs' is more full of problems than would appear at first sight. It is easy to take up a strict attitude which condemns all setting to airs other than those first intended by the poet, and, indeed, such an attitude is logically the only one which supports the view that the words always emerged from Burns's method of composing, as described to Thomson in his letter of September 1793. The passage is well known:

> . . . untill I am compleat master of a tune, in my own singing, (such as it is) I never can compose for it. My way is: I consider the poetic Sentiment, correspondent to my ideas of the musical expression; then chuse my theme; begin one Stanza . . . humming every now & then the air with the verses I have framed.
>
> (*Letters*, II, pp. 200-1)

The trouble is, that there are so many examples of the poet himself having concurred in a change of air after the words were composed. It is not merely a matter of his agreeing to or deciding on a different tune for *SMM*, because the one of his choice had already been published there to other words,[23] or of his unprotestingly accepting a suggestion of a change made by Thomson; enough cases are known of his voluntarily proposing changes of melody to make the whole of his proclaimed method of writing suspect. Of no. 181 he writes in November 1787 to Johnson, 'You will be able to tell me . . . if these words will suit the tune. If they don't suit, I must think on some other Air' (*Letters*, I, p. 138). In July 1793 he tells Thomson that if he does not like the sentiment of one song, 'there is another song of mine, Museum vol. 4th, page 340, which will suit the measure' (*Letters*, II, p. 182). Of no. 107 he wrote to Thomson, 'But there is another song of mine, a composition of early life, in the Museum, beginning "Nae gentle dames, tho' e'er sae fair" which suits the measure, & has tolerable merit' (*Letters*, II, p. 202). Again, no. 242, which had appeared in *SMM* in 1790 to the air 'The secret kiss', is recommended to Thomson in the same letter for another tune. These and other examples[24] make it clear that Burns did in fact accept, at least six years before his declaration to Thomson, that alternative airs might be suitable for the same words.

Are we then justified in condemning Thomson for his frequent habit of publishing his own choice of air in preference to that of Burns? Again, the answer is not so easy as at first would appear; it is a temptation to damn Thomson out of hand on the ground that the poet did not actually give approval to most of his choices; but what of no. 240, 'Auld lang syne'? Burns seems to have given Thomson a free choice of two airs, with an implicit preference for the first one; but Thomson printed the second, and it has become a sort of Scottish national anthem. Beside all this, it must be taken into account that among the songs of Burns which for one reason or another are today well known to airs not thought of by Burns, Thomson, or Stephen Clarke, are one or two which are manifestly the better for the change. Perhaps the most obvious case is no. 242, 'Go fetch to me a pint o' wine'. Burns published one air in *SMM*, suggested a second to Thomson, who printed it to yet a third; yet not one of the three is satisfactory. I am not certain who first put the words to the excellent tune to which they are now always sung, but it is a case, perhaps not very common, of a later editor having a happy thought which has perpetuated words which otherwise would rarely have been heard. No. 30, 'Mary Morison', and no. 213, 'A rosebud by my early walk', are similar instances. Despite these exceptional instances, it is to be deplored that a good many of Burns's songs, conceived in conjunction with lovely tunes which they fit like gloves, continue to be sung to unauthorized tunes, almost all of which are greatly inferior. Mention has been made of 'Flow gently, sweet Afton'; others are 'Ae fond kiss' and 'O my luve's like a red, red rose'.

It is difficult to know what conclusions to draw from this confused state of affairs. Since Burns himself clearly on occasion not only accepted, but actually recommended, a change of tune, it is impossible to maintain a purist attitude, especially where the original can fairly be shown to be in some measure unsatisfactory. On the other hand, where the poet has given us a good match between words and music, there can be no excuse for making a change.

I do not propose to go into the question of settings of Burns's verses, more or less in the manner of *Lieder*, by such composers as Mendelssohn and Schumann; this is a different matter altogether, the words acting as stimulus to the composer, instead of the tune inspiring the poet. I know of no case of a sophisticated setting of this kind being superior to Burns's own conception.

V

The vexed question of 'arrangements' of the air is relevant to the present discussion only so far as it sheds any light upon Burns's own work. Even since they were written, the songs have been subjected to the attentions of innumerable 'arrangers', who have brought out countless editions, many of them miserably incompetent and musically illiterate, others the work of good craftsmen working within the limitations of a formal training in harmony, and a few, a *very* few, the result of the loving labour of real musicians who understood the idiom, cared for the words and the tunes, and were sufficiently gifted to translate their feelings into settings which allowed the beauty of the songs to speak for itself. An interesting fact about 'arranging' is that it tends always to reflect the taste of the particular age in which it was undertaken, and to sound dated and old-fashioned to later generations; for this reason the splendid (for their time) arrangements of Burns's songs by Hamish McCunn are difficult for us to accept nowadays except as period-pieces. Similarly, arrangements such as those in the *Oxford Scottish Song Book*, acceptable today, will probably not be so to our successors; likewise, the fashion for accompanying the songs by primitive harmonies played on the guitar will no longer be acceptable. The only way of communicating the songs which never dates is by singing them without accompaniment, and there is much to be said for this; but it must be remembered that *this is not how Burns conceived them*. He expected them to be accompanied on the harpsichord or in some more elaborate fashion, raised no objections, and continually referred technical matters to the musical editor of *SMM*, Stephen Clarke, deeming himself incompetent to meddle where musical 'learning' was concerned, and relying on Clarke (and later on Thomson) to see that things were properly managed. 'I hope against I return, you will be able to tell me from Mr. Clarke if those words will suit the tune', he writes to Johnson in 1787 (*Letters*, I, p. 138). And again, to Thomson in 1793, 'Mr. Clarke . . . is quite an enthusiast about [air no. 340]; and I would take his taste in Scots Music against the taste of most connoisseurs' (*Letters*, II, p. 168). The following year he tells Thomson, 'I have Clarke on my side, who is a judge that I will pit against any of you' (*Letters*, II, p. 256). These and other references to Clarke make it clear that Burns relied on him absolutely to guide him in the more sophisticated musical aspect of the work; but the truth is that, even allowing for changing taste, Clarke's harmonizations (for they amount to little more) show him to have been a very dull fellow indeed, of little imagination. Moreover, Clarke was by no means above 'improving' or making changes in the detail of an air, based on his restricted ideas of harmonic and melodic propriety. For instance, I will stake any reputation I may have that the sharp against the third-last note of no. 366, 'My Collier laddie', was an unwarranted editorial addition of Clarke's. And he evidently saw nothing wrong with the absurd version of no. 344 given in *SMM*, which may indeed be his own work. There are plenty of instances. To listen to Clarke's settings today is no pleasure; they give no sense of period or of personality, and merely leave us grieving that Burns himself had so little understanding or direct interest in these matters that he accepted them with enthusiasm.

The case of Thomson, of course, is quite different. Burns lived long enough to see only six of his songs among the first twenty-five of Thomson's settings (made by Pleyel). We know nothing of his reactions except what we read in his letters. In that of July 1793 acknowledging receipt of his copy he says: 'Never did my eyes behold, in any Musical work, such elegance and correctness.' After praising Thomson's preface he continues, 'it will bind me down to double every effort in the future progress of the Work' (*Letters*, II, p. 181). Shortly afterwards, he addresses John McMurdo: 'You, I believe are a Subscriber to that Splendid Edition of Scots Music in which Pleyel presides over the musical department' (*Letters*, II, p. 184). In December 1794 he describes the collection to Mrs Dunlop as 'a superb Publication of Scotish Songs'. These quotations do not tell us much. They can be read as suggesting that Burns was enamoured more of the splendour of the format than of the contents, especially if one is right in detecting a touch of irony in his reference to Pleyel, whom at one time he suspected, not without reason, of making unwarranted alterations to some of the airs.[25] If Burns could have known how Thomson was to tamper with his work after his death, to ignore his expressed wishes, and to claim copyright in them on the most dubious legal grounds, he might have been less enthusiastic; but it would be unreasonable to expect him to be critical of the results of Thomson's misguided musical policy, in view of his repeated disclaimers of any pretence to knowledge of music other than the simple melodic beauties of the native tunes.

Nevertheless, it remains surprising, in the face of Thomson's palpable amateurishness, lack of taste and belief that he knew better than the professional poets and composers whom he employed, that Burns should have been so generally urbane and compliant. It is astonishing that he was so seldom rattled, for he cannot have been totally unaware of these failings on Thomson's part.

Time has dealt harshly but not unjustly with Thomson; his absurd dreams have faded long ago, and the much-vaunted 'symphonies and accompaniments' in his pretentious collections serve only as examples of the laughable results of asking composers, even the greatest, to undertake tasks for which they were totally unfitted.

Notes

1. Songs are referred to by the numbers in Kinsley; letters by vol. and page in De Lancey Ferguson's edition. Other abbreviations are:
   Dick—*The Songs of Robert Burns*, by James C. Dick (London, 1903)
   Notes—*Notes on Scottish Song by Robert Burns*, edited by James C. Dick (published posthumously, London 1908)
   SMM—*The Scots Musical Museum*, published by James Johnson (6 vols, Edinburgh, 1787-1803)
   Thomson—*A Select Collection of Original Scotish Airs*, ed. George Thomson (5 vols, Edinburgh, 1793-1818)
   CPC—*The Caledonian Pocket Companion*, ed. James Oswald (12 parts, London, 1743-59).

2. Another sign of Dick's circumscribed knowledge of the wider world of music is his reference (Dick, xiii) to the so-called 'peculiar scales and eccentric intervals' in Scottish music. There is nothing peculiar in any sense of the word about the scales, and there are no intervals which are not to be found in Handel. Here Dick, rather surprisingly, seems to be uncritically repeating a worn-out belief which was widely held by musicians of the early nineteenth century.

3. See, for example, no. 191 (*SMM*, 114), which is more than usually full of such slipshod work on the part of Clarke.

4. Burns actually saw only twenty-five of Thomson's published songs. These twenty-five, arranged by Pleyel, are not the worst; that distinction must be accorded to Kozeluch's dismal settings.

5. C. Hopkinson, 'Haydn and Beethoven in Thomson's Collections', *Transactions of The Edinburgh Bibliographical Society*, new series, II (1938).

6. Some issues even appear with the wrong title-page, showing Kozeluch as writing 'symphonies and accompaniments' which were actually the work of Pleyel. Was this Thomson's economical way of using up surplus sheets already printed?

7. *Commonplace Book, 1783-1785*, ed. J. C. Ewing and D. Cook (Glasgow, 1938), p. 42. Nevertheless, the holograph of no. 583, 'Although my back be at the wa', shows that he could write a beautiful, legible and entirely accurate piece of musical notation.

8　The word 'cadence' has a specific technical meaning in music, but it is often used loosely and inaccurately by writers, including Dick.

9　Nos 29, 64, 89, 138, 157, 168, 175, 176, 197, 198, 203, 208, 284, 305, 387, 397, 413.

10　I am not sure, however. It has been brought to my notice that the members of a well-known provincial choral society in Scotland, having engaged a quartet to sing in their annual *Messiah*, saw the same singers in a televised performance of 'The Jolly Beggars' a few weeks before their concert, and threatened to resign if the engagement was not immediately cancelled.

11　I will not say that this three-times-three, shown in 9/4 and 9/8 time, is unique in folk-song to the Scottish tradition, but it is certainly behind the metrical scheme of a number of our finest tunes, including those used by Burns for no. 492, 'Fy, let us a' to Kirkcudbright'; no. 381, 'Up wi' the carls of Dysart'; no. 236, 'Tam Glen'; no. 565, 'Leezie Lindsay'; and also the superb air 'The muckin' o' Geordie's byre', set to the vapid 'Adown winding Nith I did wander'.

12　As a matter of technical interest, two of the three are cadences implying subdominant harmony, unusual in contrived music but common in Scottish traditional tunes. Cf. the first cadence of 'Auld lang syne'.

13　Nos 43, 45, 80, 84a, 84d, 84e, 84f, 84g, 115, 140, 170, 179, 195, 196, 199, 200, 201, 205, 218, 240, 251, 268, 285, 293, 297, 302, 306, 311, 316, 339, 340, 344, 361, 362, 364, 365, 373, 375, 380, 383, 385, 392, 394, 420, 425, 430, 444, 453, 457, 461, 466, 484, 503, 574, 585, 588, 589, 595, 596, 600.

14　Nos 9, 65, 89, 107, 179, 183, 188, 208, 317, 388, 399, 405, 408, 421, 422, 429, 454, 496, 509, 525, 582.

15　Dick's happy expression.

16　Kinsley, p. 1438.

17　Burns's spelling here conjures up a happy if unintentional picture.

18　Besides those mentioned, the list includes nos 66, 182, 234, 341, 378, 555.

19　Nos 30, 84c, 84h, 203, 213, 232, 242, 328a, 337, 342, 349, 558.

20　Crawford defends 'Auld Sir Symon', and Daiches finds no fault with 'Jolly mortals fill your glasses'. Nevertheless, I unrepentantly condemn both as unworthy of the verses which Burns wrote for them.

21　Nos 339, 392, 394, 420, 425, 430, 456, 466.

22　The following is a summary of the whereabouts of the 'first class':

Exclusive to *SMM*	41
Exclusive to Thomson	8
Common to *SMM* and Thomson	11
In neither *SMM* nor Thomson	8
With 'wrong' air in *SMM*	2
With 'wrong' air in Thomson	3
	73

23　As in the case, for example, of nos 4 and 38.

24　See, for example, Kinsley's commentary on songs 228, 274 and 405. Also no. 2 which, read in conjunction with Dick, reveals an astonishing mix-up over the proper tune.

25　*Letters*, II, p. 172.

Select Bibliography

The best single-volume text of the *Poems and Songs* is that edited by James Kinsley (Oxford Standard Authors, 1969), which is based on his fully annotated edition in three volumes (Oxford English Texts, 1968). A useful facsimile edition of *Poems 1786-1787* was published in 1971 by the Scolar Press. J. C. Dick edited *The Songs of Robert Burns* (London, 1903), and *Notes on Scottish Song by Robert Burns* (London, 1908). These have been reprinted in one volume (Hatboro, Penn., 1962). The *Oxford Scottish Song Book* (1971), edited by Cedric Thorpe Davie and George MacVicar, includes arrangements of more than twenty songs by Burns. Burns's *Letters* were edited by J. De Lancey Ferguson in 1931 (2 vols, Oxford): a new edition by G. Ross Roy is in preparation. J. C. Ewing and Davidson Cook edited Burns's *Commonplace Book, 1783-1785* (Glasgow, 1938, reissued 1965 with an introduction by David Daiches).

The most detailed biography remains that by Franklyn B. Snyder (New York, 1932). *Robert Burns: the Man and the Poet* by Robert T. Fitzhugh (London, 1971) adds some new facts, and David Daiches's *Robert Burns and his World* (London, 1971) is a well-illustrated general study. J. W. Egerer's *A Bibliography of Robert Burns* (Edinburgh, 1964) gives full bibliographical details of editions of Burns. A helpful background book is Maurice Lindsay's *Burns Encyclopaedia* (second edition, London, 1971).

There are separate critical studies by A. Angellier (2 vols, Paris, 1893), J. De Lancey Ferguson (New York, 1939), Hans Hecht (second revised edition, London, 1950), David Daiches (London, 1950, revised 1966), and Thomas Crawford (Edinburgh, 1960, second edition, 1965). Early criticism of Burns is brought together in *Robert Burns: The Critical Heritage*, ed. D. A. Low (London, 1974). For past and current scholarly work, consult *The New Cambridge Bibliography of English Literature*, ed. G. Watson (vol. 2, 1971), and the 'Annual Bibliography of Scottish Literature' (1969-), issued as a supplement to *The Bibliotheck: A Scottish Journal of Bibliography and Allied Topics*. The annual *Burns Chronicle*, published by the Burns Federation, Kilmarnock (1892-), contains articles on all aspects of the poet's life, art and reputation.

Index

This select index lists: 1. Poems and songs of Burns, by short title or first line, and 2. Names of the main persons referred to in the text.

1. Poems and Songs of Burns

Index

To you, Sir, this summons I've sent, 178

Twa Dogs, The, 44, 59, 67, 90, 91, 101-2

Twas ev'n, the dewy fields were green, 175

Up and warn a' Willie, 148-9
Up wi' the carls of Dysart, 160-1, 185

Vision, The, 6, 61

When o'er the hill the eastern star, 172
Whistle o'er the lave o't, 67

White Cockade, The, 151
Will ye go to the Indies, my Mary, 166-7
Willie Wastle dwalls on Tweed, 67
Wilt thou be my Dearie, 161, 173, 178

Ye banks and braes o' bonie Doon, 149, 167, 169-70, 178
Ye Jacobites by name, 153
Yon wild mossy mountains, 160
Young Peggy blooms our boniest lass, 175, 178

2. Names

Aiken, R., 91, 95
Ainslie, R., 17
Alasdair, A. MacM., 148
Albany, Duchess of, 146-7
Anderson, R., 63
Armour, Jean, 73, 99
Arne, T., 132
Austen, Jane, 113-14
Aytoun, Sir R., 66

Bach, J. S., 171
Barbour, J., 8
Barlow, J., 120
Beattie, J., 76, 125-6, 134
Beethoven, L. van, 28
Blacklock, T., 2, 39
Blackwell, T., 125
Blair, H., 16, 60, 98, 126-8, 134
Blake, W., 6, 8
Bonnie Prince Charlie, see Charles Edward Stuart
Breadalbane, Earl of, 102
Brown, G. D., 44-5
Bruce, Mrs, 140
Buchan, Earl of, 20
Burke, E., 117-19
Burnes, W., 57, 141
Burness, J., 17

Burns, G., 57
Byron, Lord, 2-3

Campbell, Mary, 85, 93, 99
Carlyle, T., 11
Catullus, 116
'Clarinda', see Mrs M'Lehose
Clarke, S., 170, 181, 182
Coleridge, S. T., 5
Collins, W., 124, 128
Constable, Lady Winifred Maxwell, 140
Cowper, W., 11, 106-23
Creech, W., 16, 33
Cunningham, A., 35, 152

Drummond, W., of Hawthornden, 96
Dunlop, Mrs Frances, 19, 20, 22-3, 41, 103, 108

Ferguson, A., 125
Fergusson, R., 58-9, 63-4, 77, 80, 121, 129
Fielding, H., 50

'Gibbon, L. G.', see J. L. Mitchell
Glencairn, Earl of, 16, 35
Goldie, J., 82
Graham, D., 64-5

Index

Graham, R., of Fintry, 35
Gray, T., 1, 50
Grose, Captain F., 23

Hamilton, G., 39, 95
Hamilton, W., of Gilbertfield, 60
Handel, G. F., 124, 132
Haydn, J., 28, 173
Henryson, R., 8
Herd, D., 131, 148
Hesketh, Lady, 115
Hill, P., 33-4
Hogg, J., 52, 137
Hume, D., 56

Johnson, J., 23, 24, 27, 29, 30-1, 132, 137, 177, 178, 179, 180, 182
Johnson, Dr S., 82, 109

Keith, G., 140
Kozeluch, 28

Lapraik, J., 74
Lawrence, D. H., 74
Lewars, Jessie, 9
Lyndsay, Sir D., 8

MacDonald, Flora, 138
Mackenzie, H., 39, 91, 92, 130
M'Lehose, Mrs Nancy ('Clarinda'), 19, 20, 31-2
Macpherson, J., 126, 132
Marvell, A., 84
Maxwell, J., 112
Miller, P., 17
Mitchell, J. L. ('L. G. Gibbon'), 45-6
Moore, Dr J., 20-2, 42, 57, 92, 141
Moore, T., 165
Murdoch, J., 57, 158

Nichol, W., 17, 34, 41, 139

Paine, T., 9, 67
Paton, Elizabeth, 70, 92
Percy, T., 132-3
Pope, A., 7, 55, 75-6, 109

Ramsay, A., 55, 59, 60, 63-4, 66, 77, 97, 131, 150, 165, 167, 180
Ramsay, J., of Ochtertyre, 130, 140
Rankine, J., 70
Riddell, Mrs Maria, 4, 19, 32-3
Riddell, R., 32, 33, 137
Rose, S., 108
Rousseau, J.-J., 128-9

Schubert, F., 164, 176
Scott, W., 2-3, 11, 40, 62, 154
Shelley, P. B., 8
Shenstone, W., 14, 121
Sillar, D., 71
Simpson, W., 80
Skinner, J., 141-2
Smith, J., 83
Sterne, L., 4
Stevenson, R. L., 47, 157
Stewart, D., 16, 39-40
Stuart, Charles Edward (Bonnie Prince Charlie), 138, 146-8, 154, 156

Thomson, G., 19, 20, 23-9, 30, 36, 65-6, 132, 137, 143-4, 161-7, 172, 174-5, 177-84
Thomson, J., 114, 124
Tytler, W., 131, 139

Vico, G., 125

Walkinshaw, Clementina, 146
Watson, J., 55
Whitman, W., 36
Wordsworth, W., 2, 5-7, 108, 109-10